THE POLICE, PUBLIC ORDER, AND CIVIL LIBERTIES

The
POLICE,
PUBLIC ORDER,
and
CIVIL LIBERTIES

LEGACIES OF THE MINERS' STRIKE

Sarah McCabe *and* Peter Wallington
With John Alderson, Larry Gostin,
and Christopher Mason

Routledge
London and New York

First published in 1988 by
Routledge
11 New Fetter Lane, London EC4P 4EE

Published in the USA by
Routledge
in association with Routledge, Chapman & Hall, Inc.
29 West 35th Street, New York NY 10001

Photoset by Mayhew Typesetting, Bristol
Printed in Great Britain by Richard Clay Ltd, Bungay, Suffolk

British Library Cataloguing in Publication Data
McCabe, Sarah
    The Police, Public Order, and Civil Liberties:
    Legacies of the miners' strike.
1. Great Britain. Coal industries. Miners.
Industrial relations. Strikes. Role of
police, 1984–1985
I. Title II. Wallington, Peter
331.89'2822334'0941

ISBN 0 415 00724 0

Contents

The authors

Sarah McCabe, MA, BLitt. Leverhulme Emeritus Fellow; formerly Senior Research Officer, Centre for Criminological Studies, University of Oxford.

Peter Wallington, MA, LLM, Barrister at Law. Professor of Law, University of Lancaster.

John Alderson, CBE, QPM, LLD, DLitt, Barrister at Law. Visiting Professor of Police Studies, Strathclyde University; formerly Chief Constable of Devon and Cornwall.

Larry Gostin, BA, JD. Director, American Society for Law and Medicine; formerly General Secretary, National Council for Civil Liberties.

Christopher Mason, MA, PhD. Lecturer in International Relations, University of Glasgow; member of Strathclyde Regional Council.

Preface

This report, as its title suggests, is about three interrelated questions: the role of the police, the maintenance of public order, and civil liberties. Our study originates from the miners' strike of 1984–5. Early in the strike, in April 1984, the National Council for Civil Liberties (NCCL) resolved to establish an independent inquiry into the policing of the strike. We were subsequently appointed to conduct the inquiry. The events leading from the publication in December 1984 of our interim report to our collective resignation in May 1985 are referred to in more detail in the Introduction. In themselves they are at most of incidental interest, but they also shed light on the issues generated by the strike, and significantly influenced our own appreciation of the issues discussed in our report.

Despite our resignation as an NCCL-sponsored inquiry we decided to complete our report, under the original terms of reference, because of the importance of the issues and so that the valuable materials we had gathered should not be lost. However in the course of completion of our report, and with the benefit of some two years' hindsight on the strike, our focus has significantly altered. The miners' strike was of course the most momentous event in the post-war history of British labour relations, and its repercussions on many aspects of industrial relations and the labour movement as a whole, to say nothing of the legal framework of trade unions and industrial conflict, have been immense. In the face of such profound consequences, it is easy to misapprehend the significance of the conduct of the strike, and of its policing, as part of a major watershed in the development of the way Britain is policed. In the longer term we believe that this will prove to be the most important legacy of the strike, for both the community at large and the trade union movement. It is a depressing legacy, as we shall attempt to demonstrate in this report. But we believe it is not yet too late to reverse the direction in which the policing of industrial disputes and the preservation of public order have evolved, before it irreparably damages the fabric of our society. It is this hope which led us to develop a broader approach to the original terms of reference, away from a detailed chronology of the policing of the strike (which is now the subject of an appreciable volume of literature) and towards an overview of the issues it highlighted, seen with hindsight and in the context of continuing developments. We hope also that our report will in some way help to fulfil the passionate concerns of the very many people who at the outset gave us practical, moral, and financial support in the gestation of this report.

Our debts in the preparation of this report are many and real. We are grateful to the NCCL, and particularly to its then General Secretary, Larry Gostin, for the initial invitation to serve on the inquiry. We also gratefully acknowledge the financial support given to the NCCL by a variety of public authorities, organizations, and individuals, which enabled us to be given financial support and research assistance. Following our resignation in May 1985, and our reconstitution as a group of private individuals we received generous financial support, without which it would not have been possible to complete our work, from the Joseph Rowntree Social Services Trust, the Barrow and Geraldine S. Cadbury Trust, the University of Lancaster, and an anonymous individual donor.

Those who provided us with information, evidence, and in some cases more practical assistance are too numerous to mention individually. We would single a number out here for thanks. Sheffield Policewatch discussed their work at length with us and provided us with detailed records of what must rank as the most extensive exercise in the observation of the policing of picket lines ever undertaken. We also received invaluable help, practical as well as documentary, from the Chesterfield and North-east Derbyshire NCCL Group, and particularly Arnold Wynne; this group's observations of policing in a very sensitive area of the dispute have contributed greatly to our appreciation of what took place. The NCCL commissioned a research project, prior to our appointment, based on observers in most of the major areas of strike activity. We have benefited from seeing the conclusions of this research, although we have not seen the detailed observers' reports.

Other assistance which we would particularly mention has come from the Police Authorities of Gwent, Merseyside, and West Yorkshire; from the South Wales and Staffordshire areas of the NUM; from numerous county and district library services, whose staff in many cases went to great lengths to assemble archive material for us; from several newspaper archivists; and from many individuals, including Members of Parliament and people professionally involved in the dispute. Although the nature of our final report has meant that we do not make detailed reference to much of the material derived from these individuals and bodies, it has been invaluable in building up our general understanding of a complex history.

There is now a wealth of published materials, and we are greatly indebted to the inquiry research assistant, Ian Cram, for locating and classifying the published materials and providing us with an index system for this and the evidence submitted to the inquiry. It is our intention that the materials assembled from published (including newspaper) sources will be made available to scholars as a research archive (for details please contact Peter Wallington).

Finally our thanks are due to Joan Kokle, Pauline Bowman, Heather Watt, Sharon Walker, and Helen Whittaker for their efficient and enthusiastic secretarial services; and a special debt is owed to our respective families for their support, patience, and tolerance over a prolonged period of varying degrees of preoccupation and trauma on our part.

Unfortunately as well as the variety of help we are glad to acknowledge, we must also record the lack of assistance received from two quarters: the National Union of Mineworkers (NUM) and the police. An initial assurance of co-operation from the NUM nationally did not materialize, despite a number of reminders, and the response from NUM area offices varied from the extremely helpful to complete silence. As a private organization it is of course entirely a matter for the NUM whether it wishes to respond to an unofficial body, and we do understand the enormous organizational problems faced by the union. The lack of direct evidence from the union whose members were most directly concerned is nevertheless regrettable. The National Coal Board (NCB) also declined to offer us any assistance.

We also sought evidence from the police. All chief constables, and the police representative associations, were approached but declined to co-operate. The representative associations again declined to give evidence when we approached them after our resignation and reconstitution. A number of our respondents made the point that they were willing to give evidence to an official independent inquiry. The government, wrongly in our view, refused repeated requests to set up such an inquiry. However the issues remain important, and we find the unwillingness of the police to discuss their experiences particularly ironic in the context of an inquiry which was bound to be closely concerned with the effectiveness of police accountability. In so far as we have failed to give adequate weight in our report to the police perspective, the failure is not one of effort on our part.

A variety of alternative sources of information has helped to fill the gaps in direct evidence. These include private contacts with many police officers, miners, and representatives of other sections of the communities most affected; chief constables' annual reports and some special police reports on the strike; the observations and reports of Police Authorities; eyewitness reports; and the official police film of events at Orgreave on 18 June 1984. The statistical information on the strike collated by the National Reporting Centre was also much more comprehensive than for most strikes, and much has been published through replies to Parliamentary Questions. Armed with this material we do not feel disqualified from commenting on and evaluating in general terms the policing of the strike.

In the course of our work Ian Martin, one of the original inquiry panel, was appointed to be Secretary-General of Amnesty International. His new position precluded his continued association with the inquiry and he reluctantly resigned; we are all grateful to him for his contribution to our work during his membership of the panel. The report represents the conclusions of all of the remaining members of the panel; principal responsibility for drafting the report fell on Sarah McCabe and our chairman, Peter Wallington, but all of us accepted the analysis presented.

SFMcC, PTW, JCA, LG, CM

July 1987

PART I
Issues and background

1
Introduction

The central thesis of this report is that our system of policing is in urgent need of review. The problem has two major strands. Evidence as to the policing of the miners' strike during 1984 and 1985, supplemented by subsequent developments, indicates mistaken emphases in the approach to policing situations of potential disorder, especially industrial disputes, embracing training, assessment of priorities, and policing strategies. In short, we shall argue that the police are pursuing the wrong priorities. Underlying this is the second and more serious concern: the collapse of the tripartite system of police accountability. This, together with continuing weaknesses in the control of improper police behaviour by means of the courts and thorough, independent investigation of complaints, leaves the British police almost uniquely, and dangerously, excluded from effective democratic accountability.

We develop this thesis in the context of an examination of the policing of the miners' strike and associated issues, and put forward for discussion some possible steps towards regaining a fully accountable police force serving the public interest effectively. As will be seen, these measures pose further questions and present options. We have neither the resources nor the impertinence to put forward a model policing system as being in a fit state for implementation. But the problem is acute, the need for action urgent; hence our first recommendation is for a full government-sponsored inquiry, preferably a Royal Commission, to produce acceptable proposals for rapid implementation. Our report is in a sense an agenda for such a body and, we hope, will contribute to the public discussion that should surround its deliberations.

There is another strand to the report, and in particular to our assessment of the policing of the miners' strike. This is an examination of the most powerful criticism of the role of the police advanced during the strike, namely that they were used for the partisan political objective of defeating the strike. Much of the antagonism shown towards the police during the strike stemmed from a belief that they were acting as an organized force of strike-breakers. In our view this belief was an exaggerated, but not fundamentally erroneous, view of the situation, and the major part of the blame lies on the government for its contributions to the position in which the police were placed. This is not just a matter of history, because it sheds light on many of the problems of policing revealed by the strike and stands as a clear warning of what must be avoided in future.

Our perspective in approaching policing issues is twofold. We are committed to the support of civil liberties as a set of values which should be respected and protected for their own sake, and for the sake of the democratic society they support, rather than for the sake of the promotion of the particular policies or objectives of individuals wishing to exercise them. The other perspective is a belief in the need for the effective accountability, in a democracy, of those institutions and agencies which exercise power over individuals and make significant political choices – including on both counts the police. These perspectives are developed in Chapter 2. Here only one comment is necessary. We will inevitably be accused of producing a report which is anti-police. We are indeed critical of many aspects of the policing of the strike, but constructively, so far as we are able, and only where the evidence discloses actions which we believe merit criticism. Unfortunately some commentators appear unable to distinguish criticism of how the police do their job from attacking the police. Those who equate criticism with attack may do so simply because they strongly support the methods under scrutiny and over-react to the suggestion that there are better alternatives, but some have a more fundamental objection, that the police are entitled as public servants not to be criticized because of the prejudice to their political impartiality that this could create.[1] We unhesitatingly reject the notion that the choices, priorities, and strategies adopted by the police are immune from discussion and criticism among the public for whose benefit the police exist, and would simply add that the extent to which such discussions focus on the police, and by implication expose them to criticism, is in direct proportion to the lack of any other agency which can be called to account for such decisions on their behalf.

BACKGROUND TO THE INQUIRY

Before completing the Introduction with the traditional preview of the body of the report, we must set out briefly the circumstances which have led to a group of private individuals undertaking this inquiry. In themselves the events are not now (if they ever were) of particular significance or interest beyond the small circle of those involved. However they do give an important insight into the issues we shall be addressing, and in particular the perspectives from which they can be approached.

The genesis of the inquiry was a resolution passed at the annual general meeting of the National Council for Civil Liberties in April 1984, calling for the setting up of an independent inquiry into the policing of the miners' strike, then in its second month. After some little delay, caused in part by difficulties within NCCL in formulating appropriate terms of reference, the members of the panel were approached and appointed to serve, a field research team was established and started to gather evidence, and the inquiry formally constituted and publicly announced in August 1984, with the following terms of reference:

To inquire into and thereby establish the fullest possible account and the civil liberties implications of the role of the police, the police authorities and the criminal courts in the events arising from and relating to the NUM dispute, which began in March 1984.

The focus in the terms of reference on the actions of the police, together with the exclusion of the strikers and their supporters, led to immediate challenges to our impartiality, and was probably instrumental in the refusal of the major police associations to offer us any assistance. From the outset we regarded it as axiomatic that we should have to look at the policing in the context in which it took place, including any actual or threatened violence, and that we would be free to make our position with regard to picket-line violence and intimidation within mining communities perfectly clear. However we considered it right that the emphasis should be on policing; and since this report reflects that emphasis equally strongly, it is worth reiterating our reasons, as expressed in our interim report:

> if private individuals or organisations infringe the rights of other individuals or organisations, that is a matter for adjudication by the courts. If private individuals or organisations break the criminal law it is the responsibility of the normal agencies of law enforcement to take action. In neither case is it a matter for an independent inquiry. But the actions of the police, and the machinery of criminal justice generally, are a different matter. They are public agencies, acting on behalf of society. The actions of the police are more than just acts of individuals; they are invested with the authority of the community on whose behalf they work.
>
> (NCCL 1984: para. 1.5)

At an early stage in our deliberations we concluded that we would need considerable time to deal adequately with the issues raised by the policing of the strike, but that some contribution was needed to stress the urgency of the situation and the need for wider recognition of the civil liberties implications of what was happening. We therefore produced an interim report, which was published on 10 December 1984 (NCCL 1984).

The interim report was largely devoted to outlining the civil liberty issues raised by the policing of the dispute and the role of the courts. It was predominantly critical (we develop the criticisms in this report) and attracted attacks from police representatives and government supporters for this. The criticism was however set in the context of a brief exposition of our philosophy of the role of civil liberties (developed here in Chapter 2) and of statements of unequivocal condemnation of violence, from whatever quarter, in the dispute. This part of the interim report attracted vociferous criticism from some sections of the political left and trade union activists, in particular our statement that 'freedom not to take part in a strike is as much a fundamental right as the right to strike'.[2] Various emergency resolutions about our report were tabled for the NCCL's 1985 AGM, and the NCCL Executive Committee on 28 February 1985 approved resolutions to the effect that the inquiry had 'exceeded its terms of reference in commenting on the conduct of striking and working miners and setting out civil liberties principles which did not directly relate to the role of the police', and that the presentation of the report was 'unnecessarily damaging to the miners' cause'. These views were endorsed by the AGM on 29 April, by majorities of 325 to 206 and 290 to 236 respectively.

The AGM resolutions in our view imposed an interpretation of our terms of reference which was incompatible with the freedom of action which we had sought, and still needed, as an independent inquiry, and required us to adopt a position we had explicitly rejected in our interim report. We therefore felt obliged, reluctantly but unhesitatingly, to resign and did so two days later. Larry Gostin also felt compelled by this and other actions of the AGM to resign his post as General Secretary of NCCL.

We all agreed, however, that the issues raised by the strike and the material we had collected were too important for our work to be abandoned, and we have continued as a group of individuals for that reason. We were fortunate in obtaining funding for the inquiry (as detailed in the Preface); inevitably the events described and our new status (and in Larry Gostin's case a new post in the USA) have delayed our work. We hope the added benefits of greater hindsight partially balance this.

This report is not the place to comment on the internal affairs of the NCCL. The issues raised in the interim report are discussed more fully in Chapter 2 and in our conclusions in Chapter 10. At this juncture only a few observations are appropriate.

First, in the aftermath of the defeat of the strikers after the most significant industrial dispute in sixty years, it was inevitable that feelings on both sides would run high and that non-partisan views would be difficult to sustain. At various stages throughout the strike a similar degree of emotional partisan-ship could be witnessed in the comments of some supporters of the govern-ment. The casualty of both protagonists' emotions is likely to be the civil liberties of individuals. The response to our interim report itself helps to make the case for the clearer recognition of civil liberties as a constituency in their own right and for their own sake in the process of reconciling con-flicting political and economic interests.

Second, some of the criticism of our reference to freedom not to take part in a strike as a 'fundamental' right appears to have been the result of confu-sion between 'fundamental' and 'absolute'. We did not and do not advocate a system of absolute rights. With the most limited exceptions, individual rights and freedoms must all be subject to whatever restrictions on their exer-cise are necessary to permit the exercise of other freedoms; they may none the less be fundamental rights. Freedom of speech for example, deserves to be upheld unless its exercise may interfere with the life or liberty of others. The balancing of freedom *not* to strike with freedom *to* strike is intrinsically difficult if not ultimately a conceptual impossibility, and attempts to establish a balance are apt to draw one inexorably into taking a position on the political merits of the dispute.[3]

In any event the point of our reference to freedom not to strike was more basic. It was the premise on which most of the policing of the strike was officially based, and our analysis of the policing was and is constructed on the same basis – that those who wished to work had rights, the exercise of which the police had a duty to protect. Even had we felt otherwise, no analysis of the policing from any other premise would have been credible.

STRUCTURE OF THE REPORT

The first part of our report sets the scene for an examination of the policing of the miners' strike itself. As already foreshadowed, in Chapter 2 we address fundamental questions of civil liberty relevant to the dispute, set out our basic philosophy as to individual and collective liberties, examining briefly some of the arguments that have been advanced against this position, and then attempt to relate the philosophy to the role of the police and in particular the priorities adopted during the dispute.

Chapters 3 and 4 deal with crucial aspects of the background to the strike: in Chapter 3 the issues behind the strike, government policies, the legal background and the structure of the NUM, and in Chapter 4 developments in the policing of strikes, police organization and training, and the system of accountability. It is important to stress that in looking at the background to the strike we are not attempting to draw any conclusions as to the merits of the positions of the union, the employers, or indeed the government. There are matters of fact that need to be borne in mind, and among the facts are the firmly held beliefs of many of those involved on all sides of the strike. Whether their beliefs were well grounded or not is often beside the point: the fact is that they were held, and that fact often influenced the course of the strike. The background not only sets the scene for the strike, but also emphasizes the extent to which the strike revealed changes and trends which had already happened or were under way before it began – in policing and in the civil law particularly; the continuing movement of these trends reappears as a theme both during and after the strike.

Part II of the report (Chapters 5, 6, and 7) is an account of the strike itself and its policing, and of the response of the criminal courts. We cannot hope to do justice to the sheer scale of events, or even to identify all of the issues they raise. We have tried instead to give a broad picture, to describe the typical as well as the dramatic, and to illustrate particular features of the policing which form the subject of comments later in the book. Some supplementary material on particular incidents is included in the Appendices.

In Part III we trace some of the important developments which have occurred since the end of the strike: in Chapter 8 in the coal industry, the NUM, and the civil law, and in Chapter 9 in policing, and the extension of police powers through the Public Order Act, 1986. Here the concerns about trends in policing and their implications for civil liberties, which we advanced in our interim report, are more than substantiated by events in the two and a half years from that report to the completion of this.

The final chapter, Chapter 10 (Part IV) contains our conclusions and recommendations. We attempt to draw conclusions as to what was wrong with the policing of the strike and the extent to which more fundamental problems are highlighted. We then address the questions that these problems raise for the future reform of the structure, management, training, and especially accountability of the police. The key features of our conclusions are presented at the beginning of this Introduction.

This report is not the first or in all probability the last, and certainly not by a long chalk the most original, contribution to the literature of the strike.

Our aims are more modest: to be dispassionate, consistent, and accurate, and to provide material which may contribute to public awareness of some crucial issues of our time.

NOTES

1. A variant of this objection was put to us by some Conservative MPs whom we met in January 1985 to discuss our interim report. They argued that criticism of police methods undermined public confidence and police morale and effectiveness and should therefore not be voiced, at least during the strike. Applied to almost any other professional group or public service, this point would be summarily dismissed as special pleading.
2. The relevant paragraph in the report (para 2.6) reads as follows:

    2.6 We accept that freedom not to take part in a strike is as much a fundamental right as the right to strike. Going to work during a strike is in any case a lawful activity, and like any other lawful activity ought not to be impeded by violence, threats or physical obstruction. We have identified the freedom to travel unhindered for any lawful purpose as a fundamental liberty; this is equally so whether the purpose is peaceful picketing, taking part in a demonstration, or simply going to work.

3. The concept of fundamental freedoms, and more especially the fundamental freedom not to strike, are discussed in more detail in Chapter 2.

2
Civil liberties: principles and issues

Most people in Britain would readily agree that the rights and freedoms of the citizen are an important part of the values which they respect and which they wish to see protected. But this consensus does not always extend to the definition of these rights and freedoms nor to the apportionment of their relative value. Indeed in the miners' strike, both those who withdrew their labour and those who asserted their right to go to work maintained that only what *they* did was clearly in accordance with a just and fair apportionment of rights. Given the opportunity, however, most members of each group were prepared to argue the case for their stance and, in some instances, to abide by the results of this argument. But the historical and political context in which the argument was conducted made not only agreement, but even discussion, difficult. Economic and financial constraints had a strong influence on the government and its representative, the Coal Board, which made them favour the rights of those who chose to go to work. Among many coal-miners, on the other hand, a high value was put upon the maintenance of the unity and power of a free association of industrial workers which could help to secure the continuance of employment and good working conditions. The grievous conflict that took place in the twelve months of the strike illustrates how easily the rights and freedoms of members of any society may be distorted and abused by citizens and by governments alike.

But what meaning can be given to these notions of rights and freedoms which – though widely supported – give rise on some occasions to differing interpretations and contentious, even aggressive assertion? Until the present century, individual rights have, in general, been asserted against and claimed from the state.[1] The right to have a say in the levying of taxes, for example; the freedom to end one's own life; or the right to the free practice of the rituals of any religion – all of these rights have been won from reluctant governments.[2] Of late, however, the argument has shifted a degree or two from the balance of rights between citizen and government. It now bears rather more upon the dissonance of claims made by individuals and by the associations into which they form themselves. If the conflict which may result from such claims is not to be injurious to the community, there must be some power given to the state to arbitrate between the claimants and to enforce a settlement of the issue if arbitration fails. This is the essential meaning of the social contract between citizen and state. And it is, or should be, based upon an assessment of the value of a just and fair distribution of rights to a civilized and compassionate society.[3]

Under a general umbrella of 'civil liberties', the terms 'rights' and 'freedoms' are sometimes used interchangeably. In legal usage, however, there is a clear and crucial difference in meaning reflected in the legal status of each.[4]

A right recognized by law carries with it a corresponding duty upon others not to interfere with or prevent its exercise. The right to life, for example, is protected by the laws of homicide; the right to peaceful enjoyment of one's property and environment, by laws against theft, criminal damage, trespass, nuisance, and pollution. A freedom, on the other hand, is signified by the absence of a legal duty restraining an individual from particular actions. He is free, as we have noted, to kill himself, but not others, or to destroy his own property but not that of others.[5] More positively, an individual is free to publish his opinions (subject, of course, to such *ex post facto* restrictions as the libel laws), but others have no duty to assist him by printing or reading what he writes.

In addition to this lack of clarity about conceptions of right and freedom there are other possibilities of misunderstanding about their nature and scope. We have referred in our Introduction to the apparent confusion between 'fundamental' and 'absolute' rights. No system of law can afford to the generality of rights and freedoms the status of being absolute or inviolable. If the rights of some were to be absolute they would have the capacity to extinguish those of others. This is, in part, because the equal distribution of particular rights cannot be guaranteed in law or brought about in practice. Let us imagine a citizen who, while living with a small group of fellow citizens, claimed the right to life and annexed all of the limited supply of food and water available to the company. He would, in doing so, usurp the rights of his companions by asserting his own. In this example we see the recurrent moral problem of political philosophy and of the practice of politics, namely the limited supply of the human resources which make some rights realizable. This can be illustrated by further consideration of the company we have spoken of. If each individual in that company were to be given an equal but insufficient share of the means of survival, none would live. But must all die to preserve the balance of rights? If not, how should the right to live be decided – by lot, by might, by agreement, or by a system of priorities devised and imposed by states? This is no far-fetched question, illustrating a philosophical quibble. It is a balance measured and decided every day in the allocation of kidney machines, heart operations, and the like. That some should die and some live is a matter which is decided, for good or evil but by tacit agreement, in medical terms and by those who practise medicine. At no time, however, are the rights of each of those who are subject to these decisions obliterated. Their claim is inviolable. It is its realization which is at risk. Those who practise politics have different responsibilities as we shall see.

Sometimes the problem of allocating priority between rights arises where the rights are of a different nature. In this context a particular class of right, rather than a particular category of individual, may be accorded priority. In most systems of government, some kind of balance is maintained by the apparatus of the law, sometimes pragmatically, sometimes by reference to established orders of precedence. That this latter is so suggests that there may be some civil liberties distinguishable from others by the centrality of their importance to human life and liberty. Rights to personal safety and protection from deliberate or avoidable harm are most likely to be in this category – thus few would dispute a prohibition on smoking in a filling-station; the same rationale is advanced to justify the prohibition of racialist literature. The tacit admission of relativity does not necessarily diminish the validity of affected rights (here, to freedom of private behaviour or of expression), but underlines the great difficulty inherent in any concept of absolute rights. It also raises again the important question of how priorities are to be established. Is it to be by agreement between citizens (which could be embodied in legislation), by legal intervention at the instance of individual citizens, or by the ukase of governments?

We must also consider a third dimension in which the necessity for balance arises, that is in the choice between the exercise of civil liberty and other general or 'public' interests. It is here that an acknowledgement of the intrinsic value of civil liberty is put to the test. Any claim to exercise a purely individual right may be weighed against the cost or inconvenience of allowing it to be exercised. For example individuals joining in a demonstration may hinder traffic: speakers or journalists may embarrass the government: defending the liberties of unpopular groups may be electorally unwise; it may be operationally inconvenient for the police to provide protection for a peaceful protest on an issue which generates highly emotional responses. In cases such as these, the maintenance of individual liberties is in danger of being subordinated to the convenience or prejudices of the administration.

Yet despite all the difficulties of definition, and all the obstacles to the protection of the rights and freedoms of every citizen, the assertion of the very existence of these rights, whatever may be the effects of their expression, provides the moral basis and indeed the only justification for the willing submission of citizens to the control of any government, autocratic or popular. Such a contract demands from both citizens and government an understanding of the range of freedoms which, in a just society, should be accessible to all. Until this century, the exploration of these ideas was largely left to philosophers and men of letters. When ordinary men and women claimed access to particular rights, they did so in an instinctive rather than informed belief that the rights they sought formed a basis for a just society. Since the Second World War, however, a much clearer framework and series of bench-marks have been created for the basis on which societies should seek to regulate the relationship between citizen and state, and between one citizen and another. The United Nations Universal Declaration of Human Rights in 1948, later fleshed out in the UN Covenant on Civil and Political Rights of 1966,[6] and the European Convention on Human Rights of 1950,[7] marked the recognition that in the aftermath of war, most countries were repairing their institutions, and that agreed principles for the establishment of a just society should be the underpinning for such renewals.

Notions of rights and freedoms, therefore, are no longer inhibited by the lack of an accessible framework. The rights and freedoms enshrined in the Conventions are the core of the 'manifest fairness' of any society.

Apart from the natural tendencies of those in authority to pursue a quiet life, the great threat to civil liberties arises from the reactions of those who oppose or are offended by the purposes to which such liberties are put, and seek to be selective in the terms on which they will support or permit the exercise of particular rights and freedoms. Indeed there may be a moral *duty* on citizens to protest – against anti-democratic or tyrannical actions or the exploitation of defenceless groups and individuals, for instance – which transcends the convenience of the authorities and other citizens. The question of what liberties should have been accorded effective protection in the strike is a completely separate issue from the merits of the strike itself. This at least seems to us to be implicit in any concept of a fundamental freedom.

CONFLICTS IN RIGHTS AND FREEDOMS IN THE MINERS' STRIKE[8]

It could be said that the only benefit which accrued from the miners' strike was the opportunity it provided for the review of two issues of considerable importance to the relationship between the citizen and the state. The first is the determination of the actual rights and freedoms available to workers. The second is the responsibility – and consequently the control – of agencies of the state when they establish priorities between divergent and conflicting claims by groups of citizens. Let us take first the state of the law governing industrial action, and the nature of the rights and freedoms with which it is concerned: principally the freedom to strike, and more controversially freedom not to strike.

The question of a fundamental freedom not to strike is controversial principally because it not only conflicts with but also has the potential to frustrate the effective exercise of the freedom to strike. The issue is often posited in terms of a conflict between collective and individual rights, although as John Lloyd has pointed out, in the miners' strike it was as much a conflict between the collective interests of working miners in areas which had voted against a strike and those of the national union and the strikers.[9]

We are in no doubt that the freedom to strike is fundamental and central to the maintenance of a free society. Nor do we suggest that freedom not to strike must be equally fundamental simply as the other side of the coin – the two freedoms cannot be equated in their nature, rationale, or exercise. To understand the point of freedom *not* to strike, it is helpful to begin by restating the justification for the freedom *to* strike.

Kahn-Freund and Hepple, in their classical analysis *Laws against Strikes* (1972: 6–8), offer four justifications for freedom to strike: to promote equalization of the respective bargaining power of employers and workers; to preserve the system of industrial collective bargaining by equipping it with sanctions; as a safeguard against the corollary of denying freedom to withdraw labour, that is a legal compulsion to work; and as a necessary safety valve for the psychological tensions of employment. We regard all these reasons as powerful, and some, particularly the first, underline the essential point that as striking has an economic objective, the effective exercise of the freedom is dependent on collective solidarity.

But none of the arguments in favour of freedom to strike is generally held to justify unrestricted freedom. In some situations key workers may collectively wield such economic power, or such power to achieve their objectives through the pressure they can impose on sections of the community, that the defence of others' civil liberties demands a limit to freedom to strike – so, for instance, strikes which endanger human life are legitimately forbidden.[10] Equally the methods used in support of strike action may interfere with others' freedom to such an extent that they would generally be regarded as impermissible – such as the use of violence to extend the range of the strike, or the conscious wrecking of valuable public assets by the withdrawal of essential safety cover. These examples highlight the basic proposition that freedom to strike cannot override all other freedoms. In all western democracies the law imposes limits, and while there are, rightly, strong arguments as to the proper limits to set, the principle can hardly be in issue.

It is also generally accepted that there are, and must necessarily be, indirect as well as direct limits on freedom to strike. The employer in a dispute, and his customers, are free to make such alternative arrangements as they can to avoid the full economic effect of the strike, and to seek to persuade employees to work, just as the union tries to persuade them not to. Of course, if successful, these efforts undermine the effectiveness of the strike, but that *alone* is not a justification for forbidding them. At the same time if the legal and economic cards are stacked too heavily against the strikers, so that the freedom to strike becomes an empty formality, then we would contend that liberty has been improperly diminished.

The argument for a fundamental freedom *not* to participate in a strike derives from the general freedom to behave as one chooses within the limits of the law. Such exercise of freedom does not forfeit its entitlement to protection merely because it has adverse consequences for others or because those exercising it do so for unworthy reasons – the essence of freedom is choice. For many people who refuse to take part in a strike, their action is in any case more than simply an exercise of choice; it is an exercise of freedom of conscience. There may be the strongest conscientious objections to going on strike – if for instance it involves withdrawing care for the sick or an essential public service. But freedom of conscience is not dependent on the merits, as judged by others, of the conscientious belief, or the numbers of those exercising it; it is entitled to respect as a liberty in its own right.

The contention that refusal to take part in a strike may frustrate the legitimate collective objectives of the strikers is a powerful one, but on close analysis it can be seen that it takes the argument no further. The law sanctions freedom of collective action, not the objectives in pursuit of which the action is undertaken, and the action sanctioned is that of those who agree to act collectively. Thus the point turns out simply to be a statement of the nature and inherent limitations of the freedom to strike itself.

It is not necessary for us to consider here the argument that trade unionists should respect the traditions of democracy and solidarity within their union. We sympathize with this argument, at least where membership of the union is voluntary, but it did not arise in the miners' strike. In the absence of majority support for strike action in a ballot – indeed in those areas where a ballot had been held, it had produced a vote against strike action – the argument was not so much a two-edged sword as a boomerang. Its very boomerang qualities serve to underline the inherent limitations of the argument itself as a universal prescription.

These points lead us to affirm the view advanced in our interim report that freedom not to strike is a fundamental right (not 'absolute', for all the reasons developed in the first part of this chapter). Even were this not so, we would feel constrained to reject the suggestion that it is legitimate for strikers to use physical force to prevent others from going to work. We would also feel bound to recognize, as we do, that since the act of working during a strike and the process of travelling to work are both lawful activities, the police had a duty to protect those who chose to work during the miners' strike, and any analysis of the policing of the strike must acknowledge that fundamental point.[11]

The rights and interests of striking and working miners were necessarily in conflict much of the time, and a resolution of the conflicts, while sometimes achieved by mutual discussion, was more often the result of a framework imposed by the police. Inevitably the role of the police in balancing these conflicting rights raises the central issues of the propriety of the decisions taken and the enforcement of responsibility for them, in general as well as particular terms. To these we now turn.

There is a general assumption in the UK that the police and advocates of civil liberties are in opposing camps. This is not particularly surprising. After all, the principal national organization for the protection of the liberties of the citizen was founded as a result of protests against oppressive behaviour by the police as they operated to control unemployment marches and anti-fascist demonstrations in the 1930s. There is, therefore, an understandable difference of view between the two groups. Nevertheless there is no inherent antithesis. The police exist to uphold the law, the existing constitutional order and institutions of the state, including the principles of liberal democracy on which they are based. Successive UK governments have ratified and accepted as internationally binding obligations various human rights Conventions, in particular the European Convention on Human Rights and the more comprehensive United Nations Covenant on Civil and Political Rights referred to on p. 11; these Conventions and the civil liberties they embrace therefore form part of the framework of constitutional principles which the police are charged with upholding. Even where our domestic law may be deficient in recognizing or protecting basic liberties (as it is in a number of respects) the general duty of the police to preserve civil liberties is in our view clear.

This analysis leaves open a number of questions. Police officers themselves frequently identify their role as the protection of liberty but their emphasis does not necessarily coincide with that favoured by other civil liberties campaigners. Where should the emphasis lie? Manifestly the police should seek to protect those liberties recognized by law. We have noted that most of the rights enjoyed by citizens in this country are protected by the criminal law – the laws against homicide, theft, and obstruction, for example. In the absence of positive constitutional rights, however, there is no absolute requirement for the police to uphold freedom of peaceful assembly or association, or freedom to strike. The enactment of a Bill of Rights based on the European Convention on Human Rights would make explicit many of these matters which are at best implicit in domestic law. This would make it easier for the police to accept the positive duty to recognize and safeguard those rights and freedoms which are of particular concern to civil liberties campaigners; in this way a clearer basis for a common commitment to civil liberties could be established. However the police already in our view have a duty to recognize and safeguard those fundamental freedoms guaranteed in the international conventions to which the UK is a party.[12]

Matters are complicated by the image of the police in industrial disputes. During the nineteenth and the first half of this century the police frequently operated as little more than a private strike-breaking agency at the disposal of the employers; Geary fully and persuasively documents this.[13] Since the Second World War, matters have changed considerably, with an increasing police appreciation of the legitimate role of peaceful picketing and the establishment of norms of co-operation and tolerance, described by Geary and by Kahn.[14] This new accommodation was severely tested by the miners' strike, for reasons, at least in part, outside the control of the police themselves.

The second question is of priorities. The police have considerable discretion in establishing their own priorities in enforcing the law and protecting individual liberties. In normal circumstances the choices are constrained by a variety of influences, and policing follows a relatively common pattern in each of the forty-three nominally autonomous police forces in England and Wales. However this pattern does not necessarily reflect the priorities of local communities, although the increased emphasis on protecting ethnic minority communities from violence and more sophisticated responses to the needs of rape victims both show that community concerns can be reflected in policing. Occasional, vivid examples of the personal commitments of individual chief constables can also be seen in the diversion of police resources to particular campaigns, such as that against pornography in Greater Manchester by James Anderton, or against drunken driving in Nottinghamshire under Charles McLachlan. The question who decides priorities leads naturally to the issue of accountability, which is the final point we address in this chapter.

We start from the general proposition that in a representative democracy, public agencies exist to serve the whole body of citizens. It follows from this that there must be mechanisms by which these citizens can, either collectively or through their representatives, decide what they want to be done and the methods to be used in doing it. Put another way, this democratic accountability is the necessary precondition for the consent element of 'policing by consent' – both in principle and in practice.

Yet by the gradual erosion of the power of local police authorities the police have been allowed to become almost uniquely independent of external accountability. Moreover the nature and constitutional importance of the powers which society invests in its police make it more rather than less necessary that there should be proper accountability. There are critical decisions of policy to be taken regarding the exercise of these powers, which must be taken by the police, but which are nevertheless not private police property but matters of legitimate public concern.[15] It is for this reason that the history of the miners' strike is so important. It shows in sharp relief how civil liberties may be curtailed by the agents of a representative democracy, when those agents are free of representative control.

In our analysis of the policing of the strike, and of the developments which preceded and followed it, we shall examine the way in which and extent to which the police respected and promoted civil liberty values. In this chapter we have attempted to offer a framework of reference for an evaluation of these matters. Put simply, it is this. Freedom, both of individuals and of groups of individuals, is a fundamental value which institutions of society, including the police, should seek to promote. Where freedoms conflict, as necessarily they must on occasion, the reconciliation of the conflict should be based on the balancing factors laid down by law (including our international human rights obligations) and not on an assessment of the value of the purposes for which either party wishes to exercise that freedom. Where freedom conflicts with the institutional interests of authority, then it is the former which must be given the largest practicable latitude. Therefore when the police act to enforce general interests they should do so in ways which do not unnecessarily diminish individual or group freedoms.

NOTES

1. The early struggles of trade unionists for the right of association were an exception; in the first instance at least, claims were laid against employers. The confrontation with governments came later when the latter used the criminal law to frustrate the unionists' attempts and protect the employers' privileges.
2. Where the practice of a religious belief entails interfering with the rights and freedoms of others, there is less room for the recognition of the right to its pursuit.
3. The necessary relationship between individual claims to autonomy and the social institutions which make up the context of this claim is well expressed in a recent review of Joseph Raz's exposition of *The Morality of Freedom*:

   > It is a matter of social achievement to develop social institutions in which individuals count for something; and what individuals count for is in turn explicable or statable only in social terms not in some ineffably private language.   (MacCormick 1987)
4. Hohfeld (1923).
5. The freedom to kill oneself, given legal sanction in Britain in 1961, is a clear example of changing ideas about particular human demands. That these changes have not been wholehearted is shown by the steps taken by others to prevent or discourage suicide, and the general support given to preventive measures.
6. Ratified by the UK government in 1976.
7. Ratified by the UK government in 1951; the right of individual petition to the European Commission on Human Rights for alleged violation of the Convention was adopted by the UK in 1966 and has been renewed by successive governments since. The Convention has been the model for most of the numerous Bills of Rights introduced in Parliament in recent years.
8. The question of violence in the strike is considered in Chapter 10.
9. Lloyd (1985: 34).
10. See the Conspiracy and Protection of Property Act, 1875, section 5.
11. At the same time the legitimacy of the feelings of bitterness displayed by the striking miners towards the 'scabs' cannot be ignored. Exercise of a freedom does not entitle one to be secure against hostility for having done so. In a long and gruelling ordeal such as the strikers faced strong feelings were inevitable, and a recognition of their nature was a precondition

to effective policing of the picket lines. After we had completed our report the government published proposals (contained in the Employment Bill, 1987) to deny to unions the power to discipline members who refuse to take part in strike action, even where the strike was approved in a secret ballot. Nothing in what we have argued supports, either in logic or in practice, such an extraordinarily one-sided measure. While safeguarding absolutely the right of the dissentient, it imposes a denial of freedom on those who do not wish, for however strongly felt reasons of conscience, to associate with strike-breakers. The effective destruction of the closed shop removes any vestige of justification from such an abrupt (and unique) departure from the voluntary principle of freedom of association and will make it even harder for union members to accept the validity of our analysis.

12. See generally on the police and the European Convention, Alderson (1984).
13. Geary (1985: 7–66).
14. Kahn *et al.* (1983: ch. 5).
15. Public accountability also carries the important responsibility of being subject to criticism for the actions of those for whom the agency is accountable. Without effective public accountability for the police, it is the police themselves who are the inevitable target for such criticism.

3

Background to the strike: economic, political, and legal issues

The miners' strike was precipitated by, and primarily (though not exclusively) about, proposals for the closure of 'uneconomic' pits. It took place against a backdrop of developments in the coal industry and the political and legal environment, and its origins and progression were deeply influenced by the particular constitutional structure of the NUM. Some of these matters are peripheral to the purposes of our report, but the course of the strike and its policing cannot be intelligibly described without at least a cursory examination of them. This we attempt here, briefly and selectively, emphasizing aspects particularly relevant to our examination of the policing of the strike.

ORIGINS OF THE STRIKE[1]

The strike began officially on 12 March 1984 (some pits in South Yorkshire had struck the previous week). There was already a national overtime ban in force, called in November 1983 on the twin issues of a 5.2 per cent pay offer and the general question of pit closures; this remained in force throughout the strike and was duly observed at working pits. The precise trigger of the strike itself was the announcement of the impending closure of Cortonwood Colliery in South Yorkshire, made by Area Director George Hayes at a colliery review meeting on 1 March. Specific closure threats to Bulcliffe Wood, Herrington, Polmaise, and Snowdown were later linked with Cortonwood as issues in the strike, but the national dimension was a more generalized indication that the NCB's budget for 1984–5 envisaged a loss of 4 million tonnes of productive capacity, 20 pit closures, and the loss of 20,000 jobs, as revealed at a national consultative meeting on 6 March. Cortonwood was the first precipitate step in this closure programme.

Behind these figures, argued the NUM leadership, were undisclosed plans for the further closure of some 50 pits, with the loss altogether of 75,000 jobs, as a prelude to the privatization of the remaining profitable sections of the industry. As we shall see, although privatization seems at the time of writing to be unlikely (at least in the medium term), the actual numbers of pits closed and jobs lost within two years of the ending of the strike closely matched those suggested by the NUM; how far this can be taken as a vindication of the union's position, and how far it represents the consequences of economic damage to the industry inflicted by the dispute, are matters of controversy on which we make no comment.

Commentators on the strike have analysed closely the circumstances of the Cortonwood announcement (which was made in breach of the complex consultative procedure and with exceptionally short notice) as a political indicator of whether the strike was deliberately provoked at the instance of government. We are not persuaded that this is what happened, but in any case, in our view, it is more helpful to examine the circumstances which led to the strike being almost inevitable, in March 1984 or soon after.

THE COAL INDUSTRY 1947–79

Since nationalization, as for three decades before, the coal industry has been in a steady decline, fatefully but temporarily interrupted in the mid-1970s. The statistics of manpower, output, and pit closures are clear indicators: manpower, from some 700,000 in 1947, fell to 287,000 in 1970 and 190,000 at the start of the strike; output fell from 228 million tonnes in 1952, the post-war peak, to 135 million tonnes in 1970; after a brief revival in the late 1970s it was 125 million tonnes in 1982 (before the figures were affected by the 1983 overtime ban); the 980 pits vested in the NCB fell to 292 by 1970 and 179 at the start of the strike.

The reasons for the decline in output and consumption are easily identifiable. Major factors include the switch from manufactured to natural gas, the reduction in domestic coal consumption following the Clean Air Act, 1956, the end of steam on the railways, the growing importance of oil as an industrial fuel and latterly of nuclear power generation, and the effects of the 1980 recession and of energy-saving measures on total energy consumption.

The decline in manpower and numbers of pits reflects a process of rationalization, investment, and increasing productivity over and above the decline in output. Manpower losses and pit closures over this period were achieved with relatively little industrial conflict. Other employment opportunities were readily available in many areas and there was extensive migration to the expanding East Midlands coalfield.[2] In the later years compliance was maintained by full use of the coal industry's elaborate consultative processes and relatively generous severance payments.

In 1973–4 the process of decline was dramatically jolted by the world oil crisis. This coincided with the second strike victory in two years over miners' pay, and with the election of a government not only sensitive to the industrial power the miners now apparently had but also sympathetic to their interests and indeed politically indebted. The outcome was the famous 1974 Plan for Coal, a tripartite agreement on investment, output targets, and closures between the Department of Energy, the NCB, and the NUM. It envisaged a considerable investment in the industry, support for developing the market for coal, and production rising modestly. Pit closures necessitated by geological problems or exhaustion would be balanced by new developments. The Plan underwent some modification during the life of the 1974–9 government but in its essence was implemented over this period (and not formally rescinded thereafter). The Plan was the basis on which the NUM constructed its position throughout the strike. Production was significantly improved in 1978 when incentive bonuses were reintroduced – ironically by area agreements following the rejection of a national scheme in a ballot held in response to a High Court decision – and reached a peak in 1980 of 130 million tonnes. The regeneration of the market by the oil crisis was however relatively short-lived, and the recession soon reinforced the pressures on coal.

CONSERVATIVE GOVERNMENT POLICY

The incoming government of 1979 had the future of the nationalized industries as an important priority in its plans and its manifesto. A Conservative Party policy group on the nationalized industries produced a report, written by Nicholas Ridley MP, in 1978. (The report was never published, but it was extensively leaked in *The Economist* of 27 May 1978 and became notorious as the Ridley Report, not least for its Annex, much quoted in the strike, to which we shall return.) The report proposed a strategy of controls on subsidies, the ending of monopolies, and a rapid move towards privatization. It clearly set the scene for the government's general approach to the public sector, including coal. However the progress towards the confrontation on pit closures was chequered.

Legislation establishing new targets for external financial limits for the coal industry was passed in 1980.[3] This necessitated an acceleration of pit closure proposals which produced a conflict with the NUM in February 1981, and a very rapid government climb-down entailing some £250 million extra financial support. At that stage, it has been widely suggested, the government was not ready for a showdown; indeed the then Energy Secretary, David Howell, subsequently confirmed this.[4] Be that as it may, the issue was deferred, but in circumstances which enabled the NUM's ground to become significantly weaker. Production was maintained at nearly the 1980 peak, until the overtime ban in November 1983, whereas consumption fell sufficiently to produce an increase in pithead and power station stocks of coal from 28 million tonnes in 1979 to 58 million tonnes in 1983 – over six months' total requirements. In fact pit closures did take place on an increasing scale during the following two and a half years, but no one issue generated sufficient support for industrial action on a national scale; there were national strike ballots on pit closures in November 1982 and March 1983 which both produced majorities of 61 per cent against strike action. The one significant positive ballot result was an 86 per cent vote in support of action on pit closures achieved in the Yorkshire area in January 1981.

Two investigations of the finances of the NCB were undertaken after the events of early 1981. Both the House of Commons Select Committee on Energy, reporting in December 1982, and the Monopolies and Mergers Commission in its substantial and influential report of the following May, were critical of the industry's finances.[5] The latter report in particular recommended a major shift in emphasis for the NCB and individual managers from production-led performance criteria to a policy of value for money and tailoring output to the market. When Ian (later Sir Ian)

MacGregor was appointed Chairman of the NCB from September 1983, it was in the expectation that he would pursue the principal recommendations of the Monopolies and Mergers Commission Report. That report also emphasized the very high proportion of total losses, and the relatively very large gap between production costs and market price, in the least efficient and productive collieries. Inevitably this focused attention on pit closures, and particularly the closure of 'uneconomic' pits.

'UNECONOMIC' PITS

As the strike was presented in much of the media, the issue of 'uneconomic' pits was put crudely in terms of subsidizing jobs in one industry while others had suffered the rigours of a chill economic reality. The issue is of course more complex, and we believe it is helpful to spell out some of the alternative perspectives on this issue. We do so not to take or support any particular view but to highlight the issues involved in the strike which could have been the subject of public debate had not picketing, violence, and police actions so dominated the news.

In computing the total cost of coal produced by a particular pit, the cost of men and equipment to get the coal from seam to pithead is only one element, and probably the only one which can be stated with reasonable precision. Other elements nationally include payments of compensation for mining subsidence, the cost of redundancy payments and of topping up the pension fund, and interest charges. There is considerable room for dispute about which, if any, of these elements should properly be charged as costs of particular mining operations, and if they are, how the total should be apportioned. There is, for instance, a clear interrelationship between investment and profitability, but the allocation of costs of investment to particular output is controversial. To take another example, subsidence results in large part from past mining operations, and will occur (and still more be compensated) over widely varying periods after the actual excavations. Other costs too, such as interest and pension payments, occur independently of coal output, and any apportionment to particular activities is necessarily arbitrary. The statement, widely quoted, that coal extracted from Cortonwood cost £64 per tonne (against a sale price of £47) is not a simple fact but the product of calculations constructed on certain assumptions. In the strike, the assumptions were in dispute.

The more prominent controversy was over the total costs of closing uneconomic pits. The case for the NUM position, as argued for instance by Glyn, was that closure would not, overall, save public funds, and that there was no economic case for closure quite apart from the serious social damage which the closures would inflict on mining communities. In some degree, the argument is indisputable. The cash costs of severance payments to redundant miners, the partial continuation of costs such as interest charges and subsidence compensation which would occur irrespective of closure, and the writing-off of irrecoverable equipment are all direct costs of closure, or need to be offset against savings to produce the true net saving to the NCB. But Glyn's argument and that of the NUM went further, bringing into the equation the costs in unemployment benefits and lost tax revenue of the job losses, both in the mining industry and employment dependent on it. Glyn calculated on this basis that *no* pits could be closed without a net loss to public funds. This too was based on particular assumptions about costs and savings, and we are not qualified to judge the merits of this or any other financial analysis.[6] However it serves to highlight the range across which arguments on the issues involved in the strike were conducted.

Going beyond economic questions were the social arguments against pit closures, especially with respect to the effects of closures on mining communities heavily dependent not only for employment but also for effective survival on the local mine. Particularly in the older (and economically more marginal) coalfields, physical isolation of mining villages is a major problem and it was widely recognized that this issue was more than special pleading.[7] Supporters of the strike also presented the issue in broader terms, the miners' struggle symbolizing resistance to the wholesale loss of jobs in many traditional sectors of industry. The social arguments were supported by a conservationist one: coal as a non-renewable source of energy should be exploited to the full, and not discarded by closure of mines with workable reserves (which can rarely be exploited once a mine has been closed and workings abandoned).

These arguments are worth mentioning not to prove or disprove a point of view but simply to demonstrate the range of perspectives and the nature of the issues underlying an apparently simple (and often simplistically presented) question of whether the country could afford to subsidize uneconomic pits.

PREPARING FOR THE STRIKE

It has variously been suggested that the government wanted, or engineered, a strike in the coal industry so that it could defeat the miners. We feel this allegation is not substantiated and is inherently improbable. There is, however, clear evidence that the government planned for a major strike, which they anticipated as a real risk of the economic measures they judged to be necessary for the industry, and it is reasonable to assume that there was some attempt to influence the timing of the dispute and the issues upon which it would focus. When the strike came, the government pursued its objectives single-mindedly, according them high priority, and the NCB was seen as a mere agent of government policy (although it retained *de facto* control of much of the conduct of the campaigns for a return to work, and of such negotiations as took place). The ready identification of the government's political objectives with one party to the dispute was of course particularly important in relation to the role of the police, which most miners thought was simply to facilitate strike-breaking.

The extent to which a major coal strike had been foreseen, and strategies developed against the eventuality, is evident from the Annex to the Ridley Report. This, as published in leaked form, identified potential 'political threats' to the general denationalization strategy, of which the most likely was from the mineworkers. Ridley argued that a Conservative government should:

(a) build up maximum stocks, particularly at the power stations; (b) make contingency plans for the import of coal; (c) encourage the recruitment of non-union drivers by haulage companies to move coal when necessary; (d) introduce dual coal/oil firing in all power stations as quickly as possible. The group believes that the greatest deterrent to any strike would be to 'cut off the money to strikers, and make the union finance them'. . . . There should be a large mobile squad of police equipped and prepared to uphold the law against violent picketing. 'Good non-union drivers' should be recruited to cross picket lines with police protection.[8]

There has been some disagreement about the extent to which this document became an action plan for the government; Adeney and Lloyd, for instance, argue that it was largely forgotten in government circles.[9] The circumstantial evidence that it was a key influence is however very strong. Coal stocks, as already mentioned, more than doubled between 1979 and 1984. Coal imports during the strike were double previous levels, despite a brief dock strike and intensive picketing of incoming traffic – this probably could not have happened without *some* preparation before the strike. Many power stations were converted to burn oil (and did so during the strike). We have no evidence of systematic recruitment of non-union lorry drivers but in the event drivers prepared to cross picket lines were available in more than sufficient numbers during the strike. The 'greatest deterrent' was implemented by legislation in 1980 (as explained on p. 29). Most significantly from our point of view, the police were systematically retrained in riot control, and readily mobile Police Support Units set up in every force, following a review of police training in 1981 initiated in response to the urban riots of that year; we discuss this in Chapter 4. These developments incidentally improved the government's capacity to meet head on any major public order confrontation that might arise in the course of industrial action over its economic strategy.

The tactical climb-down by the government over pit closures in February 1981 in response to threatened industrial action is entirely consistent with the view that ministers wished to prepare their ground sufficiently, in accordance with the Ridley Report, before allowing confrontation. The appointment of Ian MacGregor as Chairman of the NCB in September 1983, whatever the industrial merits of the choice, can most easily be regarded as having been intended to bear the interpretation that miners' leaders put on it, namely that the gloves were off. If Ridley was not a plan put into effect, then it was certainly, as the Sunday Times Insight team say, 'an eerily prescient sketch' (1985: 18).

On the miners' side, preparation was less evident and systematic. Some last-minute preparations were made, particularly for the transfer of assets out of the jurisdiction of the English courts (presumably in anticipation of the sequestration of the NUM's funds which indeed occurred later in the course of the strike). Sir Ian MacGregor has argued that the timing of the strike was planned by the NUM leadership some time in advance, on the strength of a conversation in December 1983 between NUM Vice-President Mick McGahey and NCB Deputy Chairman Jimmy Cowan, but this limited evidence is not otherwise corroborated.[10] Whatever thought may have been given to the conduct of a prolonged strike, there was little evidence of effective planning of the way that picketing or spreading the impact of the strike through supporting action should be organized.

However, to some extent, just as the appointment of Ian MacGregor made it more likely that a strike would occur, so did the election of Arthur Scargill as NUM President in December 1981. We do not believe the strike can usefully be analysed in terms of personalities or a personalized conflict; but both men undoubtedly epitomized the positions which were taken up. Scargill's primary commitment to fight pit closures was not just a personal matter; he represented also the growing tide of concern that the achievements of the 1970s symbolized by the Plan for Coal were at risk. He also symbolized for many the defeat of the Heath government – as the leader of the Saltley pickets in 1972 in particular. The personalization of the dispute and his high public profile provided a secondary focus for the strike when it did come which the government must have been happy to accept.

TRADE UNIONS IN THE COAL INDUSTRY

Apart from the personality of its president, the structure, constitution, and internal politics of the NUM were all important factors in the strike, and a brief examination of these matters and of the other unions in the industry, the National Association of Colliery Overmen, Deputies and Shotfirers (NACODS) and the British Association of Colliery Managers (BACM) is necessary.

The National Union of Mineworkers was established under its present name and constitution in 1944. The central feature of its structure and constitution is federalism. As well as the national union, to which all members belong and which has its own constitution, there are nineteen separate areas, each having a constitution and each affiliated to the national union; NUM members are all also members of the area union to which their branch or lodge belongs. Areas have internal self-government and elect their own officials, and in practice have a considerable degree (and tradition) of autonomy; in particular they control their own, in some cases extensive, funds. Nearly all the areas represent geographical areas (not, incidentally, the same as the NCB's geographical divisions) but five 'areas' are in fact specialized sections of the membership, including the Colliery Officials and Staffs Area (COSA) and the Power Group.

As well as a tradition of federalism the NUM and its constituents have a long tradition of democracy, with the election of officials by secret pithead ballot and constitutional requirements for ballots prior to industrial action rarely found expressed in other union rule-books. The government of the NUM is ultimately in the hands of the Delegate Conference. Between sessions of the conference (which is normally annual, but may be specially convened ad hoc), 'the National Executive Committee [NEC] shall administer the affairs of the union and perform all duties laid down for it by resolution of conference, and it shall not at any time act contrary to, or in defiance of, any resolution of conference' (Rule 8). The Conference consists of delegates from the various area councils; the NEC is composed of national officers (the president, vice-president, and general secretary) who are elected by the entire membership, and area delegates. Although superficially the composition is similar, in fact the wide disparity in size of the various areas produces some over-representation of the smallest areas.[11] In addition the NEC members tend to be full-time area officials while Conference delegates are more likely to be rank-and-file activists. For these reasons the Delegate Conference was much more committed to the left than the NEC, a factor of some importance in the internal politics of the NUM during the strike.[12]

The provisions of the national and area rule-books on industrial action are complex; they were crucial to the course of much of the litigation during the strike. National industrial action is governed by Rule 43, which at the start of the strike provided that

> a national strike shall only be entered upon as a result of a ballot vote of the members taken in pursuance of a resolution of Conference, and a strike shall not be declared unless 55 per cent of those voting in the ballot vote in favour of such a strike.[13]

This rule applies to strikes only; other forms of industrial action can be sanctioned by the NEC. The overtime ban which began in November 1983 and continued throughout the strike was authorized in this way, and the propriety of such action was never questioned. However it is equally plain that no national strike could be called without a ballot – which was not held.

Each area has rules providing for the calling of industrial action within the area. Most require the holding of ballots and 55 per cent majorities for strike action; however Scotland, for instance, has no ballot requirement. Area action is subject to Rule 41 of the national rules, which requires the sanction of the NEC. The NEC duly gave sanction, initially to Yorkshire and Scotland on 8 March, and then to other areas and finally all areas. With the exception of Scotland, where the strike was held to be a lawful area action, legal challenges to the strike were successfully mounted on an area basis over the lack of a ballot majority, and within some areas also on the basis that in reality the dispute was a national strike called in breach of the requirements of National Rule 43 and not (as the NUM maintained) a series of area strikes validly sanctioned by Rule 41.

One other matter regarding the NUM requires mention. We have referred to the autonomy in practice of individual areas. This is reinforced by the considerable differences in tradition and background, and current circumstances, of the regions represented – such as the contrasting prospects and conditions in the rich and accessible East Midlands coal deposits as compared to the geologically difficult and declining Scottish and South Wales coalfields. As far as the East Midlands, especially Nottinghamshire, is concerned, the differences were reinforced even before the strike by a degree of distrust by miners from other areas of the successors of the men who were felt to have betrayed the 1926 strike by negotiating a separate agreement for a return to work, and whose breakaway union led by George Spencer MP split the ranks of mineworkers from 1926 until its collapse in 1937. The superficial parallels with the 1984–5 strike and its aftermath make the suspicions more readily understandable, but it is important to realize that they were there already – hence the early rush to picket out the Nottinghamshire pits when the strike began.[14]

Of the other two unions significantly represented in the coal industry, BACM, whose membership is drawn from management grades, played no part in the strike. Within the limits of the circumstances, its members attended for work throughout. NACODS, however, had a much more significant part. Its members include those responsible for key safety activities and the strict statutory regulations governing the operation of coalmines make it illegal to work underground without the presence of deputies drawn from grades represented by NACODS. In practical terms this gives NACODS the power to stop the industry. NACODS's rule-book requires a strike ballot and a two-thirds majority vote for any strike action. It held a ballot at the start of the strike and attained a majority vote for action, but less than the required percentage; its later, successful, ballot is referred to in Chapter 5.

THE LEGISLATIVE FRAMEWORK

The law impinged on the strike in three distinct ways. Most visible was the criminal law, the relevant provisions of which relating to picketing and the law of police powers to preserve order had changed very little in the decade preceding the strike. The operation of these powers had however been affected subtly but significantly by the impact of changes in the civil law – for example by the use of the Picketing Code of Practice to determine the maximum number of pickets the police would allow – and more sharply by developments in policing which are discussed in Chapter 4.

The area of the civil law most frequently invoked, and to most dramatic effect, was the largely judge-made law regulating the rights of individual trade union members against their unions. This issue had scarcely featured in litigation over previous disputes, and developments through legislation had only the most peripheral impact on its application. It was largely the special characteristics of the strike itself, combined with resourcefulness on the part of a small number of working miners and their supporters and an unusually innovative attitude displayed by some judges, which brought this aspect of the law to the fore, with the sequestration of the NUM's assets and the appointment of a Receiver.

The law regulating the civil liability of unions and their officials for organizing and prosecuting industrial action played almost no part in the strike until it neared its end, but the dramatic changes in its content during the five years before the strike and subsequently in the course of the strike exercised a powerful influence on events, not least the attitudes of the police.

Each of these aspects of the law needs to be examined briefly. What follows is necessarily only a bare outline of the law, with some indication as to its significance for the dispute. For fuller accounts reference should be made to one of the standard legal texts or to relevant journal articles on specific points.[15] The civil law is described in terms of English law; Scots law in these areas is broadly the same, and with one exception the civil actions brought during the dispute were all brought in England and Wales. There are important differences of detail between English and Scots criminal law, which we refer to in the text, and major differences in the system of law enforcement, which again are dealt with briefly below. It will be helpful to begin with the civil law, since recent developments here colour the analysis of the criminal law.

ENFORCEMENT OF UNION MEMBERS' RIGHTS

The law here can be quite simply and shortly stated, although in practice it is highly complex. The relationship between a union and each of its members is governed by a contract, the terms of which are derived from the union rule-book. Any member is entitled to enforce the rights conferred on him or her by the rule-book, for instance to benefit; the union too can in principle enforce members' obligations, for example to pay subscriptions, although in practice unions do not resort to litigation for this purpose.

This general principle is subject to certain technical legal problems which happily need not be expounded in detail here, since they influenced the form and procedures of the various actions brought during the strike rather than their substance.[16] In addition statutory restrictions on certain kinds of actions by members against their unions prior to 1971 have had a general influence by inhibiting the development of any tradition of members' taking actions against their union.

In the past the great majority of cases of union members' actions have concerned challenges to disciplinary action and disputes about eligibility for union office or the conduct of elections. In both these areas statute has recently clarified and extended members' legal rights.[17] Only very rarely has there been a challenge to a union's political or industrial actions.[18] Particularly significantly, there was no precedent at all before 1984 for the enforcement of judgements obtained by union members with which the union refused to comply.

If there was little experience of union members' resorting to law to prevent industrial action being taken in breach of the rules before 1984, there was even less of the remedies against unions which defied court orders. The most potent remedies are sequestration of the union's funds and the appointment of a Receiver. The former remedy had in principle been available for many years for disobedience to court orders. Because unions were until 1971 (and again between 1974 and 1982) largely immune from legal action by employers, sequestration was nearly unknown in practice, having been used only during the dockers' disputes under the Industrial Relations Act, 1971, and again in 1983 over the Stockport Messenger dispute; it had never been used in a case initiated by a union member. For technical reasons it was probably not possible to appoint a Receiver for a union before 1971;[19] in any event the NUM was the first union to suffer this fate.

CIVIL LIABILITY FOR INDUSTRIAL ACTION AND PICKETING

The structure of the law in this area is complex and confusing, largely for historical reasons. The liability of strike organizers and their unions was established and delineated during the second half of the nineteenth century by judges openly unsympathetic to organized labour. By the time of the land-mark *Taff Vale Railway* case in 1901, strike organizers and their unions were liable to be sued for calling virtually any kind of industrial action involving a breach of employees' contracts; peaceful picketing was treated as an actionable nuisance outside a statutory immunity that had been construed so narrowly as to be virtually meaningless, and various other forms of liability looked likely to be developed by the courts.

To this crippling liability the Asquith government responded by legislation. But the Trade Disputes Act, 1906, did not attempt to alter the substance of the common law, which is still today in many respects only marginally less rigorous than in 1901; instead it created statutory immunities for unions, and also for their officials pursuing industrial action within the limits laid down by the Act and in furtherance of a trade dispute.

The law remains based on a series of immunities or exceptions; confusion is compounded by the most recent changes being expressed in terms of exceptions to the exceptions. As well as conceptual difficulties, this approach has resulted in the debate about the law of strikes being focused on how much immunity a union should have, rather than (as is usually the case in a legal system based on positive rights) what a right to strike should entail. For completeness it should be mentioned that liability at common law is not affected by whether action is official or unofficial, or whether or not it is taken in conformity with the union's rules.

The high point of statutory immunity for strike action was reached under the 1974–9 Labour government; the Trade Union and Labour Relations Act, 1974 (TULRA), as amended in 1976, exempted unions as such from civil liability for industrial action, and gave wide immunity to officials organizing action in furtherance of a trade dispute. After several attempts by the Court of Appeal to restrict its application, the House of Lords in due course gave the law an interpretation in accordance with the parliamentary intention which all but removed the law as a significant constraint on the organizing of strike action and sympathetic or secondary boycotts.[20]

The incoming Conservative government made no secret of its intention to curtail union power. It is a moot point how far the realization of this intention has been facilitated by changes in the economic and political climate as distinct from changes in the law, but there can be no doubt that the legal changes have revolutionized the position. Although they were far from complete by the start of the miners' strike, the changes already in force exerted a profound influence on events and on how they were assessed by the strikers and the police.

The previous Conservative government's attempt to reform industrial relations law had gone badly wrong before it was cut short by the defeat of the government in February 1974. The next attempt displayed more subtlety and the hallmarks of careful long-term planning. The close interrelationship of the legislative changes with the general strategy apparently foreshadowed in the Ridley Report is clear.

Two Acts of relevance were passed in 1980. The Employment Act amended the statutory immunity for picketing, which had previously covered all purely peaceful picketing in furtherance of a trade dispute; henceforth only picketing at the pickets' own place of work was protected.[21] This does not mean, as is commonly believed, that all other forms of picketing are unlawful. However the Act expressly removed civil immunity from other forms of picketing (and from certain kinds of secondary action which might be taken in the course of a dispute). In practice it is difficult to envisage picketing which does not at least arouse fears that workers will be persuaded not to cross the picket line – which would normally be enough to obtain an injunction. Lastly, the Act gave the Secretary of State for Employment power to issue Codes of Practice with quasi-statutory force;[22] it was under this provision that the Code of Practice on Picketing was issued in 1980. It is not as such law, but section 3 provides that it can be taken into account whenever relevant in any legal proceedings. A number of paragraphs in the Code are of interest:

> 26. It is not the function of the police to take a view of the merits of a particular trade dispute. They have a general duty to uphold the law and keep the peace, whether on the picket line or elsewhere. The law gives the police discretion to take whatever measures may reasonably be considered necessary to ensure that picketing remains peaceful and orderly.
> 27. The police have *no* responsibility for enforcing the *civil* law . . . .
> 28. As regards the *criminal* law, the police have considerable discretionary powers to limit the number of pickets at any one place where they have reasonable cause to fear disorder. The law does not impose a specific limit on the number of people who may picket at any one place; nor does this Code affect in any way the discretion of the police to limit the number of people on a particular picket line . . . .
> 29. The main cause of violence and disorder on the picket line is excessive numbers . . . .
> 31. Large numbers on a picket line are also likely to give rise to fear and resentment amongst those seeking to cross that picket line even where no criminal offence is committed. . . . Accordingly pickets and their organisers should ensure that in general the number of pickets does not exceed six at any entrance to a workplace; frequently a smaller number will be appropriate. (Code of Practice, 1980; italics in original)

The other legislation in 1980 was the amendment to the Supplementary Benefits legislation affecting strikers' dependants foreshadowed by the Ridley Report.[23] Previously strikers were automatically disqualified from unemployment benefit and could claim supplementary benefit only for dependants or in cases of exceptional need. The amendment provided that in calculating dependants' needs it was to be assumed that a striker was receiving a prescribed amount of strike pay during the dispute; this amount minus a small 'disregard' is then deducted from dependants' benefits. The amount fixed for 1983–4 was £15 a week, rising to £16 in November 1984. The net result of this (and some further tightening of the exceptional needs rules) was that single strikers received no benefit and those with dependants a small fraction of the already minimal levels of benefit they would have received as longer-term unemployed.

Various attempts to obtain concessions or other benefits during the strike were usually rejected by the DHSS adjudicating authorities.[24] Some money was found from other sources, but the resentment caused by this aspect of the law, the real hardship it occasioned, and the extent to which it may have influenced strikers to act out of desperation in the later stages of the strike, should not be underestimated.

The Employment Act, 1982, made further changes, one of which is crucially relevant to the legal background to the strike. This key amendment was the ending of trade unions' immunity from civil liability. Section 14 of the Act removed the immunity for acts done by the union itself; section 15 extended liability to action authorized or endorsed by a 'responsible' person, including the president, general secretary, national executive, and in certain circumstances other officials or organs of the union.[25]

In the parliamentary debates on this part of the Bill the major concern was that employers would be able to bankrupt unions with huge damages claims; this possibility was foreshadowed and met in part by section 16, which sets a tariff of maximum awards of damages according to the size of the union membership. However in the event the effects have been markedly different. Employers are rarely interested in damages as a primary remedy; they want the action stopped. The possibility of injunctions against unions, and the consequent risk of fines (for which there is no statutory maximum) or sequestration of assets in the event of the injunction's being disobeyed, are the major weaponry of the new law. One result of the change has been an increasing willingness of the courts to grant injunctions; another has been to open up the possibility of others affected, including in the miners' strike working miners, pursuing injunctions over unlawful picketing or intimidation.

Further changes in the law were introduced by the Trade Union Act, 1984, primarily to remove statutory immunity from union-supported action taken without benefit of a secret ballot. This Act did not come into force until September 1984, and it was not clear whether it applied to strikes already in progress. In fact no attempt was made to rely on it in civil proceedings over the strike, and its relevance was largely in sharpening the political debate about the failure of the NUM to hold a strike ballot.

It may be helpful to summarize the civil law position as at the start of the strike. The organizing or calling of strike action, or inducing third parties to break contracts of employment (for example by not crossing the picket line) or otherwise to interfere with contractual rights by unlawful means are all actionable torts at common law, for which those affected can sue for damages or an injunction unless there is statutory immunity. A *quia timet* injunction can be obtained in anticipation of unlawful action, and the union can also be sued if it has authorized or endorsed the action directly or through a 'responsible person'. The statutory immunity will not apply where the alleged tort has been committed in the course of picketing other than peaceful picketing of the pickets' own place of work in furtherance of a trade dispute with their employer, nor will it apply to inducements to secondary blacking or boycotts outside the limited protection of section 17 of the Employment Act, 1980. As will become apparent from our narrative of the strike, the NUM was from the outset vulnerable to injunctions against most of the picketing at the suit of not only the NCB but also a number of other employers whose premises or employees were subjected to picketing. This is the background which makes the position of the police as described in the passages from the Code of Practice on Picketing quoted above so ambivalent.

One other aspect of the civil law, brought to prominence by an action by working miners in February 1985, is civil liability for the conduct of pickets.[26] Peaceful picketing of the pickets' work-place is probably not actionable in tort unless it involves trespass to the employer's property.[27] However any form of disorderly picketing, or picketing which obstructs access to premises, is likely to amount to the tort of nuisance, actionable at the suit of the employers. This was clearly the position well before 1984, but only since 1982 had it been possible to sue the union as organizer; moreover the removal of immunity for picketing not at the employees' place of work made it easier to argue for an injunction in many cases.

THE CRIMINAL LAW AND PICKETING

Apart from the very narrow range of peaceful picketing at the pickets' own place of work which has statutory protection, all picketing is subject to the general criminal law. The immunity given by section 15 of TULRA 1974 does not confer a *right* to picket, still less any ancillary rights such as to stop vehicles to speak to the occupants, and it may be overridden by the requirements of the police acting to preserve the peace.[28] All that it does is to declare lawful activities which might otherwise be criminal. By the same token picketing not conducted in the terms of the statutory immunity is not automatically criminal – like any other activity it remains lawful unless the participants can be shown to have committed a specific offence.

In practice, of course, the statutory immunity has a greater significance than a legal analysis would suggest, since it gives legitimacy to pickets and influences police behaviour accordingly; as we shall see, this happened during the miners' strike.

The picketing recognized as immune by TULRA is, since the 1980 amendment, confined to picketing for the purposes only of peacefully communicating information or peacefully persuading others to work or not to work, conducted in furtherance of a trade dispute by workers attending at or near their own place of work, or by their union officials accompanying them. There is no direct limitation of numbers, but aside from the indirect influence of the Code of Practice control is also achieved by the courts' readiness to infer a purpose beyond those permitted if numbers are larger than reasonably necessary for peacefully informing and persuading.[29]

The scope of the criminal law outside these narrow immunities is considerable. Naturally acts of violence against individuals, criminal damage to property, and significant incidents of collective disorder generally are matters dealt with by the general criminal law. Prosecutions for offences of varying degrees of seriousness in each of these categories were brought in respect of conduct on the picket line during the strike. However they represented a small minority of all criminal charges, especially in Scotland. Three offences commonly charged in the context of the picketing merit some discussion: obstruction of the highway, conduct likely to lead to a breach of the peace, and 'watching and besetting'.

Obstruction of the highway is an offence of considerable scope in any policeman's armoury. Although it is only a summary offence with the relatively modest maximum penalty of a £400 fine, it carries a power of arrest.[30] The elements of the offence, wilful obstruction and lack of lawful authority or reasonable excuse, are not difficult to prove. It has long been established that no intention to obstruct need be shown, and the obstruction need be only partial or even potential. Reasonable excuse has generally been construed as requiring the defendant's activity to be judged in relation to the primary purpose of the highway being that of passage, whether vehicular or pedestrian.[31] This is so open-ended in the context of a stationary activity such as picketing that the police effectively license pickets (outside the statutory immunity) by not enforcing the law strictly. This has operational advantages for the police and is not necessarily objectionable if the police use common sense and restraint, and maintain an even-handed approach. The law as such, however, must be of concern to anyone who values freedom to engage in peaceful picketing as a civil liberty.

Conduct which may give rise to a breach of the peace ranges widely from serious, deliberate attempts to provoke violence, to little more than the hurly-burly of an ebullient crowd. Not all such conduct is a criminal offence. The legal requirements (as far as England and Wales are concerned) are set out in section 5 of the Public Order Act, 1936; in 1987 this section was replaced by new and broader offences, the implications of which we examine in Chapter 9. As they were at the time of the strike, the elements of the offence were the use of threatening, abusive, or insulting words or behaviour with intent to provoke a breach of the peace, or (much more commonly charged) whereby a breach of the peace was likely to be occasioned. What is threatening, abusive, or insulting is a question of fact, as is the likelihood in the circumstances that a breach of the peace will result.[32] The term 'breach of the peace' itself is somewhat elastic, but it has recently been made clear by the Court of Appeal that some element of violence either to person or property must be involved.[33] The breach of the peace need not be the response of the person insulted – supporters of the 'verbal assailant' may be goaded to act by the verbal attack on their mutual adversary.

Translated to the picket line during a strike, breach of the peace offers a versatile artefact to police seeking to control the pickets. The shouting of 'scab' or other abuse or issuing threats to those crossing the picket line is a good example; as we shall see, during the strike some senior officers routinely used shouting 'scab' as a ground for arresting pickets, while others freely tolerated it. Practice differed not only from area to area but also from day to day in a manner which pickets could perceive only as random. Few aspects of policing show more clearly the range of discretion in maintaining order and enforcing the law, and we shall argue also that few show as sharply the damaging effects of officious or inconsistent policing.

The law on this point in Scotland is different: breach of the peace is a crime at common law covering a wide and loosely drawn range of conduct contrary to standards of good order or decency or tending to disturb the peace. It is the most heavily used instrument of public order control on the streets, and in the strike its use in some two-thirds of all charges was not unexpected (although there was less evidence of arbitrary and unpredictable use of the law in Scotland than in parts of England where heavy use of mutual aid brought members of several police forces to the same picket line, consecutively or simultaneously).

Before the strike few people can have heard of the offence of 'watching and besetting'. It had never since its enactment in 1875 been extensively used and within recent memory its use was virtually unknown. The full description of the offence is 'wrongfully' watching and besetting any place where a person works, lives, or 'happens to be' with a view to compelling that person to do something he has the lawful right not to do, or vice versa.[34] The offence has been interpreted to require at least that the conduct is independently unlawful (for example the tort of nuisance),[35] and its use has been circumscribed by the lack of a power of arrest, a matter remedied for England and Wales by the Public Order Act, 1986. The most common case in which it was used during the strike was for the picketing of working miners' homes, for which we regard it as useful and proper in principle. It was also used quite extensively in relation to picket lines, but by no means consistently.

Among the more serious offences invoked during the strike, here we need mention only riot and unlawful assembly, which were extensively used in respect of some of the major incidents during the strike, but with a spectacularly low conviction rate. This matter and its implications are best dealt with in the context of our discussion of the response of the courts (see Chapter 7).

POLICE POWERS

Control of picketing is less a question of what activities on the part of the pickets constitute criminal offences than of the exercise of police powers. This embraces arrest – in immediate importance the decision to arrest matters more than the decision whether the arrested person is guilty, which by its nature will not be taken until some time after the event. It also embraces the substantial preventive powers of the police, invested in them by virtue of their general duties.

The police (and indeed all citizens) are under a duty to prevent apprehended breaches of the peace, and to maintain freedom of passage on the public highway. In connection with the former duty the police may lawfully take such steps as they reasonably consider to be necessary to prevent a breach of the peace, provided it is imminent both in time and proximity. In connection with the latter there are particular powers to regulate traffic and a general power to prevent obstruction. The exercise of these powers is part of the execution of any police officer's duty. This has particular legal significance since it is an offence wilfully to obstruct a police officer in the execution of his duty.[36] Any deliberate act, even one otherwise lawful, which makes it more difficult for the officer to carry out his duty is sufficient; it need not be a physical obstruction.

This offence has been applied to a wide range of situations from drinking whisky to prevent an effective breathalyser test to refusing to reverse the wrong way down a one way street to make way for an ambulance.[37] In the context of picketing and breach of the peace, it covers refusal to obey the instructions of the police given in the execution of their duty to prevent a breach of the peace or an obstruction of the highway. The offence was first used in this way in the notorious case of *Duncan* v *Jones* in 1936, the first test case brought by the NCCL; a speaker's refusal to move to another site was held to be an offence where the officer instructing the move said that he believed that the speaker's use of the proposed site (outside an unemployed workers' centre) would lead to a breach of the peace. In fact the evidence for this belief was tenuous, and the case was an attempt to challenge a confidential ban on meetings outside centres for the unemployed imposed by the then Metropolitan Police Commissioner, Viscount Trenchard, but the facts as found by the magistrates prevented this issue from being properly aired in court. Since then the principle of the case has been applied in picketing situations to uphold a police instruction that there should be no more than two pickets on a gate, that pickets should not block an entrance by parading in a circle, and that all pickets should stay behind a police cordon while a bus carrying strike-breaking workers left the site.[38] The last case is particularly important because the effect of the police cordon was to eliminate all picketing at the crucial time, even though it was accepted that the pickets were within the statutory immunity. The duty to preserve the peace, the court observed, overrode the pursuit of an activity even if it was lawful.

A number of important practical points should be noted regarding obstructing the police. First, the courts allow the police the power to give orders on pain of arrest and conviction only where the orders are necessary to prevent a 'reasonably apprehended' breach of the peace, but in practice the courts are in no position to second-guess operational judgements on such matters, and so the police judgement is usually accepted at face value. Second, in the absence of a constitutionally protected right to picket there is a clear legal subordination of the pickets' freedom to the maintenance of order. Third, the cases do not differentiate whose fault the disorder would be as a factor restricting the discretionary powers of the police.

The implications of the scope of police powers and the offence of obstruction can be illustrated by the case of *Moss* v *McLachlan* (1985), an unsuccessful challenge to the legality of the turn-back policy of Nottinghamshire police during the strike (which we discuss in more detail on pp. 36 and 90). The pickets in that case were acting lawfully up to the time of being stopped, exercising their right to travel on the highway, and there was no evidence that they personally intended to act unlawfully; nevertheless their convictions were upheld.[39] This case serves to highlight that picketing is effectively conducted entirely at the discretion of the police. The wide powers of regulation and even prevention vest powerful discretion in the hands of the police, necessarily focusing attention on the way in which that discretion was exercised during the strike. This in turn leads us to the developments in police organization and training prior to the strike, which we consider in detail in the next chapter.

NOTES

1. More detailed accounts, from which we have drawn heavily for this section, are in Lloyd (1985), *Sunday Times* Insight Team (1985), Crick (1985), and particularly Adeney and Lloyd (1986). See also MacGregor (1986).
2. This may have had an important influence on the course of the strike. By and large the close-knit communities of the traditional mining villages in the older coalfields maintained more effective solidarity than those areas where miners who had moved into the area were spread thinly in established communities often some distance from the pit; the NCB skilfully exploited this factor in planning its 'return to work' campaign, especially in Derbyshire. Cf.

MacGregor (1986: 201–3; 324–6).

3. That is cash limits on the total of operating losses and interest and other charges in each year.
4. Interview quoted in Crick (1985: 88).
5. Select Committee Report (1982); Monopolies and Mergers Commission (1983).
6. A helpful summary of some of the arguments on this issue is given in Lloyd (1985: 29–31).
7. We do not suggest that the government and NCB were unaware of, or necessarily unsympathetic to, the wider economic or social considerations; indeed palliatives were offered, most importantly a guarantee of alternative employment for those displaced by the disputed pit closures who wished to stay in the industry.
8. *The Economist*, 27 May 1978; quoted in Adeney and Lloyd (1985: 73).
9. Adeney and Lloyd (1985: 72–4).
10. MacGregor (1986: 146–8).
11. Yorkshire, with one-third of the membership, is one area, as (in 1984) was Cumberland, with at that time one remaining pit. There is some weighting of representation but the NEC is too small for this to be fully effective.
12. These consequences (the most significant being the decision of a Special Delegate Conference on 19 April 1984 not to hold a national ballot) are discussed in Chapter 5.
13. The percentage needed to validate a strike was reduced to a bare majority by the April 1984 Special Delegate Conference. The rules were substantially revised in the wake of the strike: see Chapter 8, and Adeney and Lloyd (1986: 266–74).
14. For a fuller discussion of the political background within the NUM in Yorkshire in particular, see Crick (1985: chs 1 and 3). See also Allen (1981).
15. See e.g. Kidner (1983), Riddall (1984), Rideout and Dyson (1983), I.T. Smith and Wood (1986); for public order and police powers see S.H. Bailey, Harris, and Jones (1985: ch. 3) and Supperstone (1981). Useful articles include: on union members' rights, Ewing (1985); on the civil law, Bercusson (1980); on secondary picketing and secondary action, S. Evans (1983); on social security benefits, Partington (1980); on injunctions against unions, Ewing (1982); on strike ballots, Hutton (1984); and on tort actions during the strike, Benedictus (1985). On the police and criminal law see Bennion (1985), Kidner (1985), and Wallington (1985).
16. The problem is a rule (known from a nineteenth-century case in which it was formulated as 'the rule in *Foss* v *Harbottle*') which prevents individuals from challenging irregular decisions by trade union governing bodies unless the decision is outside the legal capacity of the union or directly affects some personal right of the member. Claims that the strike was in breach of the rules and challenges to disciplinary moves against working miners fell within the respective exceptions.
17. Sections 4 and 5 of the Employment Act, 1980, giving a statutory right not to be arbitrarily or unreasonably expelled from a union where a closed shop operates, and Part I of the Trade Union Act, 1984, requiring members of union executive committees to be elected by secret ballot.
18. A significant exception, ironically, was litigation between the Kent and Yorkshire areas of the NUM and the national president over the holding of a national ballot on incentive payments in 1977 (McIlroy 1985: 93–4).
19. Ewing (1985: 171).
20. See particularly *NWL Ltd* v *Woods* (1979) and *Express Newspapers Ltd* v *MacShane* (1980).
21. Section 16(1), amending the previous statutory provision, TULRA section 15. Union officials are allowed to accompany members on the picket line, and dismissed strikers may picket their former place of work. The section as such imposes no limits on numbers of pickets.
22. The Act also contained several other provisions not relevant to this analysis.
23. Social Security (No. 2) Act, 1980, section 6.
24. Mesher (1985).
25. Section 15 applies only to torts involved in organizing and calling industrial action; for torts such as nuisance or intimidation the union's liability can be much wider, depending on common law concepts of custom and practice.
26. *Thomas* v *NUM (South Wales Area)* (1985).
27. Wallington (1976); the 'probably' is because of a lingering doubt over the Court of Appeal decision to the opposite effect in *Lyons & Co* v *Wilkins* (1896).

28. See respectively *Broome* v *DPP* (1974) and *Kavanagh* v *Hiscock* (1974). The latter case was taken a stage further to uphold police actions in preventing miners travelling to picket lines during the strike in *Moss* v *McLachlan* (1985); see p. 141.
29. See Lord Reid's analysis in *Broome* v *DPP* (1974) at p. 90.
30. Highways Act, 1980, section 137(2). From 1 January 1986 the power of arrest became subject to the stricter preconditions of section 25 of the Police and Criminal Evidence Act, 1984, but in the context of a picket's refusal to move on, where a power of arrest is most useful, the law still sanctions arrest. This offence applies only in England and Wales, but in Scotland its absence is compensated for by the much broader offence of breach of the peace.
31. *Hubbard* v *Pitt* (1976); Wallington (1976). A case since the end of the strike makes a significant shift towards recognizing the legitimacy of peaceful picketing on the highway: *Hirst* v *Chief Constable of West Yorkshire* (1986).
32. *Brutus* v *Cozens* (1973) and *Jordan* v *Burgoyne* (1963) respectively.
33. *R* v *Howell* (1982).
34. There is also an offence, subject to the same conditions, of intimidating any person. Probably this requires at least a threat of violence. Because both offences are under the same section (section 7 of the Conspiracy and Protection of Property Act) statistics from the strike do not differentiate them, but a more detailed report given in a Parliamentary Answer suggests, surprisingly, that intimidation was scarcely charged at all during the strike: HC Debates, 31 January 1985, cols *231–2*.
35. *Ward, Lock & Co* v *OPAS* (1906); see Bennion (1985) on this but also the remarks of Scott J in *Thomas* v *NUM (South Wales Area)* (1985) at p. 18.
36. Police Act, 1964, section 51; Police (Scotland) Act, 1967, section 41. In Scotland this offence is regarded as confined to physical obstruction: *Curlett* v *McKechnie* (1938). Although the police frequently arrest people for obstructing them, there was until the coming into force of section 25 of the Police and Criminal Evidence Act, 1984 (on 1 January 1986) no such power: *Wershof* v *Metropolitan Police Commissioner* (1978). However the police could exercise the same common law power to prevent a breach of the peace by arresting, instructions having failed to produce results.
37. *Dibble* v *Ingleton* (1972) and *Johnson* v *Phillips* (1975).
38. See respectively *Piddington* v *Bates* (1960), *Tynan* v *Balmer* (1967), and *Kavanagh* v *Hiscock* (1974).
39. If the police can legally prevent lawful acts by prospective pickets, it follows that they can similarly restrain those seeking to cross picket lines – a point to which we must return in due course. See also, on the duties of the police to prevent a breach of the peace, *R* v *Chief Constable of Devon and Cornwall* (1981).

4

Background to the strike: police and policing

Two interrelated aspects of the recent development of policing are examined in this chapter: the weakening of the tripartite structure of accountability and the shifting emphasis in policing, and police training and organization, on the prevention of disorder. Both aspects assumed a high visibility during the strike, but both had undergone significant changes which were exposed to view by the enormous strains which the policing of the strike imposed on the system and on individual officers.

A detailed history of these matters would be out of place, but fortunately we can refer readers to a range of excellent recent publications in a field which until recently had been sadly neglected by most academic disciplines.[1] Here the focus is upon developments which help to make clear the issues of policing which are of greatest concern. The analysis of the structure of policing relates only to England and Wales; the Scottish system has important differences to which we refer shortly, and suffered less trauma from the strains of the dispute.

THE STRUCTURE OF POLICE

In this century there has been four Royal Commission Reports on the functions and practices of the police, each of which throws some light on the public perception of police activities and beliefs and on the reasons for the organizational changes that have taken place.[2] The first, the Report of the Royal Commission on the Duties of the Metropolitan Police (1908), includes an interesting comparison between the independence of the police constable and the total subjection to authority of the private soldier. 'The police force', it said, 'in its organisational structure is quite unlike the army which does its work through groups of units . . . and the responsibility of the private soldier is reduced to such a point that he becomes little more than an automatic "machine".' This comparison is of some importance in an understanding of the current arguments about police organization and we shall return to it later. At this point it is sufficient to note that the comparison was made eighty years ago at the start of the long haul to achieve a reasonable degree of police accountability.

A second Royal Commission was appointed in 1928 not to review the heavy police control of the industrial and political disturbances of the time but to consider the malpractices in arrest, detention, and investigation that had been revealed by the case of Miss Savidge.[3] The members of the Commission accepted the argument that the abuses that had undoubtedly taken place were due to occasional departure from the normal high standards of police behaviour. It concluded that the conduct, tone, and efficiency of the police were well established. Citizens themselves must do everything in their power to remove all avoidable causes of friction and misunderstanding.[4]

This emollient report, which laid upon the citizen the duty to maintain good relations with the police, helped to delay for thirty years any further consideration of priorities in police functions, despite the confrontations between the police and large bodies of citizens during the unemployment marches and public disturbances caused by fascist demonstrations in the 1930s. In the exhausted stability of the post-war years these were forgotten or pushed aside, for the next Royal Commission was set up in 1960 as the result of disturbing events which seemed to call in question the wide power with which chief police officers could determine their policies and carry out their duties without rendering an account of what they did. Between 1956 and 1959 chief officers in Cardiganshire, Brighton, and Worcester had been arraigned not only for maladministration but also for criminal offences.[5] The Chief Constable of Nottingham was sacked by his Watch Committee and reinstated by the Home Secretary. In the House of Commons the Home Secretary himself was criticized for trying to buy off a litigant who had brought an action against a Metropolitan police officer. During the parliamentary exchanges that followed these events the appointment of a Royal Commission was announced.

The Commissioners, while acknowledging the low morale of the police and making a gesture of publishing an interim report on police pay and conditions, remained convinced that public anxiety about increases in crime was the starting-point in their discussions.[6] But the *terminus ad quem* was the construction of a satisfactory system of accountability and control that would allay public unease while reassuring the police themselves that their necessary discretion would not be unduly fettered. In their final report in 1962, in the development of their argument about the appropriate measures to be taken, they noted that the 'problem of controlling the police can be restated as the problem of controlling Chief Constables'.[7] About how this should be done they seemed to be in two minds. The fact that crime was largely local suggested local accountability and control but there was already a strong move towards larger units of organization evidenced in the proposals for regional crime squads. Besides, as the report puts it, 'local forces, all the while diminishing in number, have come, in modern times to assume the character of a nation-wide police service' (para 41). Hedging their bets, the Commissioners recommended a central unit to provide technical and managerial assistance while advocating as the constitutional base for the police service a local structure and administration based on existing counties. A powerful note of dissent from Dr A.L. Goodhart put forward arguments for central or national control that cannot be lightly dismissed. He noted, among other things, that local organization did not necessarily mean local control or accountability; if provincial forces were to be made constitutionally accountable that must mean that they should answer to Parliament through the Home Secretary. In the event, the Police Act, 1964, was modelled on the recommendations of the majority of the Commission.

The remodelled tripartite structure of governance and control which was now formulated, of local government, central government, and the police themselves, showed a further distinct shift in favour of central government and chief officers of police at the expense of local police authorities. Yet no central *responsibility* was built into the system to match the shift in power. Indeed the formal responsibility for policing remained firmly in the hands of the police authorities: section 4 of the Act states quite simply, 'It shall be the duty of the police authority for every police area . . . to secure the maintenance of an adequate and efficient police force for the area'. But the subordinate clauses in the syntax of the Act show how strong an influence was intended for central government and how extensively the powers of the local police authorities necessary to carry out their responsibilities were thereby circumscribed. Thus the appointment of chief constables, their deputies, and assistants lies in the hands of the local police committees under section 5, which also empowers them to require such an officer to retire in the interests of efficiency. In each case however the Home Secretary has the final say in approving the appointment or requirement, and indeed he can himself institute a procedure leading to a requirement to retire; before doing so he must hear representations from the officer concerned, but not from the authority.[8] If a police committee is dissatisfied with any aspect of the policing of its area, section 11 enables it to ask the chief constable to submit a report on the matter. The chief officer, however, may appeal to the secretary of state who will decide whether such a report is necessary or desirable. But if the secretary of state himself wishes to be satisfied on any policing matter, either within the general responsibility of the local police committee or outside it, he may call for a report which the chief officer is bound to submit.[9]

The ambiguities and weaknesses in the statutory provisions for the management of police forces went largely unremarked for some time after the implementation of the 1964 legislation. County administrations saw little reason to criticize the policing of their areas so long as there were no open conflicts between local interests and the views of chief constables. Alterations in local authority boundaries, however, and the amalgamation policies of central government changed the nature of these local interests by introducing the problems of urban policing to the consideration of hitherto untroubled county authorities. Two organizations, therefore, the Association of Metropolitan Authorities and the Association of County Councils, turned their attention to the proper role of the police authority. The (unpublished) report of a seminar in 1977 organized jointly by these associations revealed some slight concern about the strength of a police authority's position in relation to the wide discretion of its chief officer. The matter was taken further by the Merseyside Police Committee which reviewed the history of the 1964 legislation and, in particular, the pronouncements of ministers during its passage through Parliament. Thus the Home Secretary (Henry Brooke) had listed as legitimate questions which an authority might address to its chief police officer:

> the allocation of the force between crime prevention and traffic policing.
> . . . It could ask about the extent of police protection provided in a certain
> district and it could call for a report and comment on it. . . . What the
> police authority cannot do . . . is to bombard the chief constable with
> innumerable questions about exactly how a particular police constable is
> to act on a certain beat.[10]

This suggests that Parliament wished to distinguish between operational
matters of a major and a minor character. In matters of importance, it would
seem, the local authority had some part to play. This view was reiterated by
a later Home Secretary (Merlyn Rees) in 1978. In answer to a Parliamentary
Question about the function of the police authority in the determination of
local police policy, he had this to say:

> The chief constable has the direction and control of his force; local policing
> is his responsibility. On the other hand, the Police Act in no way inhibits
> discussion of operational issues between the chief constable and his police
> authority, whether in the context of a review of the resources or more
> generally. The chief constable is generally accountable to his police
> authority for his policy.[11]

This strong view of the power of oversight of the police authority has in
recent years been subtly and progressively modified so that most chief
constables and many politicians would now restrict the police authority's
remit to the determination of manpower and the provision of adequate funds.
This process can be seen in the gradual enlargement of the concept of 'operational' matters (a word, incidentally, not used at all in the 1964 Act) which
are the preserve of the chief constable, from being the converse of 'policy'
to embracing it. By the time of the miners' strike the view of chief constables
on this point was probably in accord with that expressed by the Chief
Constable of South Yorkshire in his report to the South Yorkshire police
authority on the strike:

> One of the purposes of the Police Act 1964 is to maintain a distinction
> between operational matters, which are defined to be the responsibilities
> of Chief Constables, and administrative and financial responsibilities,
> which are under the control of police authorities and the Home Secretary.
> (South Yorkshire Police 1985: 107)

The reference to 'responsibilities' of police authorities, whether precisely
chosen or not, is singularly apt, since, as we shall see, even in the attenuated
areas allotted to them, their powers and even their influence were quickly
nullified by the pressures of the strike. But well before then, the writing was
on the wall, especially in the conurbations. The early 1980s saw a serious
decline in relationships between the chief constable and his police committee
on Merseyside in the aftermath of the 1981 Toxteth riots, and in Greater
Manchester following the election in 1981 of a Labour administration
committed to an active role in policing policy and opposed on many matters
of policing to their outspoken chief constable. In London, where the
particular circumstances of the capital have always been held to justify the

Home Secretary's dual responsibility as the police authority as well as the representative of central government, an increasing anxiety among a number of London borough councils, as well as the Greater London Council, over the services provided by the police, led to a proliferation of police monitoring and information units, intended by their progenitors as the first step towards instituting the democratic local accountability of the Metropolitan Police. As police chiefs railed against what they saw to be sectional, politically motivated interference by local representatives who professed to be seeking no more than a right on behalf of the communities they represented to influence the tone and priorities of policing, it was already clear that the situation was at danger point.

A parallel reformulation of tripartite responsibility had been essayed in Scotland in the wake of the 1962 Royal Commission. The legislation – initially and rather insultingly a Schedule to the English Act, later codified in the Police (Scotland) Act, 1967 – reflects significant differences in the legal framework of policing. In particular, the decision to prosecute has since the establishment of professional police been in the hands of the Lord Advocate (a Minister of the Crown) and his staff of Procurators-Fiscal. The latter have extensive theoretical powers to direct police investigations into crime (almost never exercised) as well as a practical veto on criminal proceedings. The 1967 Act imposes no equivalent on the police authorities of the general duty on their English counterparts to maintain an adequate and efficient force; but the specific duties, functions, and powers, and their circumscription by the powers of the Secretary of State for Scotland, are essentially the same.

By comparison with England and Wales, the constitutional arrangements in Scotland have survived relatively unscathed. It is an open question how far this reflects lesser expectations of power amongst police authorities, and fewer of the problems of inner-city conflict and alienation between police and sections of the community. Perhaps a combination of these factors enabled a greater consensus to be maintained north of the border on policing methods and priorities. During the coal strike, the arrangements for mutual aid were on a lesser scale and caused less serious problems institutionally.[12]

As we have seen, members of the Willink Commission, seeing the need for some sort of control over police activity, thought that this could best be done by controlling chief constables. The discretion of subordinate officers as they exercised their function of law enforcement was not directly addressed largely because the sweep of this discretion had never been clearly defined (though comfortable myths abounded). Two much-quoted cases made both negative and positive statements that were strong in eloquence but weak in a fine delineation of a difficult constitutional idea: the absolute power of every constable to enforce – or, more significantly, not to enforce – the law. Thus in *Fisher* v *Oldham Corporation* (1930) it was held that a constable is not the servant of any organ of government. More resoundingly and more positively, in the second case Lord Denning declared that the constable's authority 'is original, not delegated and is exercised at his own discretion, by virtue of his office'.[13] In a modern bureaucratic system of government this huge autonomy causes problems of legitimacy. In some respects, section 48 of the Police Act, 1964, seems to set matters straight. The provisions of this section make each chief constable responsible for any wrongs done by his subordinates.[14]

This is logical enough, since they must obey his instructions or submit to his discipline if they do not. There is no ambiguity about this definition of the relationship between chief officers and their subordinates.[15]

Yet the vagueness of the concept of the enforcement of law (and, by implication, of its non-enforcement) together with the fact that, for a good part of his working day, the constable operates on his own – or only in pairs – weakens the force of this part of the legislation. Chief officers have not therefore had signal success in using the provisions of the 1964 Act to punish or deter the misconduct of their officers; nor have they been able significantly to restrict their discretion. Besides, the statute which legislated for the submission of the police constable to the discipline and control of his superiors redressed the balance by defining in fairly wide terms the protection offered to him in his encounters with ordinary citizens. Section 51 of the 1964 Act, replacing and to some extent broadening the previous nineteenth-century law,[16] creates offences of assaulting, resisting, or obstructing a constable in the execution of his duty. Although these are not new offences, their grouping in the Police Act of itself served a symbolic purpose in raising their profile in the eyes of the police themselves. The wide interpretation of this provision in respect of obstruction in particular now enables even lawful activities recognized as such by statute to become subject to police prohibition and licensing, thereby offering the possibility of extensive police control by the arrest of citizens in the street, if it can be shown that a breach of the peace was reasonably anticipated. Commentators have (rightly in our view) expressed increasing concern at the ready extension of the law by judicial decisions to a point where 'nothing less than a duty to co-operate with the police is required of the citizen'.[17] We shall see how bitterly this 'because I say so' policing was resented by those who were subjected to it during the coal dispute.

POLICING AND PUBLIC DISORDER

Although the Police Act was generally thought to establish a sound constitutional framework for an important public service, there was, as yet, scant knowledge of what this service really was and who was served by its operations. There were, of course, myths about the fight against crime, matched by complaints when the fight involved questionable methods of obtaining evidence or heavy-handedness in procedures for arrest and search. The range of police activities was, however, not adequately explored in any official inquiry until the Royal Commission on Criminal Procedure which reported in 1981. However the concentration on criminal procedure in the terms of reference of that Commission did not encourage extensive consideration of other police activities, such as their crowd control or public order functions or their provision of social assistance. Yet, in the last twenty years or so, there has been an explosion of information, not only about what police officers actually do but also about the reality of what is called crime.

One well-known police study, backed by others, revealed that police officers on routine patrol do not actually 'do' very much at all, for a great deal of time is spent in watching and waiting for something to turn up.[18]

Since this relative inactivity, while an important part of police duties, is tedious, it is understandable that any excuse is sufficient to undertake more significant operations like stopping people in the street, checking cars, joining in any chase that may be taking place, and so on. Such police initiative may create the usual street crimes of obstruction or assault, but it rarely prevents or detects the more serious offences which would remain invisible if they were not reported to the police by members of the public, principally by the victims of the offences themselves. Thus high crime rates may reflect nothing more than better communication between the police and the public, together with some pressure from insurance companies who are reluctant to meet claims for theft or burglary unless they have been reported to the police. It is the knowledge of this contribution by members of the public to the creation of crime that has been one of the most important factors in the recent reassessment of police functions and responsibilities. For the 'fight against crime' has been shown not to be a matter for the police alone; it is an enterprise shared by police officers and citizens who play the major part in the construction of the crime figures. This limitation of police importance in the discovery of crime and the difficulties experienced in the detection of all save the most serious offences may have helped to persuade police officers to accept other tasks. The 'social assistance' spoken of by the Willink Commission had, of course, been canvassed for many years. Indeed a *Times* leader in 1908 claimed that the policeman in London was an integral part of its social life, 'in many a back street and slum he not merely stands for law and order, he is the true handyman of our streets, the best friend of the mass of people who have no other counsellor or protector'.[19] But the population of the streets, in the north at least, were wary of this social role and responded to it with uneasy and grudging suspicion.[20] At a later date the expansion of the 999 emergency telephone system extended police helpfulness well beyond the 'dangerous and perishing classes'. There are many millions of calls upon the time and energy of police officers; but much of this work seems to many of them to be trivial and unsatisfying. It is usually given a low priority in the ranking of jobs to be done. Not so that other function which the Metropolitan Police was, in 1829, established to perform – the maintenance of the degree of public order and tranquillity that is required for stable government.

Large-scale political and social protests took place in the United Kingdom, as they did elsewhere, in the 1960s and 1970s. As police organization and training were adapted to meet the needs of the time, some police officers undertook their new tasks of policing these activities with enthusiasm, for they gave to uniformed officers some of the excitement which was thought to be the prerogative of the CID. Indeed in most police training establishments, practice in the 'trudge and wedge' which is intended to separate elements in a riotous demonstration gave both recruits and observers some impression of the strength, cohesion, and power of a large, uniformed police presence moving forward together. Such developments in training and the social and political agitation that brought them about compelled many police forces to find not only new skills but also new stereotypes to supplant, for the uniformed officer at least, the 'villains' of earlier days. These stereotypes derive not only from their own experiences and mythology but also from the enemies put before them, from time to time, by popular fears, by the media, or by politicians. Thus communists, leftists, and subversives of all sorts find their place in a hierarchy of awkward citizens who may have to be contained on occasion if their assemblies are thought to be unstable or threatening.

The increasing importance of public order concerns in police planning and organization is evident in the formation of special units for deployment in emergencies. The first essay in this regard, in 1965, was the creation of the Special Patrol Group of the Metropolitan Police, a headquarters unit specially trained and held in constant readiness for rapid deployment in emergencies. At first – and perhaps with tongue in cheek – their function was explained as being an aid to crime control, for example in response to reports of serious robberies. Their employment in the restraint of crowds or control of street violence was more frequent. Similar units were set up in many provincial forces. There were, however, disadvantages in the use of such highly specialized groups. Kitted out as they were, for riot control, they became feared and hated, so that their use sparked off complaints and even counter-violence.[21] Besides, they used up a manpower reserve that could be ill spared from other police work. A more flexible unit, first introduced in the early 1970s and extended to all police forces in the 1981–2 reforms of public order training, is the Police Support Unit (PSU) – made up of two (occasionally three) 'serials' each of ten constables and a sergeant, headed by an inspector. Each unit has transport, special riot control equipment such as short and long shields and NATO helmets; each trains for two or three days each month; each is summoned for duty together and goes into action together. But when not employed on PSU training or activity the unit becomes its constituent parts, on normal duty on the streets, in patrol cars, or at the station. It is an ingenious use of resources. Forces in need of aid from a neighbour – or further afield – calculate the strength required in terms of these units. They are ready equipped with transport for the purpose and, of course, with the pride and purpose of a group that is trained and activated together. In such units individual discretion should have no part to play. Each constable is under orders so that the contrast between the constable and the private soldier, so clearly expressed in 1908, should no longer exist when the PSU has been called into being. Manifestly these units have come to stay. They have shown themselves to be efficient, as we shall see in the account of events during the miners' dispute; to what extent their existence will bring about a more permanent change in the attitudes and political posture of the police will depend upon the economic and social forces that are at work in the body politic. These will determine whether crime detection, crime prevention and social assistance, or the maintenance of public order come first in the police agenda.

RESPONSES TO INDUSTRIAL ACTION

In the 1960s and early 1970s the most frequent source of public protest was political rather than industrial. The issue of nuclear arms brought many people into the streets while activities of the National Front and the opposition to them caused marches and processions to be banned, re-routed, or contained. In all of these circumstances, heavy police resources were mobilized. From the early 1970s, however, the unrest generated by economic policies of restraint together with disturbing changes in the industrial structures of the country reintroduced to chief officers their function of law enforcement in the picketing and demonstrations that frequently accompany strikes and lock-outs.

In February 1972 a pay claim by the National Union of Mineworkers led to a complete shut-down of the coalfields. The dispute was effectively ended by the police failure to maintain free passage to the coking plant at Saltley in Birmingham.[22] Tens of thousands of miners and their supporters assembled at the gates; on the police side the muster was never more than 800 officers. The Chief Constable of Birmingham, anxious for the safety of his men, asked for the gates to be shut since he could no longer guarantee to protect the plant. Miners and police withdrew and the government, alarmed by the threat to electricity supplies, agreed to arbitration over the miners' pay demands. Since the reason for this defeat, as police and government thought the Saltley incident to be, was the failure to mobilize mutual aid effectively, the Association of Chief Police Officers and the Home Office consulted together and agreed that if, in any police emergency, mutual aid on a large scale seemed to be necessary, there must be some special mechanism for the co-ordination of police requests for help and for the provision of that help. Neither the chief officers nor the Home Office had a permanent organization in mind. What was envisaged was the setting up of a temporary headquarters, whether at the instance of the chief constables, the Home Office, or the Chief Inspector of Constabulary is not entirely clear. This office or headquarters would be directed by the current President of the Association of Chief Police Officers, who would himself be advised by the Home Office and the Chief Inspector. A small temporary staff would be lodged at New Scotland Yard (which is readily accessible to Home Office officials and the Inspectorate staff). The new arrangements, not the subject of any statutory enactment, were given the title National Reporting Centre (NRC).[23]

Mutual aid between police forces has been provided for by law since 1890 but its use and scope had not been clearly visible until the present decade.[24] Indeed until 1964, police officers only had the status of constable (and thus the power of arrest) for their own and adjoining police areas. The legislation (now section 14 of the 1964 Act) provides for bilateral arrangements, leaving the Home Secretary a reserve power to direct a chief constable to furnish aid if it is not offered voluntarily, and also empowers the Home Secretary to settle disputes about payment by the receiving authority. The need for more than bilateral mutual aid had not been seriously anticipated at the time of the Willink Commission. Because the Commission found it unnecessary to address the details of the question, two further erosions of police authorities' powers became possible when the NRC was conceived. The retention by the Home Secretary of ultimate financial adjudication was crucial in removing local financial influence and undermining budgetary sanctions; and the wording of the 1964 Act enabled the NRC to operate without any reference to or input from the police authorities or their representatives. Indeed, at no time during the creation of the NRC were the police authorities brought into the discussion about the necessity for this development, nor were they even notified of the decisions reached.

There were a number of national disputes in the years following Saltley: a second miners' strike, a road haulage dispute, a dispute in the building industry, and stoppages by local government employees and firemen.[25] The consequence of these disputes, however, was not so much public disorder as the disruption of industries and public services. Chief constables therefore had no need to flex the muscles of their developing organization for the maintenance of public order, except perhaps during the Grunwick dispute of 1976–8, the circumstances of which were more overtly political than any of the others that had gone before.[26] Thousands of pickets, who had no connection with the work-force, gathered to claim the right of the employees of the company to join a trade union. Political passions ran high and the control of those who tried to stop the passage of buses carrying non-union employees could be effected only by very large numbers of police officers. Many of them, however, and certainly many chief constables, believed that the massive demonstrations seen in this dispute were untypical. Whether or not this was so, the conflicts made a significant contribution to the political climate in which the 1980 picketing legislation was put forward.

The steel strike of 1980 came closer to the model of picketing and policing that most senior police officers had in mind. In this dispute picketing was country-wide, since the Iron and Steel Trades Confederation believed that stock-holders as well as steelworks should be picketed to prevent the movement of steel. But the scale of disorder was not great. Indeed some senior police officers expressed the opinion that the more violent and bitter forms of confrontation which did take place were associated with the visits of prominent politicians to areas where the strike was dominant; South Wales and South Yorkshire were cases in point. As in the later coal strike, South Yorkshire bore the brunt of the disturbances. There, the steelworkers in the state-owned sector of the industry sought to persuade those in the private sector to join them. There was heavy picketing of the principal private steelworks (Hadfields) in Sheffield. At one point, the employees of this firm agreed to join the strike, although they soon abandoned this position and returned to work. The decision to join the strike was seen by some to be another defeat for the police and the strategy of the Chief Constable of South Yorkshire came in for adverse comment. He was criticized, too, for refusing to move about 400 pickets who had blocked off a street in Sheffield at the approach to the Hadfields plant. In a report to his police committee, however, the chief constable gave a masterly account of his stewardship, pointing out that the gates of Hadfields had been closed not because the police had been unable to defend them but because the employees themselves had voted to join the strike. About the charge that he had countenanced obstruction of the roadway, he said that 400 pickets had been allowed to block a single road in Sheffield because the workers whose movement they wished to stop had already gone into the steel plant and

> as they were passive and the workers had entered the premises, a decision was taken not to try to move them. This, in my view, was sensible police

strategy and permitted the breach of a relatively minor law in preference to creating violent scenes. For a period of half-an-hour, one of hundreds of streets in Sheffield was blocked and all around the public travelled unhindered and in peace. (South Yorkshire Police 1980: App. F, p. 5)

Throughout the thirteen weeks of this dispute there were 159 arrests in South Yorkshire, most of them for obstruction or breach of the peace. There were no custodial sentences handed down for offences connected with the dispute; fines and conditional discharges satisfied the courts in this area.[27] There was no commissioning of the National Reporting Centre although the then Chief Constable of South Yorkshire, John Brownlow, on his own initiative, requested and received assistance from seven neighbouring police forces. Some Police Support Units were deployed but not in riot gear. This dispute ended before the first Employment Act was on the statute book. It was, therefore, different not only in degree but also in kind from the coal dispute that followed it, when legislation was available to the National Coal Board for relief.[28]

The relative success of the South Yorkshire (and other) police in maintaining order and access during the steel strike should not be seen as having completely removed the disquiet in police and government circles about the ability to cope with mass picketing or disorder and maintain the peace at all times. The Hadfields incident must have kindled memories of the deep scar of Saltley; it was to be more sharply recalled very shortly afterwards during an outbreak of rioting in the St Paul's district of Bristol in April 1980. Sparked off by a police raid on a cafe, the riot caught the police unprepared, and the chief constable had to authorize the temporary withdrawal of his hopelessly outnumbered men until reinforcements could be obtained from neighbouring forces.[29] In police and government eyes these incidents were defeats. A characteristic of much of the policing of the miners' strike was a determination that there should be no more defeats.

As we have already noted, the Conservative government, returned to office in 1979, had a mandate to curtail trade union immunities. Large-scale picketing was one of the first targets for legislative restraint. The question was whether picketing numbers should be restricted by tight legal definition of admissible numbers or whether and to what extent the police should be used to marshal and control whatever number of pickets and their supporters might gather at a picketed plant or institution. The Select Committee on Employment discussed this matter with a number of chief constables in February 1980, while the steel strike was still in progress. The exploration of the problems posed for the police by industrial disputes (and the picketing that might accompany them) throws shafts of light on the issues raised by the coal dispute. The chief constables were agreed that the law as it stood, that is the criminal law, was 'sufficiently firm and clear to enable the police to maintain order'. Difficulties sometimes arose because 'ordinary persons on strike or picketing believe they can mass and literally prevent people and vehicles doing things they have the right to do in law'. But these difficulties would be overcome if trade union members were instructed in their behaviour as pickets. This had been done by the National Union of Mineworkers at the time of the 1974 strike and few problems arose for the police at that time. Then one of the chief officers, John Woodcock, reflected on the matter of mass picketing:

> One should not first of all imagine that on occasions when one has large numbers of pickets there is a lawless situation. Quite frequently there are occasions when pickets are there in large numbers and all is peaceful . . . they are sometimes there for comradeship or solidarity.

Among the police chiefs present there was agreement that large crowds could be intimidatory, but that police powers and, often, the good sense of the mass pickets made police control effective. Sir Phillip Knights added:

> we have a responsibility to enforce the law and also a responsibility to maintain public order. A balance sometimes has to be struck between the two. That is a very difficult balance to strike sometimes, but it is done with all sincerity by any chief officer of police faced with that situation.[30]

Pressed further by the members of the committee to pronounce on the lawfulness of mass picketing, the chief constables, although seeming a little harassed by the questioning, maintained that mass pickets might *become* provocative if the *conduct* of people, as pickets or as demonstrators, were to be such that there was danger to people or property.

As we have seen, when the employment legislation took final shape, the determination of picketing numbers was left in the hands of the police, although the Code of Practice on Picketing rapidly came to be regarded as authority for imposing a maximum of six official pickets. Initial unwillingness by employers to make use of their new civil remedies meant that picketing regulation and control remained a matter of policing. As a rule this posed no problem; industrial disputes were few and short-lived and police attitudes to intervention in the expression of industrial disagreements were relaxed if not distant.[31] The dispute between Eddie Shah, owner of the *Stockport Messenger*, and the print unions in the autumn of 1983 obscured this truth for the police and for the public. But when it was over, policing returned to the normality of crime prevention and problems of small-scale public order.

As the threat of unemployment reduced the incidence of strikes in the two or three years before the coal dispute, its reality had a considerable part to play in the riots of 1981 in Toxteth, Brixton, and Moss Side. Here, police officers were faced with crowds who, for the time being, had totally withdrawn their consent from the institutions of government, from the police, and from most of the rest of society. Even riot shields, NATO helmets, and well-rehearsed police formations and tactical manoeuvres seemed to be insufficient to combat the violence which occurred at some stages in the Toxteth disturbances. CS gas was therefore used for the first time in mainland Britain. For the police, the inner city riots of 1981 could well have reinforced the opinions expressed by senior officers in their discussions with the members of the Select Committee little over a year before, that the policing of industrial disputes did not make the same demands as the policing of riotous assemblies and demonstrations and even football crowds. Yet the experience of the riots and the developments in organization and management which they forced upon the police were largely instrumental in making effective the police control of the coalfields during the twelve months of the miners' strike.

There were, however, other consequences which have developed in counterpoint to the main theme of increased organization and efficiency for all police forces. Lord Scarman, called in to head a public inquiry into the disturbances in April 1981, reported on the growing alienation of the black populations in run-down inner cities. He drew attention to the lack of communication between police institutions and community organizations and made proposals for remedying the situation.[32] These were accepted by the government and incorporated into the body of legislation governing the structure and functions of the police.

The more significant response to the experience of the riots was in the reappraisal of organization, training, and tactics which swiftly followed. Lord Scarman's Report recommended a review of public order training among other and more positive proposals for improving the capabilities of the police in inner city areas. His recommendation was not further particularized, and he was in any case probably pushing an open door.[33] The Home Office, together with the chief constables through their association, ACPO, took up the initiative. Within a short period, the institution of PSUs had been extended to all police forces; by the beginning of 1984 just over 10 per cent of all serving police officers were members of a unit, a high proportion given the restricted recruiting categories of young, fit males with sufficient police experience. Riot equipment was more extensively provided. Most important, in effective secrecy broken only subsequently by a forced disclosure in the course of the Orgreave riot trial in 1985, an ACPO committee prepared a Tactical Options Manual setting out a range of 'manoeuvres' and general tactics for controlling and repressing disorder. The issue of the manual in 1982 – on a very restricted circulation to the most senior officers only – marked the consummation of the process of redirecting police methods from the individual-oriented tradition to that of the team, from the minimum profile to the maximum, towards the readier use of defensive and offensive equipment, and from the reactive to the proactive. Parts of the manual are still secret, despite Police Federation protests, but those which have become known describe manoeuvres of an essentially military character involving formations of long and short shield serials and mounted police breaking up and driving back groups of demonstrators and affording cover for snatch squads to undertake arrests. These manoeuvres include one headed 'show of force', describing the initial entry of formations of officers with long shields from a concealed location, so as to achieve a 'formidable appearance' and 'convince the crowd that the police are determined to control the situation and are in a position to do so' (Long Shield Manoeuvre 1). Another is self-descriptively headed 'Mounted officers advance on a crowd in a way indicating that they do not intend to stop' (Manoeuvre 10). Manoeuvre 6 is worth setting out in full.

Long shield officers deployed into crowd and deployed across the road. Behind long shield units are deployed all the short and round shield officers with batons. On the command the short shield officers run forward either through and/or round the flanks of long shields into the crowd for not more than 30 yards. They disperse the crowd and *incapacitate* missile throwers and ring leaders by striking in a controlled manner with batons about the arms and legs or torso so as not to cause serious injury. Following the short shield units the long shield units advance quickly beyond short shields to provide additional protection. Link men from long shield units move in and take prisoners. (Italics in original)

It is not surprising that defence counsel at the Orgreave trial described this as an incitement to commit criminal assaults.

The style of policing reflected in the Tactical Options Manual was consciously copied from the crowd control methods developed in colonial police forces (such as Hong Kong) and in Northern Ireland. The manual gives little indication of any variation in approach where the circumstances of the disorder are an industrial dispute, and it is clear that this question was incidental to the perceived need for the manual.

While the 1981 riots may have been the principal catalyst to the drawing up of the manual, and perhaps future urban riots the main intended occasion for its practical implementation, in the event the first full-scale use of the type of manoeuvres envisaged was during the miners' strike, most spectacularly during the confrontations at Orgreave.

The rapidity and significance of the changes reflected in the Tactical Options Manual can be seen by contrasting the government's comment on the policing of disorder only two years previously, in the Green Paper on Public Order:

The British Police do not have sophisticated riot equipment – such as tear gas or water cannon – to handle demonstrations. Their traditional approach is to deploy large numbers of officers in ordinary uniform in the passive containment of a crowd. Neither the Government nor the police wish to see this approach abandoned in favour of more aggressive methods.

(Home Office 1980: para 15)

The end of this approach occurred without parliamentary discussion or any significant publicity.

Industrial events before the dispute gave to the police few signals of the upheavals that were to come. Senior officers knew, however, from the very specific recommendations of the Ridley Report, that the coal industry and the mining unions were to be the principal targets of government attention. Past history indicated that this would mean trouble. A year-long struggle may not have been foreseen by the police, the miners, or by the government, but the new organization and efficiency of the police in the matter of public order made it possible for them to sustain for twelve months a major disruption of their forces and to face down huge manifestations of protest that were generated by the bitterness of the dispute.

NOTES

1. Particularly useful are Marshall (1965) on the 1962 Royal Commission and its history, and the 1964 Act; Critchley (1978), a helpful if uncritical history; Jefferson and Grimshaw (1984) and especially Reiner (1985) and Lustgarten (1986). On the particular issue of the policing of industrial disputes Geary (1985) is an invaluable history and Kahn *et al.* (1983: ch. 5) a useful empirical study of recent practice.
2. Reporting in 1908, 1929, 1962, and 1981.
3. Miss Savidge was arrested for soliciting and subjected to oppressive interrogation by Metropolitan police officers. The tribunal which considered her allegations reported in 1928 and the Royal Commission was set up immediately afterwards to review police practices. See Royal Commission (1929), Minutes of Evidence 1469–71, 6269, 6232.
4. Royal Commission (1929: para 293).
5. The Chief Constable of Brighton, although acquitted, was dismissed by the Watch Committee. His successful legal challenge to this became, as the case of *Ridge* v *Baldwin* (1964), the watershed in the post-war history of judicial review of public bodies from which the modern expansion of this important area of the law started.
6. Cmnd 1222, 1960.
7. Royal Commission (1962: para 102).
8. Section 29. Disciplinary proceedings which might result in dismissal may now be instituted by a Police Authority under Part IX of the Police and Criminal Evidence Act, 1984.
9. Police Act, 1964, section 30. The Home Secretary may also set up a local inquiry under section 32, although this power is rarely used.
10. HC Debates: Standing Committee D, 17 December 1963, vol. II, cols 236–7.
11. HC Debates: vol. 952, cols *113–14*.
12. The National Reporting Centre did not operate in relation to Scotland; all mutual aid was arranged bilaterally. Half of the Scottish population, and a good deal of the disorder requiring extra police resources during the miners' strike, fell within the jurisdiction of a single police force (Strathclyde).
13. *R* v *Metropolitan Police Commissioner, ex parte Blackburn* (1968).
14. Not surprisingly it is the Police Authority which has to pay any damages awarded against the chief constable, but this does have the advantage that the Authority's approval has to be obtained for out-of-court settlements – section 48(2). There is a discretion to indemnify individual officers successfully sued for damages.
15. One qualification to this, important in practice during the strike, is that police officers seconded to another area under mutual aid are regarded as under the direction and control of the receiving chief constable (who can therefore be sued for their wrongful acts), but the sending chief constable retains responsibility for investigating complaints and for disciplinary action – Police Act, 1964, section 14(3); Police and Criminal Evidence Act, 1984, section 84(4).
16. Offences against the Person Act, 1861, section 38, and Prevention of Crimes Act, 1871, section 12 (as extended by section 2 of the Prevention of Crimes Amendment Act, 1885).
17. Gibbons (1983: 21).
18. Cain (1973); see also McCabe and Sutcliffe (1978); Heal, Tarling, and Burrows (1985); Martin (1974); Smith and Gray (1983).
19. *The Times*, 1908, quoted in Roberts (1971: 100).
20. Roberts (1971: 99–100).
21. The SPG was used during the mass picketing at the Grunwick factories in north-west London in 1976–8. Its officers were actively engaged in the suppression of disorder in the vicinity of a National Front meeting in Southall on 23 April 1979, during which Blair Peach was killed. On each occasion there were complaints about its violent tactics. See NCCL (1980).
22. For a full account see Crick (1985: ch. 4) and Geary (1985: 70–8).
23. For a fuller description of the background see Kettle (1985).
24. Hart (1951: 181).
25. The last-mentioned dispute, in 1977, has a symbolic significance in that it is the last occasion to date on which troops have been used in an industrial dispute; however their role was purely to provide an alternative fire service. As they used army fire tenders ('Green

Goddesses') it was unnecessary to cross official picket lines and the police experienced no significant public order problems.

26. The dispute itself was the subject of an extremely lucid Report by a Court of Inquiry, chaired by Lord Scarman (Scarman: 1977), the recommendations of which were however rejected by Grunwick. See also Rogaly (1977) and Ward (1978).
27. A sentence of twenty-eight days' imprisonment was imposed in the West Midlands for an offence of criminal damage.
28. Private steel companies did obtain a temporary injunction to prevent union officials from calling their staff out in support of the strike, but the injunction was overturned on appeal to the House of Lords as incompatible with the immunities enjoyed by union officials under the then law: *Duport Steels* v *Sirs* (1980).
29. Kettle and Hodges (1982: 23–38).
30. House of Commons Employment Committee, Minutes of Evidence, 27 February 1980, HC (1979–80) 462 – ii.
31. See Kahn *et al.* (1983: ch. 5) for a detailed analysis of police practice during this period, and S. Evans (1983) for an examination of employers' attitudes.
32. Scarman (1981).
33. However, while accepting the need for a small mobile force to be at the disposal of the Metropolitan Police Commissioner, he added 'a regular turnover of officers is essential to prevent too inward looking and self-conscious an *esprit de corps* developing' (Scarman 1981: para 5.53).

PART II

The miners' strike
March 1984–March 1985

Prologue

We have considered the issues of principle relevant to the policing of the miners' strike, and various background issues relating to the strike itself and to the structure, accountability, and training of the police. These issues must necessarily to some extent be examined first in isolation, as abstract concepts or phenomena are detached from their context. But we must now relate these matters to one of the most important and dramatic episodes of British post-war life.

The course of the miners' strike was exceedingly complex, with a close interweaving of several plots and subplots, personalities, events, and external circumstances; central to the array of developments, however, was the role of the police and the manner of its execution. It will be seen how the newly equipped and trained PSUs, backed by the relatively new NRC, put policing to its severest test, and by the standards and objectives they set were successful: but only at the expense of a grave distortion of police priorities, the final collapse of the local authority limb of the tripartite supervision of policing, the serious depletion of normal policing across the country, major damage to police–community relationships, and massive and often unnecessary assaults on fundamental liberties. These consequences represent the realization of the changes we have described and, as will be seen, have since, so far from leading to a national reappraisal of police, been continued, facilitated, and reinforced.

5

The progress of the strike

There is little agreement between the participants in the miners' strike – the government, the Coal Board, the police, the miners and their unions, and, to some extent, the general public – about its purpose, its conduct, and its prospects. Consequently any narrative of its course must seem one-sided or inadequate to one or more of these participants. Besides, much of the business of the strike – arrangements about policing and picketing, for example, or about negotiations for a settlement, or about the financial priorities of the government which determined policing costs and the scale of inducements to miners to return to work – was conducted in secret. Concealment and dissembling were practised by the principal parties to the dispute throughout its course. It is only the publication after the strike of various accounts, memoirs, and sporadic reminiscences that has made it possible to have a more comprehensive view of the actions and motives of the protagonists.[1]

The aims of the NUM leadership were not always coincident with those of their members. They were certainly not always in accord with the views of the leaders and members of some other unions. Coal Board and government, too, seemed at times to have divergent views. The discussions of ministers at Cabinet level are, of course, inaccessible but Parliamentary Questions and Answers were frequently used to give guidance and warnings to police and pickets or to justify expenditure. Police strategies, formulated at some unidentified level, frequently ran counter to the preferred practices of police officers on the ground. This complex web of concordances and disagreements can now be seen to have ensnared the purposes of the protagonists. It certainly prevents, at this stage, any attempt to define the aims and conduct of the strike in terms of single issues or principles.

INDECISION AND DIVISION AS THE STRIKE BEGINS

The decision to close the Cortonwood pit in Yorkshire was announced at a colliery review meeting on 1 March 1984. It was an announcement of closure, not, as was usual at such meetings, a proposal for review. Some miners stopped work immediately in protest at the announcement. The Yorkshire Area Council of the NUM responded on 5 March by calling a strike for the whole area from 12 March and asking for support from other areas. The members of the council justified the immediate strike call by referring to an area ballot of January 1981 which authorized strike action if pits in the area were threatened. Elsewhere the initial pattern of events was not consistent. A local strike at Polmaise colliery in Scotland had been going on since the end of February. In response to the appeal from Yorkshire, however, all of the Scottish coalfields were now ordered by their area union to stop work on 9 March. The Welsh miners were more careful. They had asked for and been refused support when their own pits were threatened. They were unwilling to make sacrifices for someone else now.

Under Rule 41 of the NUM rule-book, area stoppages must receive the sanction of the National Executive.[2] This was given on 8 March together with authorization and support for any other area wishing to join Yorkshire in a protest against pit closures. There was, as yet, no clear wish on the part of the union leaders to take on the Coal Board in a national strike. A report in *The Times* had already noted this hesitation:

> In view of the worsening situation in Yorkshire and the demands for action from Lancashire, the NUM will be under strong pressure to step up industrial action. Scargill and his supporters think this unnecessary because they believe the overtime ban is being effective.
>
> (*The Times*, 6 March 1984)

This may have been true in the immediate aftermath of the Cortonwood announcement. But the firm statement on the need for reduced output and pit closures which was made at the meeting between the NCB and the NUM executive on 6 March altered the context of the Yorkshire dispute and provided the grounds for a national stoppage.

By 12 March, the day on which the Yorkshire strike began, some pits were already closed. Miners from these pits were allocating picketing duties in other coalfields. The area executive, however, ordered that picketing should be restricted to Yorkshire with six pickets at each pit in accordance with the NUM and TUC guidelines. Yet the eagerness of rank-and-file union members in Yorkshire and the more considered unanimity of their officials was not evident elsewhere. Miners in Nottinghamshire, Lancashire, Derbyshire, and Leicestershire had many reservations about strike action. South Wales was sulking and not yet on strike. Only Kent and Durham joined the Scottish and Yorkshire miners. On the first day of the strike, therefore, fewer than half (83,000) of 180,000 miners in the industry had stopped work.

Pithead ballots were held in the early days of the strike in Northumberland and Staffordshire, resulting in votes not to strike. In Nottinghamshire the union officials, who supported industrial action throughout, called a ballot based on a recommendation for strike action, and asked that the Nottinghamshire miners should be left to make their decision without being harassed by pickets from Yorkshire. This request was unheeded, and the pits at Harworth, Bevercotes, and Ollerton came under siege from the first day of the strike. They remained so for many months thereafter.

The crucial importance of the coalfields in the Midlands was recognized by the NCB as well as by the striking miners. The pits there were rich in coal and worked at a profit; moreover they supplied the fuel for the electricity generating plants throughout the area. Sir Ian MacGregor described them as 'the jewel in the crown' of the Board. The Coal Board demonstrated its determination to keep them in production by applying to the High Court on 14 March for an injunction to prevent the picketing of Nottinghamshire pits by miners from elsewhere; the injunction was granted. But, it would seem, government ministers were advised that the use of their new and little-tested industrial legislation would inflame the tempers of the miners and induce strong support for the strike in areas where such support had been weak or non-existent, and the Coal Board came under pressure not to pursue its rights by applying to have the NUM held in contempt of court for ignoring the injunction.[3] Before recommending the abandonment of the injunction, however, steps had to be taken to ensure protection for the Nottinghamshire coalfields. This was done by enlisting the help of the police. The Home Secretary had already announced two days before the ballot in that area that 3,000 extra police officers from 17 forces were already stationed in Nottinghamshire to prevent trouble in the coalfields. To co-ordinate further action throughout the mining areas the National Reporting Centre was activated on 14 March. Reports coming in from areas which were holding a ballot showed that votes against a stoppage were high (South Derbyshire 83 per cent, Nottinghamshire 73 per cent, Midlands 73 per cent, Lancashire 59 per cent). Leicestershire had remained at work throughout this period and continued to do so, with little trouble, to the end, for only thirty men (the 'Dirty Thirty') went on strike, too small a number for effective action against their colleagues.

After the first week of the stoppage the NCB pulled back from the legal action which it had initiated on the grounds that police operations had been successful and 44 pits out of 176 were working normally. These were principally in Leicestershire, Nottinghamshire, and South Derbyshire. Anti-strike ballots in other areas were not always the end of the matter. In some, the local union rules gave the authority to call a strike to the area executive or to a special conference. The Staffordshire union, for example, could authorize a strike only by the vote of a special conference. Thus, although there was a no-strike vote (in the first ballot in the union's history), a special conference on 26 March voted for strike action throughout the area. This decision was not obeyed by all miners in the area and at least two pits were able to work throughout the strike. The Lancashire area, which had voted by a small majority for continued working, was heavily picketed by Yorkshire miners and was finally authorized by its area officers to join the strike on 23 March.

Such differences in policy and practice reflected the differing views of union members and of their leaders. In areas threatened by the plans of the Coal Board, fear, frustration, and anger prompted precipitate action. Where there were few possibilities of closure, miners, whose earnings were already reduced as a result of the overtime ban, were reluctant to risk loss of pay, perhaps permanent loss of employment, by joining a strike. Clearly there was no single purpose, no co-ordinated plan of campaign to defeat the Board, much less to bring down the government. Yet by the end of the second week of the strike almost 90 per cent of the pits were affected by strike action in one way or another.

THE GOVERNMENT, THE POLICE, AND THE ROAD-BLOCKS

Both government ministers and the police were seized of the importance of modern transport in the industrial disputes of the late twentieth century. Each had experience of the rapid movement of pickets from one area of operations to another; the coal dispute and building workers' strike of 1972 and 1973 had been marked by the challenging – and successful – use of flying pickets. By 1984, however, the network of motorways and urban ring-roads enormously increased the capacity of pickets – and of thieves and burglars, for that matter – to frustrate attempts to contain their movements. It was primarily to deal with this mobility of 'flying pickets' that the 1980 legislation on secondary picketing was introduced. In the miners' strike, however, since the use of these provisions was thought to be impolitic, police powers of control of the road system had to be brought into play. These powers were not generally questioned when they were used for the prevention and detection of crime: the setting up of road-blocks in murder inquiries, for example. Would they be questioned if they were extended to prevent the assembly of pickets? In the early days of the strike government ministers spelled out their view and, in doing so, publicly instructed police officers to use their powers to obstruct traffic on motorways and other arteries in such a way as to prevent the congregation of pickets at working pits. If this were to be successful, remedies by way of the civil law could be left aside.

On 15 March, the day after the NCB obtained an injunction against secondary picketing in Nottinghamshire, the Home Secretary set out what he saw to be the position in so far as the criminal law and police powers were concerned:

> The legal position is clear. Any attempt to obstruct or intimidate those who wish to go to work is a breach of the criminal law. The mere presence of large numbers of pickets can be intimidating. The police have a duty to prevent obstruction and intimidation and enable those who wish to go to work to do so. They have the power to stop and disperse large numbers of pickets and to take preventive action by stopping vehicles and people.[4]

Although this statement is, in the main, a fair summary of paragraphs 28, 29, and 31 of the statutory Code of Practice on Picketing,[5] it went further and directed the attention of chief constables to their control of the road transport system throughout the country. A fuller statement of the legal position by the Attorney General in a written Parliamentary Answer the following day encouraged the Chief Constable of Kent to chance his arm and authorize the setting up of a road-block at the entrance to the Dartford Tunnel.[6] Some miners on their way north were turned back, as were a number of other people. The Kent miners immediately sought legal redress for this restriction upon their freedom of movement, but the High Court refused to issue an injunction. Among the general public, however, there was a certain amount of disquiet about such exercise of police power where no criminal action or breach of the peace was imminent.

By the end of March the position of the NCB and the government in relation to their handling of the strike seemed to be well defined. They had reached agreement that the civil law was not to be involved but the full array of police powers would be used to keep the coalfields in the Midlands open. This was the short-term aim. There was and always had been complete unanimity about their ultimate objective, namely to change the balance of power in one of the largest state-controlled industries in the country.

Within the local and national leadership of the NUM there was considerable disagreement about the way in which union policies should be expressed. Although all the areas in which a ballot was held rejected strike action, many of the area officials thought the situation to be so grave that a strike was the only solution. As we have seen, some of them used their area rules to reverse the results of ballots. The National Executive, for reasons of pride, perhaps, or uncertainty about the outcome of a national ballot, continued to rely on Rule 41 of the NUM rule-book, namely authorization of strike action area by area. At a National Executive meeting on 12 April a number of area officials, from Leicestershire and elsewhere, pressed for an immediate national ballot. A lobby of striking miners outside the meeting made very clear that men from Yorkshire, at least, were voting with their feet and had no time for a formal ballot. The president's ruling that the motion was out of order was affirmed by thirteen votes to eight but the matter was referred to a special delegate conference to be held a week later. At this conference four separate motions calling for a national ballot were defeated. A proposal for strike action throughout all British coalfields was carried by sixty-nine votes to fifty-four. There was a hint that a ballot might be held some time in the future since the qualifying majority in any national ballot for strike action was reduced from 55 per cent to a simple majority. For the time being, however, there would be no ballot at national level.

These two meetings on 12 and 19 April put an end to the ballot question as far as the NUM leadership was concerned. But they revealed and exacerbated the divisions in the coalfields and, as we shall see, gave to some disenchanted union members the excuse and the opportunity to make use of the law against their fellows.

ORGREAVE AND AFTER

The events which led up to the major picketing at Orgreave were, for the NUM, a tragic accident. For the police, and for the government as well, it was a circumstance which was put to good use by the establishment of a clear and visible superiority over the mass pickets of the NUM. In doing so they expunged a previous, shameful defeat.

The coking plant at Orgreave, like the steelworks at Ravenscraig, Scunthorpe, Llanwern, and Port Talbot (significantly less in the case of Redcar) was one of the pawns in the negotiations between the NUM and the principal steelworkers' union, the ISTC, for support for the miners' strike by the reduction of steelmaking at the major plants. At the beginning of the strike the Scottish miners seemed confident that the Triple Alliance of steelworkers, railwaymen, and mineworkers would bring to a rapid conclusion the dispute in the coal industry. On the whole, the railwaymen (represented by ASLEF and the NUR) met most of the demands made upon them by the NUM. The steelworkers were not so compliant, since they were acutely aware of the contraction in their own industry, of the threat to one or more of the five large steel plants that remained after the 1980 steel strike, and of the poor prospects of employment elsewhere. Besides, their union leaders were critical of the NUM strategy of avoiding a ballot and relying on picketing alone to compel a shut-down of operations in the coalfields. Yet the mineworkers had lent their support for the thirteen weeks of the steel strike in 1980. Some repayment had to be made. This was slowly negotiated and early in May steel and mining union leaders agreed that a limited supply of coal should be transported by rail and not by road to the principal steel plants. The shift to transport by rail alone was considered necessary because, at the beginning of the strike, miners had had great difficulty in stopping the road transport of coal and coke. The TGWU had indeed promised full support but many hauliers were not unionized and even TGWU members were sometimes reluctant to obey instructions not to cross picket lines. A stable agreement for a regular supply by rail (enough, it was estimated, to allow production of 50 per cent of the normal output of steel) would avoid the need for heavy picketing at road entrances to the steelworks.

These arrangements were disrupted by an unfortunate accident at the Scunthorpe steelworks in May. One of the blast furnaces there began to give trouble, perhaps because it was (by agreement with the NUM) being fuelled by coal from neighbouring pits and not by high quality coke from Orgreave which was normally the source of fuel. Further damage to the furnace could be avoided only by a return to Orgreave fuel. In the third week of May the ISTC therefore approached the NUM and asked for permission to remove from Orgreave a specified amount of the fuel needed. For some reason there was a delay of two or three days in the NUM response to this request. British Steel management therefore decided to act without an agreement with the unions. Hauliers were offered large financial inducements to ferry the coke to Scunthorpe and from 23 May convoys of coke lorries began to roll in and out of Orgreave twice a day.

A conspiracy theorist might claim that the Scunthorpe plant failure may have been over-emphasized by British Steel to force the opening of the Orgreave plant and incidentally to compel the reduction of picketing at working pits. This, however, is one of the many factors which deeply influenced the course of the strike but which remains a matter for speculation.

The policing of the month-long operation at Orgreave will be dealt with later. Here it is sufficient to say that the final convoys of lorries on 18 June and the two days following reactivated the bitterness between the ISTC and the NUM and brought about the final disintegration of the Triple Alliance. The NUM, backed by the rail unions, announced that coal supplies to the five major steel plants would, from 19 June, be limited to that amount which was essential for the prevention of permanent damage to the blast furnaces. Moreover, the transport of iron ore to these plants would be blocked from the end of June. These moves were clearly intended to reduce steel operations to a level of maintenance only. Neither management nor unions in the steel industry would accept such arrangements. With some cosmetic expressions of goodwill towards the miners, the steel unions declared themselves willing to accept coal and iron from any source and however delivered.

OTHER INDUSTRIAL DISPUTES ARISING OUT OF THE MINERS' STRIKE

The clash of interest between the steelworkers and the miners which resulted in the attempt to restrict supplies to the steel plants was followed by two other disputes between transport workers and the steel industry. These arose not so much because the transport unions wished to help the striking miners as because hard-won agreements that registered dock-workers alone should unload ship cargoes had been or might be breached.

At Immingham in early July, an employee of the British Steel Corporation began to unload a cargo of iron-ore on to the waiting lorries, in circumstances which allegedly contravened established procedures. The registered dock-workers (members of the TGWU) objected and a full-blown dock strike followed. It was high summer and the ports were crammed with holiday traffic as well as the usual cross-channel lorry and container traffic. The frustrations inevitably created by these circumstances rapidly brought the strike to a head. Lorry drivers at one port showed their impatience by threatening to break up the customs sheds on the docks. At another, a group of lorry drivers used their horse-power and vehicle strength to push their way on to cross-channel ferries. A settlement was reached by the reaffirmation of the inviolability of the dock labour scheme and a temperate apology from the management of British Steel.

A second dispute erupted at Hunterston on the Clyde in August when a ship attempted to bring in supplies of iron ore for the steel plant at Ravenscraig. For two weeks the ship lay at anchor while British Steel and the dock-workers argued about the reception of the cargo, which the TGWU would not allow its members to receive or to unload. Again there was a threat of a dock strike but the issue this time was not so clear cut, dockers were reluctant to strike again, and the British Steel management in Scotland conducted a skilful and successful campaign to win round the transport union. A settlement was reached which was sufficiently embroidered to avoid the appearance of a complete climb-down by the unions (unionized labour from another area was used to moor the ship). The cargo was unloaded and Ravenscraig received its supplies.

The third dispute was closely bound up with the last realistic attempts at a settlement between the NUM and the Coal Board. It is, therefore, dealt with below, in our account of the search for peace in the coalfields (pp. 65–6). First we must consider the impact of the legal processes initiated by the various groups of people, miners and others, who thought themselves to be injured by the actions of the striking miners and their leaders.

LEGAL ACTIONS AGAINST THE NUM

Throughout their battle to survive the strike – a battle fought against the Coal Board, the government, the police, and other unions – the local and national miners' unions suffered their most crippling blows at the hands of individuals who used the courts to bring them to heel. It can, of course, be argued that the defeat of the NUM was brought about by the refusal or the inability of other unions to support the strike rather than by the loss of control of the union's funds to which the litigation led.[7] Nevertheless the symbolism of the successful legal actions brought by individuals (however much they were financed and supported by powerful interests) affected the attitudes and responses of the TUC and of sympathetic unions who were unwilling to defy the judgements of the courts simply to help their friends.

The first case to be tried was initiated by two hauliers (George and Richard Read) whose business was usually engaged in hauling coke to the Port Talbot Steelworks.[8] When their lorries were repeatedly stopped at the Port Talbot gates, the Read brothers decided to use the recent industrial legislation to obtain redress. An injunction to prevent unlawful picketing was issued on 17 April 1984. Picketing did not stop and an action for non-compliance with the order and for damages was heard in the High Court on 30 July. Mr Justice Park imposed two fines of £25,000 each on the South Wales area union, holding that it had not acted effectively to stop the unlawful picketing.[9] The Reads also applied for a writ of sequestration on the ground that the South Wales area officials were planning to evade the consequences of the court's orders. The evidence for this claim was a report in the *Daily Express* that the union was transferring its funds to the accounts of its officials. This press report was accepted by the judge and sequestration ordered. The order was not challenged by the NUM as a result of the union's policy of non-cooperation with the courts. This attack upon area funds was a precedent for the later and well-nigh fatal action against the national union.

The first legal action initiated by working miners has since been described by David Negus, a Nottinghamshire solicitor who was first approached by two working miners (Colin Clarke and John Liptrot) who were branch officials in that area.[10] They appeared at his office and asked if he could help them to force the Nottinghamshire officials to retract their ruling that the strike in their area was official. When Negus said this would be a costly proceeding the miners produced piles of notes and buckets of coins contributed by working miners to pay for legal advice and assistance. Proceedings were begun in early May and on 25 May the Vice-Chancellor, Sir Robert Megarry, ruled that the area officials in Nottingham must reverse their instruction that the strike should be regarded as official and must arrange to hold area elections. The area officials complied, area elections were held, and a number of pro-strike officers at branch level were replaced by working miners.[11]

Clearly the use of the ordinary civil law had been effective in Nottinghamshire in this case. Those who were active in pursuit of the NUM and its leadership were encouraged to support with advice, professional assistance, and money all those who wished to take action against it.[12]

Cases multiplied. Three Derbyshire miners, Taylor, Roberts, and Phillips adopted the same task as Clarke and Liptrot, namely to prevent their area officials from calling Derbyshire miners out on a strike which was unauthorized, and from disciplining those who disobeyed.[13] The judgement in this case, given on 29 September 1984, went against the union on two counts – that the strike in Derbyshire was unofficial and that a national strike was also in breach of NUM rules. Attempts to enforce strike action in Derbyshire were therefore unlawful and must cease.

For striking miners in Yorkshire the action which generated fiercest anger was that brought by Robert Taylor and Ken Foulstone, men who lived in Nottinghamshire but worked in Yorkshire, in which they claimed that no disciplinary proceedings should be taken against working miners, that the strike in Yorkshire should be declared unofficial, and that there should be a national ballot.

In his judgement in this case Mr Justice Nicholls (who had heard the Derbyshire case as well) found for the plaintiffs. Moreover he went further in his judgement in this case by ruling that both Yorkshire area and national NUM officials must be restrained from describing either the national or the area strike as official. This decision and the NUM's defiance of it led directly to the sequestration of NUM funds and the appointment of a Receiver.

Another case, which may have long-term effects on the law of industrial disputes, although it was decided too late in the day to have any great practical impact on the course of the strike, was the action brought by some of the first miners to return to work in South Wales. They complained that their right to work was being frustrated by the behaviour of pickets who were acting unlawfully. Mr Justice Scott gave an interesting and controversial judgement. Having rejected most of the grounds raised by the plaintiffs, his Lordship nevertheless found that the picketing was an unlawful harassment of them in the exercise of their right to travel to work. This – legally novel – conclusion was backed up with an injunction restricting the pickets to six at each colliery entrance, effectively adopting the purely non-statutory guidance on numbers contained in the Code of Practice, which now therefore had the authority of judicial support.

The full impact of the litigation on the finances of the union occurred quite late in the strike, following the sequestration of its assets and the appointment of a Receiver at the end of November to locate and recover the bulk of the funding which had been exported at the outset of the strike precisely in anticipation of court action. By then the possibilities of successful strike action were rapidly disintegrating and the courts may not have contributed much to the process. However the effect on the morale of working miners and those striking miners who were weakening under increasing financial pressure must have been very powerful.

NEGOTIATING FOR A SETTLEMENT

A relative stalemate after two months of intensive picketing and firm policing prompted the first negotiations for a settlement in late May. The two sides met in London on 23 May but each was apprehensive about seeming to sue for peace. The meeting broke the ice, however, and negotiations began in earnest at the end of the month. There were meetings in London, in Edinburgh, and in Yorkshire between 31 May and 13 June – a period which covered some of the most bitter confrontations at Orgreave. There appeared to be some 'give' on both sides. On the occasion of the final discussions in Rotherham, however, the miners' leaders were suspicious and angry about the content of an interview with the Chairman of the Coal Board which had been published in *The Times* the day before the meeting. In it he talked of 'regaining management of the industry'. A declaration of intent of this kind was bound to arouse the suspicions of the union leaders. There was no possibility of agreement in such a climate and negotiations came to an end. The NUM leadership claimed that government pressure had been exerted to prevent a resolution of the strike that was not wholly favourable to the Coal Board's policies of pit closures and effective economic management. Such a belief loses credibility in view of the rapid resumption of negotiations in early July.

The second round of talks during 5–18 July seemed to bring the parties near to agreement. With different forms of words it was possible to discuss the proposals of 6 March which had sparked off the strike. Thus the pits which had been designated for immediate closure might be considered again and other changes made. About 'uneconomic pits' there was a wide difference of view which was expressed by the use of the word 'beneficially' by the Coal Board and its deliberate omission by the NUM in the definition of a colliery which could be deemed to be exhausted.[14] The proposals worked out in the July meeting were considered and rejected by a special delegate conference in August. Negotiations were once more at an end.

A third set of negotiations followed the intervention of Robert Maxwell, the newspaper proprietor. He had tried to use the TUC Congress in September as a base for the establishment of some kind of communication between the two sides. This caused alarm in the Coal Board but talks did actually get under way in early September. Meetings were held, again in Edinburgh and in Yorkshire, but talks broke down, after long discussions, simply because neither side could accept the principles and purposes of the other.

The last real opportunity to reach a negotiated settlement arose out of a dispute between the NCB and NACODS. As men began to return to work in a slow stream, the Coal Board found itself in a difficulty in arranging for the opening of pits hitherto strike bound. Members of NACODS, who had the statutory duty to supervise the safe condition of underground workings, had extracted an agreement from the Coal Board that they would continue to be paid despite refusing to cross NUM picket lines to report for work, if the picketing was heavy. In mid-August the Coal Board rescinded this agreement and insisted that NACODS members must travel into beleaguered pits in protected vehicles along with the returning miners. If they did not do this, they would not be paid. Angered by this breach of an agreement the NACODS executive arranged for a ballot to decide whether strike action should be taken. The ballot showed a majority of 82 per cent for a stoppage of work.

Government and Coal Board dared not risk a strike, legalized by a ballot, which would bring the coalfields to a standstill. The union's conditions were rapidly accepted by the Board but its general secretary, Peter McNestry, saw an opportunity to bring about a reasonable settlement to the whole dispute. At his request the issues at the heart of the strike – pit closures, review procedures, and the promises given to the miners in the Plan for Coal – were put before ACAS in September and October. At the urging of the TUC the NUM was brought to the ACAS talks but the executive of NACODS had already accepted the Board's terms – their own freedom not to cross NUM picket lines without loss of pay and a revision of the Colliery Review procedure which would include reference to an independent body in cases where there was no agreement on the reasons for closure of individual pits.[15] NACODS had got what they wanted and a complete shut-down of the coalfields was averted, largely because of government insistence on a settlement. The Chairman of the Coal Board is on record as saying that he would have been prepared to face down the NACODS executive by arranging for supervision of the underground workings by using managers and others.[16] For the government the risks were too great and the settlement was made – but without the NUM, whose spokesmen could not accept an agreement which did not deal specifically with 'uneconomic' pits and the reaffirmation of the arrangements made in the Plan for Coal. Painstaking work by ACAS kept the talks going till the end of October. It was clear then that no settlement was possible.[17] The last chance of peace in the coalfields was over, although the TUC made efforts early in 1985.

The terms offered by the Coal Board on this occasion were such that the NUM felt unable even to begin discussions under their shadow. Peace was not now the language of Coal Board and government, nor had it been since the sequestration of the assets of the NUM in late October had made it inevitable that the miners' union as well as the miners themselves would be hopelessly crippled by lack of money.

THE RETURN TO WORK AND THE END OF THE STRIKE

Throughout the period of intermittent negotiations, the NCB were pursuing another, parallel strategy, closely entwined with the court actions by working miners and the incipient groupings of miners opposed to the strike whom the actions had brought together. The idea was simple: if enough of those miners, who had voted against the strike, or did not now support it, or could no longer afford to stay out of work, could be enticed back, the strike would progressively collapse. The strategy depended on skilful publicity and detailed work 'targeting' likely returnees and organizing transport; above all it depended on a guarantee of safe carriage to and from work. That in turn made the police the key to a central management strategy in the defeat of the strike.

The return to work began early, but fitfully, in the spring of 1984, carefully planned by the NCB's area director in North Derbyshire, Ken Moses. Data on individual miners were assembled, and those felt most susceptible to encouragement – those living away from mining communities, with family commitments, not known union activists – were approached.[18] The process was soon followed in Scotland, and later copied more widely, but it was not until the autumn that matters began to move more significantly. The first return to work in the crucial Yorkshire area happened in late August; likewise in Durham. It was not until November that the first Welsh miner returned, but by then numbers going back and pits 'opening' (often in no meaningful sense because there were too few men to start mining operations as such) increased steadily amid a welter of contradictory statistics issued by the NCB and NUM and widely publicized. The period before Christmas saw particular pressure exerted on hard-pressed miners as the Board publicized the substantial benefits to be gained from bonus payments to those who returned before the deadline. Many men who had survived nearly a year without an income felt forced to give up; others were simply disillusioned or saw the inevitability of failure much sooner than their leaders. The NCB let it be known that in their view once more than half of all the miners had returned to work, they would consider that the strike was over. They would be able to ignore the remaining strikers, who might not be needed in a restructured industry. In the event, on Coal Board figures, the numbers back at work exceeded 50 per cent for the first time the week before the strike was formally called off.[19]

After the ending of negotiations, and the sequestration of the NUM's funds, in late October, and the surge in the return to work in November, the strike seemed to most observers to be all but over; but it was a remarkably long time a-dying.

After a period of effective stalemate through the heart of winter, the NUM leadership, particularly its area executives, showed signs of disagreement in the final weeks about how the strike should be brought to an end. The South Wales miners (prompted by their research officer, Dr Kim Howells) floated the idea of a return to work without any settlement at all. The miners would sign nothing and therefore be held to no agreement. The NUM leadership dismissed this suggestion but it was the only alternative to continuance of the strike which was now supported by little more than half the NUM membership. The TUC was still working for a peace formula but knew that it had no hope of persuading the NUM leadership to accept the terms which had been dictated by the Coal Board.[20] Their final rejection on 20 February 1985 by the NUM executive led to a serious consideration of the South Wales proposals for a return to work on no conditions.

On 3 March a special delegate conference voted by ninety-eight to ninety-one to return to work without an agreement. The strike was over and men prepared to march back under their union banners on 5 March, twelve long months after the strike was called.[21] Whatever ultimately brought about the miners' failure, heavy policing, financial pressure, bad tactics, clever opposition, or long continued obstinacy, there is no doubt that the effects of this industrial dispute have been and will be of great national importance.

NOTES

1. The most useful narrative of the events of the strike is Adeney and Lloyd (1986). See also *Sunday Times* Insight Team (1985) and the very personalized account in MacGregor (1986). A useful chronological summary of the major events in the strike was published in the *Guardian*, 5 March 1985. We have drawn on these and other sources in producing this summary of events.

2. See Chapter 3, p. 25, for an account of the relevant rules.
3. Adeney and Lloyd (1986: 181–2); cf. MacGregor (1986: 216–18).
4. HC Debates, 15 March 1984, col. 512.
5. These are set out in Chapter 3, p. 29.
6. HC Debates, 16 March 1984, cols *279–80*.
7. Equally it can be argued that the litigation itself was the self-inflicted consequence of the tactics chosen by the NUM leadership; but we are here concerned with the consequences rather than the causes of the litigation.
8. This was the first case apart from the NCB's own abortive injunction against secondary picketing in March 1984.
9. *Richard Read (Transport) Ltd* v *NUM (South Wales Area)* (1985). See Benedictus (1985: 177–9) for accounts of this and the handful of other actions brought by employers.
10. Address given at a meeting of the Industrial Law Society at the University College, London in June 1985.
11. For details of this and other cases brought by working miners see Ewing (1985).
12. In his address (see note 10), Negus admitted the financial backing given to potential plaintiffs. Later accounts, particularly Adeney and Lloyd (1986: 104) say that an appeal to British business men for funds to help with legal costs was organized by Sir Hector Laing, an active member of the Conservative Party and friend of the Prime Minister.
13. The Taylor in this case, one Albert Taylor of Shirebrook Colliery, was not the Taylor who brought the even more significant action against the Yorkshire area union. Significantly none of the three plaintiffs was an underground worker; they were closer to the managerial and supervisory side of the industry.
14. A colliery would be deemed exhausted if a mining engineer's investigation by both sides showed that there were no mineable reserves 'that are workable or could be beneficially developed' (NCB). It was in this phrase that the word 'beneficially' was omitted by the NUM.
15. For a full (if partisan) account of the NACODS episode see MacGregor (1986: ch. 12).
16. MacGregor (1986: 280–1).
17. In the final discussions of this series of talks the NUM held firmly to their view that the Plan for Coal must remain as the blueprint for the industry. ACAS suggested a reformulation which might have satisfied the NUM. The Coal Board was not however eager for a settlement after staving off the threat from NACODS. In reality therefore it was the confidence of the Coal Board rather than the intransigence of the NUM which halted the talks on 31 October.
18. MacGregor (1986: 201–5); *Sunday Times* Insight Team (1985: 200–3).
19. *Sunday Times* Insight Team (1985: 249).
20. Adeney and Lloyd (1986: 217) claim that in the last discussions with the TUC about an agreement the Energy Secretary would have been prepared to soften the terms of an agreement. The Chairman of the NCB threatened to resign and the tough conditions remained.
21. The return to work was not immediate in all areas. Kent in particular held out for a further week in protest at the failure to secure an amnesty for the 1,000-plus miners dismissed for misconduct during the strike, and some of the formal mass march-backs were disrupted by the arrival of flying pickets.

6
Policing the strike[1]

To those who might argue that the control of picketing and demonstrating miners was an abuse of the police function, the response must be that the first duty of the police in this, as in any other country, is to maintain the order and stability that will allow an elected government to pursue the purposes for which it was elected. During the miners' strike a number of government ministers in public and in private (cf. MacGregor 1986) expressed the conviction not only that their industrial and economic policies would be frustrated by a successful pit strike but also that widespread public disorder was the inevitable outcome of mass picketing. Police involvement was constitutionally justifiable on the second ground. The defeat of well-supported industrial action by the wide sweep of the criminal law is of more doubtful legitimacy. In the event, although individual chief police officers adopted their own methods of control, there was a massive and sustained police operation to bring about an end to the strike. Heavy financial pressures upon striking miners and upon their union may indeed have contributed more to its collapse but it was the operational policies of senior police officers and the activities of those who carried them out which were crucial; these matters are the subject of this chapter.

Most of the picketing that took place during the coal dispute was peaceably conducted and as peaceably policed. Clear evidence of this is to be found in official police reports, the accounts of observers, and the testimony of striking miners themselves. Yet there were in England and Wales 9,808 arrests during the twelve months of the dispute, proportionately as well as absolutely more than in any previous industrial dispute in the last half-century.[2] Serious charges, even those carrying the possibility of a sentence of life imprisonment, were levelled against some of those who had been engaged in picketing or demonstrations.[3] Many of the arrests, however, were for minor offences of obstruction, breach of the peace, or offensive words and behaviour.[4] In our examination of the implications of the policing of pickets and demonstrations in support of picketing we shall refer, of necessity, to examples of conflict and confrontation. But all of these must be placed in the context of picketing and policing that for the most part gave rise to no greater physical confrontation than each of the parties to the struggle had been led to expect.

THE OPENING STAGES

For police officers there was little reason to think that the coal dispute would be different from others which they had encountered. Even those who remembered the earlier miners' strike in 1972 were aware that, apart from one or two exceptional battles, picketing was vigorous but non-violent. The Employment Act, 1980, which made secondary picketing unlawful, did not seek to prevent the gathering of demonstrations, which police chiefs had declared themselves able and willing to contain.[5] Moreover, that containment did not seem to involve an unacceptable level of aggression for police officers on the ground. A Metropolitan police officer remembered with a measure of delight the shoulder-to-shoulder struggle at the Grunwick photographic processing plant in 1977:

> That Grunwick dispute, I liked that one best of all. It was such a fair, clean fight. This union got all these blokes in from all over the country. They were a real tough lot, not rubbish, mind you, but a really good class of demonstrator. . . . When it was all over I felt like shaking hands with the opposition and thanking them for such a good contest.[6]

For their part, most miners looked forward to the customary give and take of the picket line – intermittent pushing and shoving and occasional arrests when police officers thought things were getting out of hand. They were, of course, aware of the indications of new and different police strategies. After all, the dispute between the National Graphical Association and Mr Eddie Shah at the Warrington printing works had shown how effective were the new methods of organization, training, and equipment which had been introduced following the inner city riots of 1981. But generally it was accepted that picketing did not and would not occasion the use of police in riot gear nor the use of dogs and horses. The first death on the picket line, however, and the persistent articulation of ministerial support for any measure, particularly the setting up of road-blocks, that police chiefs might wish to take to control striking miners made clear to them that successful picketing would not be easy.[7] In Nottinghamshire, for example, although as we have noted there were 3,000 police officers from 17 forces stationed in the county by 14 March 1984, some days before the area ballot was held, these were not enough to provide sufficient cover for each of the NCB properties where picketing miners might gather. Good intelligence, a road-block policy, or both would be necessary to keep the Nottinghamshire pits at work.[8] Although the threat of litigation and a subsequent court judgement indicated that some limits might be set to a proper apprehension of a breach of the peace, the chief constable exercised a continuing control over his domain by impeding the access of unwelcome citizens to the county.[9] By October 1984 police figures indicated that close on 200,000 striking miners had been kept away from the Nottinghamshire pits.

The turn-back strategy was adopted elsewhere in the coal-mining areas and was enthusiastically pursued by police officers on the ground, who frequently prevented the free passage of those whose destination was far from being a picketed colliery. Three women in Derbyshire, for example, who were walking together to buy fish and chips at midday were turned back by police officers who were on duty at a roundabout. A complaint to the chief constable which was passed to the Police Complaints Board elicited the reply that the action complained of was not capable of redress since it was force policy to exercise control over free passage on the highway during the coal dispute.[10] There may have been some specious justification for this police action, at least to the officers concerned. The husband of one of the women who was stopped was a striking miner and she had herself appeared among the unofficial pickets. A more cynical cruelty was shown in a report of events during the strike which was compiled by a probation officer in Nottinghamshire. He writes of a man who went to visit his wife in a maternity unit. He was returning on foot to his home which was some miles away. The report goes on:

> He had actually walked some six miles when [he was] stopped by the police and questioned about his intentions. He gave a full explanation but this was not accepted and a check was made with the maternity unit. . . .The police still did not accept that he was not a picket and took him by car back to the hospital. There, the Ward Sister identified him. He then alleges that when he asked the police how he was to get home, he was told that it would have to be 'the same way as he got to where they found him'. He had already walked two-thirds of the distance but had to walk again, arriving home in the early morning with his feet bleeding from the chafing. At 8.00 am he was awoken by the police who were yet again checking that he was not on the picket line.

Police control of the highways, demonstrated so clearly in the road-block policy, was evidenced also in the denial of passage to normal traffic when convoys of lorries and their police escorts occupied all three lanes of some motorways. This practice was widely criticized and later discontinued. There were, too, more aggressive police actions, the searching of persons and vehicles for the most specious of reasons, the diversion of drivers to strange routes and places; even the deliberate smashing of car windows (which was admitted – and justified – by some police officers).

By comparison, the setting up by Kent police of a road-block at the Dartford Tunnel entrance, while highly publicized and in the light of the later court decision almost certainly outside the lawful powers of the police, was relatively brief (it ended on 26 March) and nobody was prosecuted – although many miners were turned back.[11] However this extraordinary police action, and its endorsement by the Attorney-General, raised further disquiet about the policing.

For all these reasons there was concern about priorities in police policies and their highly discretionary implementation which caused frustration and anxiety not confined to striking miners and their families. This resulted in the setting up, in various parts of the country, of observer groups (and a subcommittee of at least one police authority) to monitor the policing of the strike and its consequences for police organization and control.

In the early days of the strike the development of picketing tactics and police response at the colliery gates ran true to form. Large numbers of striking miners sought to persuade working miners, particularly in the Midlands, to join the strike, chiefly by displays of strength and solidarity. These were met by considerable numbers of police officers in conventional dress. On two occasions, however, there were serious consequences. On 14 March, in a confused mêlée at Ollerton pit, David Jones, a striking miner, collapsed and died from an injury sustained at some point during the struggle between the police, the miners seeking to enter the pit, and the pickets who sought to prevent them. This tragedy may have hardened the attitude of the police; it certainly increased the suspicion and distrust of striking miners, some of whom were unwilling to accept the open verdict of the coroner's inquest. Indeed, twelve months later, at the end of the strike, the event was occasionally remembered as the first example of a police cover-up – whether of their own behaviour or that of the working miners mattered little.

Less tragic, but serious in its consequences, was the picketing of Cresswell Colliery on 2 April.[12] Some striking miners moved into the mining village beside the pit and caused damage and considerable alarm there by harassing working miners and their families. Henry Richardson, the NUM area secretary, who was campaigning hard to bring the Nottinghamshire miners into line with their striking colleagues, lamented the violence, saying that the cause of the strike had been greatly injured by the events of that day.

The effectiveness of the road-block policy together with the determination of miners in the Midlands to stay at work ensured that most working pits were free from the serious attention of pickets after the first four or five weeks of the strike. A few, Harworth, Ollerton, Rufford and Cresswell, in particular, were readily accessible to striking miners from Yorkshire and North Derbyshire. They were therefore heavily picketed from time to time but, although there were a number of fairly arbitrary arrests, there were no serious incidents at colliery gates. Thus when a picket said to number some 10,000 men gathered at Harworth in early May, the colliery manager showed little anxiety. He sent for extra police protection but noted that 'picketing was well-ordered. More of a demonstration than a picket line'.[13] The police response was swift; a contingent from Hampshire, for instance, arrived by plane. Neither police nor pickets, however, showed much inclination to depart from the traditional push and shove, although mounted police were present.

In Staffordshire a fairly even balance between striking and working miners meant that picketing continued; but it was largely conducted by the striking miners of the area. Moreover, policing in Staffordshire was generally more cautious than in some other areas. Union officials were in frequent touch with senior police officers and were often present on the picket line. Sheffield Policewatch recorded the beneficial effects of this policy on 4 June at Lea Hall:

> The official pickets (6) were allowed to stand in the middle of the road and stopped most working miners (only two cars turned back). After about 45 minutes there were approximately 350 miners and 400 police and 4 horses. The picketing that was allowed was the best I have seen even if it was not successful. (Best in terms of what the police allowed.) They stopped cars and spoke to the drivers, causing long queues down the road. One policeman organised the traffic . . . . The pickets were allowed to shout everything. Not one word was censored or regarded as an offence.
>
> (Sheffield Policewatch Daily Report: 4 June 1984)

The first phase of picketing throughout the coalfields could therefore be said to have ended in stalemate. In some areas working miners reached their pits; pickets were diverted, arrested, or ignored. Elsewhere the coalfields were silent, the solidarity of striking miners being broken only rarely in the early part of the dispute.

THE SECOND PHASE OF PICKETING AND ITS CONTROL

The second phase was marked by attempts by both working and striking miners to mobilize support by rallies and demonstrations at union and area headquarters. For the police this presented problems not only of strategy but also of legitimacy. Wives, families, and friends were present at some of the demonstrations which had the general character of peaceful parades for which the tight control exerted over demonstrating pickets in the coalfields was inappropriate. The events of three particular days showed that the breakdown of police discipline that occasionally happened on the picket line was also possible when miners took their case to the city streets. On 19 April strikers lobbied a Special Delegate Conference being held in Sheffield. After a noisy but reasonably peaceful demonstration, a number of Durham miners together with one or two Members of Parliament gathered at the Trades and Labour Club. There are two accounts of what happened as the miners left the club to make their way home. The chief constable, reporting to his Police Authority, described how a small number of police officers were deployed to answer a call for assistance from a public house near to the Labour Club.[14] Two of these officers found themselves surrounded by demonstrators and they were forced to draw their truncheons to defend themselves. This was obviously the account of the incident given by the officers involved. Quite another story is given in the affidavit of Richard Caborn MP, who was present throughout the incident and made a formal complaint to the chief constable. He spoke of an unprovoked attack upon those who were leaving the club by a group of officers who swooped out of a transit van and laid about them. Two of them had drawn truncheons. There was no superior officer in control. An inspector ultimately found by Mr Caborn denied all connection with the group from the transit van. He tried to calm the situation, but the damage had been done; police officers, on their own initiative, had exercised a degree of violent control that their chief constable clearly knew nothing about. An interesting aspect of police practice was revealed in this account. Mr Caborn asked one of the officers for his number. The officer gave it but added, 'You can have it now. You won't get it on the picket line.' Of the dismissive attitude of some officers towards those who seemed to them to support the striking miners, there is evidence in another exchange on this occasion. Mr Bill Michie MP was also present at the Trades and Labour Club. He, too, made a complaint to the chief constable. This is part of his affidavit:

> I noticed that some of the miners had spilled over into the roadway and police officers were trying to get them back on to the footpath. I went on to the road asking the miners to get off the road on to the footpath. Suddenly a police officer approached me from behind and put his arm

around my body. A second officer took hold of my left upper arm and together they started pulling me backwards on to the road. I could see Richard Caborn MP in the crowd in front of me and I heard him shout – 'He's an MP.' At that both police officers let go of me . . . as I was pushed back into the crowd I turned to remonstrate with them and one of them said – 'I don't give a shit whether you are an MP or not. Get out of the way or else!'

There was a second incident in the centre of the town for which we do not have an independent account. The police report, however, notes the use of truncheons:

outbreaks of disorder . . . culminating in an attack on a caterer's van near to the City Hall at 3.30 that afternoon. Drunken demonstrators had attempted to steal food from the van but had been prevented from doing so by a handful of officers . . . the attacks upon the police officers were so violent that the officers were required to draw their truncheons to protect themselves. Several police officers were surrounded by drunken, violent demonstrators and beaten severely, their colleagues being forced to mount rescues, and having to use their truncheons to do so.

The report ends with statistics for the day's events – 64 Police Support Units deployed (approximately 1,470 men), 42 police officers and 9 other persons injured, and 69 arrests.

As we have pointed out, working miners in Nottinghamshire were opposed to the policies of their officials. In an effort to bring about a change in these policies, rank-and-file members of the union staged a May Day rally at their area offices in Mansfield. Some say that working miners were given encouragement, support, and an extra day off by the Coal Board. Of this there is no proof; but an unending stream of buses and cars arriving in Mansfield suggested to the suspicious strikers that the police, at least, were assisting those who remained at work, for striking miners from outside the county were having great difficulty in reaching the scene of the rally. A large force of police mounted and on foot managed to keep the opposing sides apart for most of the day but bricks, stones, and clods of earth flew from all directions causing injuries to a number of miners, both those at work and those on strike. There were, of course, arrests. Many of these, however, were made at the borders of the county when striking miners tried to pierce the cordon which had been thrown round it. Local newspaper reports tell of the village of Pleasley being a battle-ground between the police and striking miners from Yorkshire who were assembling for the march to Mansfield. Nottinghamshire police waited in considerable numbers just inside the borders of the county and turned the striking miners back.[15]

A second rally in Mansfield was organized by the NUM on 14 May. Early on that day police management of the crowds was restrained. Few police officers were in evidence and, although the route of the procession had been clearly defined by the police, its conduct was left to NUM marshals. After the procession was over there was a change in policing tactics which may have been due to the lack of sympathy for striking miners in a community where most men had decided to work. Reports in the local press give the strong impression that shopkeepers on the route of the procession complained of the noise and disarray that resulted from it. Whether or not police officers were reacting to these complaints, they gathered in considerable force in the centre of the city and especially at the point where the cars and buses that had brought the demonstrators to the town were parked. As they went towards their transport, some of the striking miners and their supporters began to taunt the lines of police officers. A few missiles were hurled and the police moved in to make arrests. Police and demonstrators were reinforced and there was a considerable scuffle. A cordon of officers was thrown around the demonstrators who responded by trying to push their way out. Arrests were made and fifty-five of those who were arrested during the day were charged with riot.[16] Of the other incidents in the centre of the town there were conflicting reports. Some said that mounted police charged into the crowds. Indeed there is a graphic description by one miner of the confusion and terror of some incidents:

> One copper went and stood with some of the women so that they wouldn't get hit because they were just going mad. . . . I never felt so frightened or so angry in my life. You've got horses, then policemen, then people chucking bricks. . . . In the middle of it three or four, probably six police- men kicking hell out of a youth of probably 17 or 18. . . . He managed to stagger to his feet and his face was covered in blood. . . . Then one of them got out his stick about a yard long and whacked him across the face with it.   (Samuel, Bloomfield, and Boanas 1985: 118–19)

A probation officer, however, who was present in the town twenty minutes after the pubs closed, wrote: 'There was no indication that there was any undue disturbance in the town . . . the scenes there would have drawn no comment had they been taking place on a Saturday night'.

Despite the rallies and counter-rallies of April and May, picketing continued at pits where men were working or attempting to work. For the most part it was a kind of ritual. Pickets had to be posted so that deputies, clerical staff, and others, who had agreed not to cross picket lines, would not enter striking pits. Larger demonstrations were held to encourage and sustain those on strike as well as to shame those who were still at work. The culmina- tion of this second stage of the coal dispute was the mass picketing of the coking plant at Orgreave, which lasted from 23 May to 18 June.

When it became known, towards the end of May, that the British Steel Corporation was intent on moving the coke stored there, the plant and its contents became the focus of police activity as well as an object of interest to striking miners. There had, of course, been a police and picketing presence at the plant since the strike began. The British Steel Corporation, which had already encountered difficulties in moving coal and coke in and out of Ravenscraig in Scotland, had taken the precaution of providing South Yorkshire police with premises at the main gate of the plant. These furnished an adequate base for the deployment of very large numbers of men and the reception and management of dogs and horses. Convoys of lorries loaded with coke first left Orgreave on 23 May. There was a small picket (twenty- five) and a minimal police presence. In the following days the number of pickets increased. Police reinforcements were brought in and by 25 May there were more than 800 police at hand. On 29 May, however, the number of pickets increased dramatically. It was met by a large force of 2,000-odd police officers. The official police account of events says that riot gear (long shields and NATO helmets) was used for the first time on that day 'but only after officers in normal uniform had been subjected to a prolonged barrage of missiles'.[17] Other accounts from observers, miners, and less official police sources suggest other possibilities, one of which is that despite their presence in strength the police may have been caught off-guard in the early stages of the 'demonstration'. Pickets advanced on the gate before the police lines were in place. Dogs chased off the threatening advance and, to give time for the marshalling of police forces protecting the convoys, mounted officers repeatedly chased back the waves of miners who were angered by the unaccustomed use of dogs, charging horses, and the wholly unexpected appearance of riot squads. Stones were certainly thrown after the first charge of mounted officers; there were scuffles, arrests, and many attempts by the miners to re-establish their positions. On the two following days thousands of police officers and pickets faced each other and there were some unpleasant incidents, such as the throwing of paint stripper over three police officers. A number of pickets were arrested; but the convoys continued to go through.

The last confrontation on 18 June seemed, on the part of the police at least, to be a calculated and orderly re-enactment of the haphazard events of 29 May.[18] Miners had been summoned from far and wide. Some of them, particularly those from South Wales, were quite unfamiliar with the new police vestments – the long shields and formidable helmets. They had come, on a bright summer morning, to join in a demonstration of solidarity. Clad in the lightest of clothes they were prepared for the usual pushing and shoving. Although their first sight of the massed ranks of police officers, the way in which they were ushered in to the area, given parking space, and almost a welcome aroused suspicion among some, most of the pickets awaited the arrival of the convoys in holiday mood.[19] The struggle that followed was violent but unequal. Nearly 5,000 police officers with 50 mounted men and 58 dogs not only held the advancing pickets but also dispersed them through the streets and gardens of the residential areas near the plant. Short shields, devised for protection as police officers scatter, with truncheons, crowds which are deemed to be threatening or dangerous, were used for the first time during the coal dispute.

There is little evidence of serious stone-throwing before the first police advance. Indeed the official report is guarded.[20] Referring only to the deployment of the shielded and helmeted police, it says, 'There had already been some scenes of violence and police officers in protective headgear and with shields had to be deployed to protect the police cordon from missiles being thrown by the pickets.' But as the official police film of the encounter makes clear (contrary to the image of much of the media coverage), there were no 'scenes of violence' before mounted officers rode into the pickets and drove them away from the police line. Only after they had been attacked in this way did the pickets retaliate. Then barricades were built and set alight and missiles hurled at the advancing police. In the end, however, the pickets were no match for them. They abandoned the field on that day and never again attempted battle at Orgreave. For miners this confrontation with the police had been not only a terrifying but also a shaming experience for, unaccustomed to fear, they felt afraid. One miner from South Wales describes how he and some of his fellows got out of the fighting and shot down the motorway at 100 miles an hour in sheer terror.

> Orgreave was a bloody battle-ground. We left about lunch-time. We'd had a gutsful. The police got out of hand. They were beating us, kicking us; the way they brought the horses in. That's why we took the bridge. It was the only way out. They had us trapped and they kept coming in and beating the shit out of us.
> (Welsh Council for Civil and Political Liberties 1985: 105)

For the police it was a victory – but a dangerous one. For television coverage of the violent treatment of fleeing miners remains as a testimony to the retribution exacted by police officers whose task is the maintenance of order and nothing more. The chief constable's account of the day ends with the acknowledgement of one incident shown on television which involved a police officer apparently hitting a picket with his truncheon.

> Within 48 hours the results of the investigation into the incident had been considered by the Director of Public Prosecutions, who stated that a criminal prosecution was inappropriate and the matter should be dealt with by the officer's Chief Constable. A private prosecution has since been commenced.
> (South Yorkshire Police 1985: 12)

But why was Orgreave so important? The coking plant presented no great challenge to the purposes of the striking miners, for the resumption of coking convoys to Scunthorpe was an insignificant event in comparison with the necessity to keep struck pits closed and the CEGB starved of coal. Here we see the importance of symbolism for striking miners who had already endured considerable financial hardship and were fearful of its continuance. An expensive, even foolish, demonstration here would help them along. For the police – perhaps for the government as well – the Orgreave incident had historic significance. It redeemed the Saltley coke depot affair and wiped the slate clean.[21]

THE THIRD PHASE OF PICKETING AND ITS CONTROL

The admission of defeat by the miners at Orgreave did not end the strike. It simply opened the door for the use of heavier police tactics at colliery gates. For the third phase of the strike, which began in late July and early August, was marked by the slow return to work in coalfields hitherto strike-bound. During this phase police activity was concentrated on the containment of pickets at colliery gates and on the policing of mining villages now rent with discord between striking miners and those who had returned to work. Attacks on the persons and property of working miners, although they may not have been so numerous as hostile critics suggest, occurred with sufficient frequency to warrant the deployment of additional police officers in areas of greatest tension. The Chief Constable of Derbyshire, for example, formed a special squad to deal with reports of intimidation and criminal damage. This 'gave confidence to those who were victimised and reports of offences increased'.[22] Indeed this increase in reported offences had the effect of 'creating' some crimes which had not been the subject of complaint at the time they were committed. Thus a working miner reported to the police investigation unit damage to his car windscreen. In the enquiries which followed he brought up an incident that had happened six weeks before. He and a striking miner had had a scuffle in a miners' welfare club. There was not a great deal of harm done and neither man made any complaint to the police at the time. Now, however, the striking miner was charged with, and subsequently convicted of, assault. The criminal damage complaint was taken no further.

In South Yorkshire special squads of detectives were formed to investigate the incidence of assault or threats of assault upon working miners. A large number of cases of intimidation were noted (904) but whether these were discovered by the detectives themselves or reported by others is not clear. The small number of arrests, which the chief constable attributed to fear on the part of witnesses, suggests that actual complaints may have been fewer than incidents recorded by the police.[23]

An increased police presence in the mining villages, whether as special investigating officers or preventive patrols, was thought by striking miners and many other inhabitants to be oppressive, distorting normal relationships and inhibiting necessary activity. Union officials wishing to communicate with those of their members who had returned to work could do so only by grace and favour of the patrolling force. A sizeable number of police officers outside public houses and miners' welfare institutions was an unwelcome substitute for the more accommodating style of familiar local officers operating as community policemen. Yet there were heavy pressures upon those who wished to return to work. We received numbers of accounts of working miners being set upon and of their houses being damaged. Less frequently, working miners (especially in areas where they were dominant) attacked striking miners and suffered the consequences of arrest and conviction, for police officers seemed anxious to be seen to be impartial in this aspect of their control of the strike. These local tensions had been demonstrated earlier in the dispute in the Nottinghamshire village of Blidworth. There were a number of striking miners in this village, although the colliery was at work. They and their families gave hospitality to Yorkshire miners who were in the area hoping to rally support for the strike. These miners lived in tents and caravans in the gardens of their hosts and were given food and other assistance when it was necessary. The wife of one of the striking miners described a series of events which took place on 25 May 1984 as the Yorkshire men were packing up and preparing to leave. Her description was forwarded to us in the hope that the distress and anxiety suffered by her family and friends would become known. Her account, which is given some colour by reports in the local press, describes the arrest of a young Yorkshire miner who was living in a caravan in her garden.[24] He had come to borrow a loaf of bread and as he was returning to the caravan he was seized by police officers who swarmed into the garden in considerable numbers. The officers then went to neighbouring houses, roused the inhabitants, abused those who protested, and threatened arrest for any Yorkshire miner – or anyone else for that matter – who picketed next day. She ended her description of a night of disturbance and anxiety:

> We kept watch all the early hours of the morning. Police riot vans passed at intervals of every five minutes until about 3.30 and [then] they passed every three minutes, but instead of one or two vans there were at least four and sometimes five and police walked by my house very often in twos and threes.

Saturation policing of this kind was not common in the early days of the dispute. It increased as miners began to respond to the campaign of the National Coal Board for a return to work. In areas where the strike had been solid, the return of one or two men was carefully planned and protected by large contingents of police. The most extreme example of such protectiveness was at Easington in Durham where a single miner caused the sealing off of a whole village.[25] On 20 August Paul Wilkinson of Easington Colliery turned up for work supported by several columns of police. Large numbers of pickets prevented his entrance and he was driven away. Next day barricades had been built but Wilkinson did not come. Union officials and management reached an agreement that if he did return he would enter by the main gate or not at all. For the remainder of the week there was no attempt to bring him in but, after four days, large reinforcements of police arrived. Wilkinson set off for the colliery again and the pickets prepared for a tussle. But he was whisked in a back door avoiding the pickets (who were nevertheless faced by large numbers of police). Thereafter there were violent scenes as the police in riot gear moved into the village, which for the three succeeding days was completely sealed off in the morning. No one was allowed in or out. Police control of the roads ensured that men from Easington, at least, did not reach the colliery gates.

Difficulties in the mining communities were not always due to the presence of unusual numbers of police, frequently drawn from 'foreign' forces. Disorderly behaviour, vandalism, and occasionally serious violence was noted in the summer and early autumn months, particularly in some Yorkshire villages. Unemployed youngsters, even schoolboys on vacation, sometimes used the divisions between the police and community, and within the community itself, as an excuse for causing a little extra trouble. This could be, and sometimes was, attributed to striking miners by those who were out of sympathy with their conduct of the dispute. On the whole, however, complaints of riotous behaviour or police harassment had reference to occasions when pickets left the colliery gates. Well-authenticated reports of retreating pickets being pursued by police officers through their villages justify the claim of the South Yorkshire Police Authority that much of the trouble that resulted from mass picketing during the last phase of the strike was due to police policies of pursuit as pickets returned home. Events at Armthorpe, Stainforth, and Wath-on-Dearne were all of this nature. What happened at Grimethorpe was rather different. It was the violent response of a community which felt itself to be over-policed. The arrest of miners and their families who were taking coal from NCB coal dumps lit a fuse which caused an explosion of disorder and a torrent of complaint from people in the village about their subjection to police control. The Chief Constable of South Yorkshire, in his report on the strike (South Yorkshire Police 1985: 35) underplays the incidents at Grimethorpe. He mentions only the attack on the local police station by a number of young men. But the proceedings of a meeting held subsequently in Grimethorpe between villagers and senior police officers make it clear that the trouble was more deep-rooted. Complaints voiced by local residents on that occasion included references to the persistent presence of unusual numbers of police officers in the village and the injustice of the over-zealous enforcement of the law against those stealing from Coal Board stores of coal which were dotted around the village. One man passionately denounced the practice of arresting and prosecuting everybody found removing the coal; it was, he said, *their* coal, mined by *their* labour. Pointing to the local cemetery, he said that some of the men there had given their lives to dig this coal. It belonged, therefore, to the community. However wrong in law he was, this man still voiced the deep feelings of a mining community struggling to survive.

The slow return to work continued. Despite the spread of the effort needed to maintain picketing throughout the coalfields, striking miners managed, in the autumn and winter months, to post considerable numbers of men at the gates of pits where men were abandoning the strike. In the early weeks of the return in Yorkshire and other initially solid areas, only handfuls of miners were escorted into the colliery buildings under heavy police escort and frequently in vehicles with blacked-out windows and protective mesh. In many cases, therefore, there was no possibility of 'peaceful persuasion'. Pickets were not merely resentful of this frustration of their functions; they argued, too, that a police effort dedicated to ensuring that one or two miners entered a pit where work was impossible was wasteful and provocative. Moreover, an unfortunate police practice of locating their vehicles within the colliery gates and frequently directing operations from there suggested to the striking miners that the police were 'MacGregor's Men', taking instructions from the Coal Board and promoting its interest. There may have been sound reasons for this practice during the miners' strike. The Chief Constable of South Yorkshire argues in his report on the strike (South Yorkshire Police 1985: 70) that this method of directing the policing enabled maximum protection to be provided to persons and property with the minimum of manpower, and the establishment of maximum control. Previous industrial disputes had not usually been policed in this way.

Although the policing of the return to work was, in general, not marked by major confrontation, there were some instances of police provocation and picketing excesses that gave rise to the belief, nurtured by the media, that the coalfields were aflame with violence. Certainly some police officers accepted the stereotypes of picketing violence offered to them and reacted with unacceptable violence themselves.

For this third and last phase of the dispute, however, there is a great deal of concrete evidence about the policing of picketing at colliery gates. Groups of observers provided full reports of events at many collieries. They were able to assess the temper of the pickets and the police, to estimate their numbers and give a general account of police strategy and picket response. Occasionally in these reports there are accounts of arrests and their apparent justification. All are agreed that the incidence of violent picketing or intemperate policing was relatively small. Even very large pickets (or demonstrations) were possible without unacceptable levels of aggression. The group of observers from Chesterfield NCCL conclude from their observations, however, that during the last three months of the strike the ratio of police to pickets was reduced. During this period, in their experience at least, violence on the picket lines virtually disappeared. But observers did not always see the whole of the game.[26] For an appreciation of what some pickets suffered we have also had recourse to the many individual accounts which we received from occasional bystanders, pickets themselves, or their friends and relatives. Many of these reports reached us through Members of Parliament to whom constituents had written in default of any other reasonable outlet for their complaints.

From these accounts it would seem that striking miners were convinced that some police officers attacked peaceful pickets with unnecessary and unjustifiable force. Whatever may be the expectations of the 'dangerous and perishing classes' in their relations with the police, the ordinary citizen does not expect, even in an argument with a police officer, to be thumped with a truncheon or kicked with a sturdy black boot. Yet this is what happened to some striking miners. One observer witnessed an incident at Kiveton Park Colliery on 22 August 1984.[27] He was on his way to the nearby railway station and stopped at the picket line to speak to a friend. Seeing the police bearing down on the pickets he moved off but heard and saw one policeman kicking a youth to the ground. This police officer was joined by three others who kicked the youth for fully three or four minutes. He went on:

> Another collier was on the ground being kicked by another group of policemen. After they had had a good kicking the two pickets were dragged back down towards the colliery gates.

He ends his report:

> I did think for a moment of stopping one of the officers and asking why none of them were displaying their numbers, but I was honestly under the impression that anyone who got in the way of the police on that particular morning would have been flattened.

Another incident at the beginning of the return to work in South Yorkshire was described by a member of NACODS who happened to be helping his wife at Hatfield Main Miners' Club. Seeing a large number of police and pickets he locked up the club but watched what was happening from inside:

> Pickets who were sitting down near the colliery gates were attacked by police officers in riot gear and beaten. One man was carried away unconscious. He saw an old man knocked off a wall and women and children running away in terror.
>
> (South Yorkshire Police Authority 1985: 94)

Every senior police officer has, at some time in his career, had experience of street policing and the pressures upon junior officers that are its accompaniment. But transfer to management level may well modify the effects of that experience and induce the belief that a wholly disciplined force is a reality; that the production of reports and the immediate supervision of police officers on the ground is proof against the power of the traditional myths, self-images, and self-interest which influence the behaviour of those who enforce the law on the streets.[28] For the lower-ranking police officer, the uniform he wears conveys an authority he will not willingly see questioned or diminished.[29] If a reduction of that authority is the price of neutrality as between one group of citizens and another, he will not normally pay that price. Of course the degree of sensitivity to the impairment of his rights and duties varies between individual policemen. It is also deeply affected by the nature of the area in which each officer operates. Thus the dilemma for working policemen is particularly acute in the urban and inner city areas where much of life, for the younger population at least, is spent in the street. Policing is therefore heavily concentrated there. But law enforcement in the shape of such an open exercise of authority meets with resistance from members of the public. In reply police officers are frequently tempted to exert their constitutional authority, even their physical strength. In their view they cannot afford to lose any moral or physical confrontation. It is for this reason that public expressions of concern about police behaviour during the coal strike frequently fastened on officers from Merseyside, Greater Manchester, and the Metropolitan police. In these areas control of the 'residual' population is frequently marked by abusive and derogatory language of the kind to which the mining communities took particular exception. They did not see themselves as worthless citizens, the 'rubbish' of the population of whom urban police officers are frequently contemptuous and dismissive. They were top wage-earners in a proud and self-sufficient industrial class whose contacts with law enforcement agencies were on their own terms. The armlocks, indiscriminate arrests, abuse, and baton blows had been, for them, a matter of history, not present-day reality.[30] The conduct of some police officers on and off the picket lines convinced them that history was repeating itself.

Disciplinary control of the street behaviour of police officers is extremely hard to effect, since supervision is infrequent.[31] During the strike, however, there was usually a sufficient number of supervisory officers on the normal picket line to ensure a fair level of responsible behaviour. After all, the control of picket lines at colliery gates was organized in support units each of which had a supervisory officer of inspector rank assisted by two sergeants. Moreover, the tactics of forward movement had, as we have shown, been clearly laid down. It was, no doubt, well-practised; but there were difficulties. Some of these were given expression during the Joint Central Conference of the Police Federation in May 1985. In a heated discussion about policing of the miners' strike, police officers spoke of the lack of leadership on the part of senior officers. What this complaint amounted to was a lack of clarity in tactics. This weakness had apparently been noted since new 'packages' had been drawn up by the ACPO training committee. The Police Federation had not been involved. Apparently, said one speaker, members of the federation are not to be trusted. They were not even allowed to have copies of the Tactical Options Manual. All attempts to secure its distribution to members of the federation had failed. There were problems too about communication at the picket line. On the occasions when there was trouble between police and pickets and the degree of noise and tumult was great senior officers found it difficult to communicate with those who were in the thick of the pushing and shoving. It should be possible, continued the speaker, to fit radio receivers into the NATO helmets worn as part of the police officers' protective clothing.

Striking miners also complained of lack of supervision and control on the part of supervisory officers. Actions which in normal circumstances would be restrained or which might even attract a disciplinary sanction went unnoticed. Complaints by pickets or their supporters were hampered by a rapid sequence of events which made the recognition of individual officers difficult, if not impossible. Besides this, a number of police officers did not display their official numbers. There was, indeed, another more general obstacle to citizen control over the unacceptable behaviour of working policemen. When the Merseyside police were on duty at Markham Main Colliery in the week beginning 20 August they seem to have behaved with unusual arrogance and insensitivity. Residents of the adjoining village of Armthorpe met on 14 September to discuss the violent events at Markham and in the village itself in that week. There were complaints that the Merseyside police had hurled coins as well as abuse at the pickets and that they were drunk; that when pickets dispersed they followed them into the village, assaulted them, forced their way into houses, and damaged property. The complaints were levelled not at individual officers but at a detachment of men known to be from Merseyside police. Some of the complaints were of criminal assault, others were of such a general nature that it is unlikely that they would fall within the provisions of section 49 of the Police Act, 1964. Yet there was clearly ground for complaint; the problem was one of whose responsibility extended to these circumstances. Police officers seconded under mutual aid are under the direction and control of the chief constable of the host area, and thus the latter should have been the proper target for complaints. Indeed the Chief Constable of South Yorkshire was asked for a report on the matter although the Special Subcommittee repeated their belief that he was not to blame for what happened. The South Yorkshire Police Authority had no standing to question the Chief Constable of Merseyside, who as the sending chief officer retained full disciplinary authority over his men – his South Yorkshire counterpart had none. To add to the rather confusing split of power and responsibility it was the South Yorkshire Chief Constable who would be liable to be sued for any individual wrongful actions of officers under his direction and control, if any could be proved. This discloses a serious problem – the split between operational and disciplinary control means neither is fully effective and even the usual, inadequate channels of accountability are foreclosed. Chief officers assume that the control of their forces – even when they are operating outside their own areas – is comprehensive. What happened during the coal strike showed them to be in error.

VIOLENCE BY STRIKING MINERS

Although the behaviour of the police may have justified criticism, the actions of some striking miners could not be excused either by their colleagues or by the general public. In the autumn and winter months, as financial hardship goaded men to return to work, there was fierce pressure upon those who did so by those who were determined to stick it out. Despite the presence of police patrols and the activities of the CID, houses were vandalized, men were threatened, and families abused. There were serious attacks upon Coal Board property, the cutting of conveyor belts for example, or the destruction of vehicles and huts. Unmanned police stations received attention also, although here the damage was less serious and may have been the work of youths who had nothing better to do. Many of these actions were the reckless and extravagant response of young men to the frustrations of the strike and the failure of their efforts. (Indeed the same gloss may be put on policing activities, since the pressures upon young police officers were also considerable.) Whatever the explanation of the violence of striking miners, its consequences on one occasion were outrageous and tragic. In South Wales attempts to disrupt the convoys of coal lorries to the Port Talbot steel works involved a watch being set on some of the bridges over the M4 motorway. Missiles were then hurled down, some of which caused damage to lorries and apprehension among drivers. A senior police officer gave a public warning about the danger of this practice. It was unheeded for, when the first handful of miners returned to work at Merthyr, two young men dropped a concrete block upon the taxi which was driving one miner to work. The driver of the taxi was killed.[32] There had been other fatalities: two strikers killed at the picket line, two young boys engulfed by coal on a tip which they were raiding, and at least one adult killed while 'picking' for coal; but this South Wales killing was the most awesome single consequence of the strike. It will always obscure the fact that the year passed in a kind of armed neutrality between pickets and police, each of whom maintained for the most part a correct, if distant relationship.

THE ORGANIZATION AND FINANCING OF THE POLICING

The total scale of policing involved in the strike was enormous. Clearly it was beyond the resources of those police forces in whose areas most of the serious conflict occurred. The system of mutual aid laid down by the Police Act, 1964, was rapidly put to its most severe test; the experience raised serious questions to which we return later.

Mutual aid was co-ordinated through the National Reporting Centre, which was brought into active service on 14 March. The NRC operated from a room in New Scotland Yard, under the operational control of the current president of the Association of Chief Police Officers – initially Mr David Hall of Humberside, succeeded in the summer of 1984 by Nottinghamshire's Charles McLachlan. Throughout the dispute the NRC gathered and collated information about all aspects of the picketing and police responses, received requests for mutual aid, and arranged the dispatch of the necessary officers.

Its critics ascribed to it powers of direction over chief constables. Although this was regularly denied by police spokesmen, there was some evidence to support the charge, and there was certainly very little sign of effective resistance by chief constables to its requests for assistance.[33] The local police committees were not brought into the process at all. Only the Home Secretary, as Police Authority for the Metropolis, had any effective involvement, but this was informal and indeterminate; officially the NRC was a creature of the chief constables – literally a mutual assistance facility – its evident power notwithstanding.

The financial rules for mutual aid are as skeletal as the legal powers themselves. Under section 14 of the 1964 Act the Police Authorities involved in a mutual aid arrangement may agree the financial arrangements themselves; in default of agreement (as in the strike) the Home Secretary has power to determine the amounts to be paid. Because of previous difficulties over the application of these principles, the Home Office had issued more detailed rules in a circular of 1973, which classified mutual aid into three levels (small, larger scale, and major) with different methods of calculating the cost to be reimbursed by the receiving area. For major aid the full economic cost – including for instance the basic salaries of the aiding officers – is payable, whereas for larger-scale aid only the *additional* costs (overtime, transport, and so on) are covered.

The Home Secretary classified the miners' strike as 'larger scale'.[34] This reduced the amounts payable by areas such as South Yorkshire, Derbyshire, and Nottinghamshire, the three principal recipients of aid. But the amounts payable were still enormous, and way beyond the budget limits of the police committees or their parent councils. The early months of the strike saw a series of unedifying disputes between the local authorities and the Home Office – which eventually met 90 per cent of additional expenditure, plus everything in excess of a 0.75p rate. There were also disputes between the police authorities themselves – Derbyshire refused to pay the bills it received and litigation was threatened – and between police committees and their chief constables. Desperate searches for budget savings led to a proposal in Nottinghamshire to opt out of the Regional Crime Squad, while in South Yorkshire a proposal to abolish the Mounted Section nearly led to litigation. A resolution that the chief constable be required to seek prior approval for virtually all expenditure did lead to action, brought by the Attorney-General, and a rapid retreat by the authority.[35]

Eventually a system for billing and reimbursing was worked out, and some £200 million was repaid to the police authorities to meet the costs for which they had been charged. This represents only the Home Office share of the *additional* costs of policing; the total cost has not been accurately calculated but was greatly in excess of this amount.[36]

PUBLIC CONCERN AND COMPLAINTS ABOUT POLICING DURING THE DISPUTE

CONCERNS OF THE POLICE AUTHORITIES

At the end of the strike the tripartite structure of responsibility for the policing of the country was seen to be in ruins. The Chief Constable of Greater Manchester voiced the frustration of chief constables; the police authorities had already recognized the impossibility of their position; only the government seemed satisfied with an arrangement which gave it the power it needed while remaining free of formal responsibility.

It was clear that the principal concern for all authorities, and especially those whose police chiefs were compelled to ask for aid from other forces, was the money that would have to be found, over and above the police budget, for the policing of the strike.[37] The elucidation of the police authorities' weakness in the control of spending by their chief officers is powerfully expressed in Spencer's account of the police authorities' experience.[38] During a meeting between members of the Merseyside Authority and the Deputy Under-Secretary of State for the Home Office, it was maintained by Home Office representatives that in the operation of mutual aid, chief constables were responsible to the police authorities only to the extent of 'rendering an account'. Authorities could set no limit to their chief constables' spending; they could ask only for an account. This interpretation of the position was formally confirmed by the Home Secretary on 18 June 1984 in the following terms:

> A chief constable, acting reasonably, cannot be required to obtain police authority approval for the expenditure involved, but responsible chief constables and responsible authorities would meet to discuss the situation thereafter.

Clearly, when section 14 of the Police Act, 1964, is invoked, the control of any authority affected by its operation is reduced to zero.

Most authorities were anxious, too, about the effect upon crime prevention and detection of the concentration of effort upon this policing. In resolving these problems, they faced not their chief officers but the Home Secretary since, as we have shown, it was he who put into effect the central government's policy in the matter of finance. Indirectly therefore he was responsible for the efficiency of police forces throughout the country.

Confronted with the realization of their constitutional weakness, a few police authorities did their best to mediate between 'national' policing policies and community needs. Of these, the South Yorkshire Authority had some success. On many occasions during the strike, members of the Special Subcommittee of the authority met in various parts of the county together with police officers, officials of the NUM, and members of the community. The complaints of miners, their wives and families, and others affected by police action were put to senior officers of the force. On one occasion the deputy chief constable attended a meeting in Grimethorpe after the incidents referred to earlier between the police and the villagers when arrests were made for theft of coal from NCB stockpiles – to which the villagers, in their difficulties, thought they had a moral right. He apologized unreservedly for any improper action taken by the officers of his force but pointed out that the law must be upheld.[39] This simplification of police responsibility is frequently used to justify a tough reaction to the misdemeanours of citizens. Police officers know, however, that the most important political function is to distinguish between circumstances in which action should be taken against apparent law-breaking and where advice, negotiation, or even turning a blind eye should be preferred. During the coal dispute the enforcement of the letter of the law seemed to be the most frequently chosen option. In the case of coal thefts at Grimethorpe, police officers' political choice may have been influenced by the National Coal Board. In the light of its consequences, it was insensitive and short-sighted.

Throughout these meetings there was a clear expression of the need felt by members of all the mining communities that the use of police officers from other forces should be avoided. There would be no trouble, it was claimed, if officers living in the area or known to people living there were returned to their normal function of policing the community. But the conflict between community feeling and national policy was evident. In answer to a complaint about numbers of police officers stationed at one of the Yorkshire pits, a superintendent replied that the police were present 'because they were under the impression that some miners were intending to return to work and, *in accordance with policy laid down nationally*, they were ensuring that men who wished to return to work could do so'.[40] The Report of the Special Sub-committee which recorded the recognition of this restraint upon local initiative also recorded the confidence of the police authority in the South Yorkshire chief constable. The terms in which this is expressed are of some interest: 'there have been . . . differences of opinion over police tactics, but he has listened to what people had to say to him and *whenever he was able to* he has acted on what was said'.[41]

CONCERNS OF ORDINARY CITIZENS

The unease of ordinary citizens about developments in the organization and management of police forces was at the beginning of the strike focused in part on a perceived move towards a national police force. It derived also from accounts of road-blocks and the arrests that followed from their use. Disquieting as this volume of criticism is, it cannot match the torrent of complaints from striking miners, their families, and their friends in the later stages of the dispute, that is when the return to work had begun – or perhaps from Orgreave onwards. These complaints, voiced to MPs, police authorities, the media, and ourselves, referred in almost every case to the behaviour of individual police officers and their unpredictable judgements. Even the method of applying handcuffs varied from one officer to another. Some 'prisoners' had their hands behind their back, some in front. Some were handcuffed with a particularly vicious plastic contraption that caused some pain. On one occasion an arrested miner complained to one police sergeant that these plastic bands were too tight and causing his hands to swell. The sergeant replied, 'Too bad'. Another officer, passing the police van, released the tight bands and replaced them in a more comfortable position. 'Is that better, son?' he asked. Random arrests were, it was said, accompanied by unnecessary violence, which was usually witnessed or experienced when supervising officers were not present. If complaints were made by those who were victimized, their accounts had little chance of surviving in the face of self-justification by police officers. Besides, complaints were frequently out of the question since it was impossible to identify the particular officer or officers who were said to have struck the blow or made the offensive remark.

But the difficulties encountered in pressing to a conclusion complaints about police strategies and their consequences were acknowledged by the Police Complaints Board in its (valedictory) Annual Report for 1984:

> Such complaints have not been regarded by chief officers as matters to be recorded and investigated under section 49 of the Police Act 1964. We accept this view.   (Police Complaints Board 1985: para 6.3)

Here is a clear example of the powerlessness of the citizen to have his complaint even considered by those to whom, in the first instance, it must be made. The Police and Criminal Evidence Act, 1984, which substituted a new complaints procedure, retains this feature, with an explicit exclusion of complaints about policy decisions from the remit of the Police Complaints Authority. Redress may be obtained only through the courts. Attempts to restrain the use of road-blocks and the restriction of movement of ordinary citizens were frustrated by the judicial view that mass picketing was, in itself, intimidatory and could not be allowed the protection of the courts.[42] Yet, as we have seen, the official view of the Association of Chief Police Officers was that picketing was not always intimidatory and it could always be contained by the police. This view was echoed at the Police Federation Conference in 1985 where a delegate from Wales insisted that many striking miners behaved with dignity and restraint.

The few complaints that reached the formal complaints procedure (551) seemed to have little chance of surviving the course. Thus 111 were later withdrawn, for what reason is not at all clear, though some miners suspected that contamination with a complaint might give rise to difficulties in present or future court proceedings. In Yorkshire, as noted in the first Annual Report of the Police Complaints Authority, members of the NUM were advised not to lodge complaints until the strike was over. This distrust of the system seems to be justified by the failure of any complaint alleging assault (and there were 257 complaints of this kind) to bring about the public prosecution of a single police officer. We have already made reference to the violent attack upon a fleeing picket by a police officer at Orgreave. The truncheon blow appeared to be quite gratuitous and without the justification of self-defence which police officers can put forward in less public circumstances. Yet no official action was taken, apart from a swift reference to the Director of Public Prosecutions, who advised that the evidence available was not strong enough for a conviction.[43] (It is, of course, generally accepted that the prosecution of members of the police force is not undertaken without much stronger evidence than is thought to be appropriate in other cases.) Even among the complaints that reached the Police Complaints Board, and later its successor the Police Complaints Authority, none was considered to justify disciplinary action. A total of 150 complaints were processed by the Board and Authority, but no disciplinary proceedings were taken; as the Authority said in its Annual Report for 1986 'various officers were admonished and advised about their behaviour', but for the rest, where there were grounds for complaint the offending officers could not be identified.[44] We discuss the general implications of this in Chapter 10.

It is arguable that the most important lesson of the miners' strike and its policing is the inability of any citizen or body of citizens to make an effective complaint against policing policy. Lord Scarman's pallid recommendation that a subcommittee of the police authority could be used for consideration of such complaints was tried by the South Yorkshire authority, which was occasionally able to moderate the more serious effects of some high-level decisions or at least to provide a forum for open discussion of grievances.[45] It declared itself, however, utterly powerless to affect the national decision to use the police to ensure, at any cost, the symbolic entry into strike-bound pits of single miners who wished to give up the strike. This policy – an open reversal of the majoritarian principle upon which police power usually rests – stood utilitarian arithmetic on its head and gave the colour of superior moral and political principle to the apportionment of protection between one set of citizens and another.[46] But the cost, in terms of civil liberties, public peace, and police morale, has been heavy indeed.

NOTES

1. For a full review of the legal implications of police policies and procedure in the coal dispute see Wallington (1985).
2. In the 1972 coal strike, which lasted six weeks, arrests for the five weeks for which there are records totalled 263. In the 13-week steel strike in 1980, arrests in South Yorkshire alone (which was the centre of the strike) amounted to 159. In South Yorkshire in the 52 weeks of the coal strike, arrests totalled 1,533. On steel-strike standards, the figure should have been around 650.
3. Riot charges in Nottinghamshire and South Yorkshire had been preferred some considerable time before the Home Secretary gave public approval to this policy in his speech at Worksop in September 1984.
4. Detailed statistics of charges are given in Appendix 1.
5. See evidence of a number of chief officers of police to the Select Committee on Employment in February and October 1980, quoted in Chapter 4. Police insistence on the difference between a 'picket' and a 'demonstration', together with their existing power to limit the numbers on a picket line, weakened the case for the picketing provisions in the 1980 legislation and ensured that mass picketing could remain, on specific occasions, a matter to be controlled or sanctioned by the police.
6. Policy Studies Institute (1983: vol. 4, p. 88). This may not have been the view of the demonstrators who faced the ranks of police during this dispute.
7. See p. 134.
8. The use of the Special Branch to provide intelligence about the conduct and potential for disorder of major industrial disputes is well known and documented in police records. Trade union leaders acknowledge this as a fact of life, but those who are striking and picketing react badly to the suspicion that their movements are being watched and their strike committees and meetings infiltrated by police officers. The acquisition of Special Branch information may often be more simple than this, but there is no denying that the information is obtained and passed from force to force. In the miners' strike, Special Branch officers from each force would certainly pass it on to the National Reporting Centre. The strike also

produced numerous allegations of telephone tapping, in some cases backed by strong circumstantial evidence. It is impossible to say how far strike organizers' telephones *were* tapped; however we regard it as almost inevitable that some such activity did take place. The adequacy of safeguards in this field is discussed in Chapter 10.

9. *Moss* v *McLachlan* (1985). It took some time (until November 1984) for the court to hear this test case, in the form of an appeal from the decision of Mansfield magistrates to convict a group of striking miners for trying to force their way through a police road-block.

10. This incident was reported to us by one of the women to whom passage was denied.

11. See also Chapter 5.

12. This pit was in the Nottinghamshire NCB area which was not on strike. It fell within the Derbyshire police area, where miners *were* on strike.

13. *Retford Times*, 4 May 1984. Throughout the dispute, figures were bandied about to score points for one side or another. The numbers of police officers are usually fairly accurate, since they are provided by the police information service. Estimates of picketing numbers are also given by the police. They were frequently on the high side. There is, too, the possibility of inaccurate transmission of information. A newsflash in the *Leicester Mercury* about the incident at Harworth refers to 1,000 pickets, not 10,000.

14. South Yorkshire Police (1985: 6).

15. *Nottingham Evening Post*, 2 May 1984.

16. Not one of these was convicted of riot. See *Legal Action*, September 1985, for details of the riot cases arising from the strike.

17. South Yorkshire Police (1985: 9).

18. Some pickets, however, complicated matters by effecting an entry to the plant itself in the early hours of the morning. There was some diversion of police resources to deal with this problem.

19. Some accounts (including those of South Wales miners) have suggested that the striking miners were enticed into Orgreave to make a better killing at the battle the South Yorkshire commander had prepared for. (See for example Welsh Council for Civil and Political Liberties (WCCPL) 1985: 93–4). But this is scarcely credible. What is true is that the policy of the South Yorkshire Chief Constable was unlike that of his colleague in Nottinghamshire. He did not cordon off his area with road-blocks.

20. South Yorkshire Police (1985: 12).

21. For accounts of Orgreave see also Adeney and Lloyd (1986: 112–18); *Sunday Times* Insight Team (1985: 83–106); WCCPL (1985: 85–106); and the accounts of observers from Sheffield Policewatch, some of which are reprinted in Appendix 3. See also MacGregor (1986: 205); Sir Ian MacGregor there indicates the importance of Orgreave as a diversion of the pickets' efforts from the Nottinghamshire coalfields.

22. Annual Report of the Chief Constable of Derbyshire, 1984.

23. South Yorkshire Police (1985: 33).

24. Particularly *Nottingham Evening Post*, 25 May 1984.

25. See the excellent account of this incident in Beynon (1984).

26. The reports of the Chesterfield NCCL observers are sensitive to this weakness. Their general accounts do, however, carry conviction. Some specimen reports and their general conclusions are reprinted in Appendix 2.

27. The final report of the observers from Chesterfield NCCL notes that 'over a fairly extended period the policing at Kiveton Park Colliery in South Yorkshire, with mounted police, police dogs and police wearing riot gear very much in evidence, was much heavier than normally seen in Derbyshire'.

28. Junior officers are warned of this by the repeated advice of older men: 'Never put it on paper.'

29. See the helpful discussion on the self-image of police officers in the Metropolitan police in Policy Studies Institute (1983: vol. 4, pp. 87 ff. and 173 ff.).

30. Robert Roberts recalls strike-torn Salford in 1911: 'I saw an officer lean forward on his horse and hit a neighbour with his truncheon above the eyes, heard the blow like a thump of wood on a swede-turnip. . . . The man ran crouching, hands to his face, into a wall and collapsed.' (Roberts 1971: 94; cf. Samuel, Bloomfield, and Boanas 1985: 119.)

31. See Policy Studies Institute (1983: vol. 4, pp. 274 ff.) for evidence of this.

32. Two striking miners were convicted of the murder of the taxi driver. Their convictions were later reduced to manslaughter by the Court of Appeal, and sentences of eight years' imprisonment substituted for the earlier life sentences; the House of Lords later dismissed

a prosecution appeal on the murder charge – *R* v *Hancock and Shankland* (1986).
33. cf. Kettle (1985).
34. Spencer (1985a) – an excellent account of this aspect of the strike; 1.4 million days of mutual aid were worked. What would be needed to justify the 'major' classification?
35. See Spencer (1985a: 13–14); South Yorkshire Police (1985).
36. See Appendix 1 for figures on this.
37. Spencer (1985a: 18).
38. Spencer (1985a: 17).
39. South Yorkshire Police Authority (1985: 112).
40. South Yorkshire Police Authority (1985: 96).
41. South Yorkshire Police Authority (1985: 12).
42. cf. Newbold (1985).
43. The Police Complaints Authority records as one reason for this failure to act the refusal of a victim to give evidence against the police (1987: para 3.6). We do not regard this as a reason for not taking disciplinary action, at the least, in the wider public interest. We understand that a private prosecution was brought but its outcome has not (so far as we are aware) been made public.
44. Police Complaints Authority (1987: paras 3.4–3.7); cf. also Police Complaints Board (1985: para 6.2). In three cases an apology was sent to the complainant 'if the conduct of the officers (none of whom could be identified from the available information) had given cause for complaint'.
45. Scarman (1981: para 7.27).
46. The flight from majoritarian principles in many political philosophies and practices of the present day is given the moral justification of individual rights. The policing of the miners' strike showed how easily and speciously the rights of some may be defended at the price of grave injustice to large bodies of citizens.

7

The use of the criminal process in the miners' strike

Not all striking miners and their supporters on the picket lines or at rallies and street collections suffered the blunt edge of police methods of control. Since the end of the strike, therefore, those police activities which had no enduring consequences for mining communities may now be remembered without rancour. Only the financial consequences of the stoppage of work, such as heavy loans and mortgage repayments, rent arrears and fuel bills, or the summary dismissal which sometimes followed arrest remain as a grievous testimony to the twelve months' struggle. It is true that the events at Orgreave may pass into coal-mining history, but as a landmark, rather like Saltley, with overtones of myth and legend which will affect the attitudes of the miners' union as a whole, rather than of its individual members. Those who endured the rigours of the criminal process are in a different category.

Few of the men and women who were arrested and brought before the courts had any experience of the consequences of law-breaking. They were not 'villains' in the police sense, although one or two may have been involved in law-breaking as children or motoring offences at a later stage. This relative innocence accounts, in part, for the shocked dismay with which they recounted what had happened to them.

THE PROCESS OF ARREST

There were 11,312 men and women arrested in the course of the strike.[1] A relatively high proportion of arrests occurred in Nottinghamshire, where the road-block policy of the chief constable allowed and encouraged his subordinates to turn back those who were thought to be travelling to picket Nottinghamshire pits. Those who challenged or resisted police orders were, of course, liable to arrest. A number of incidents occurring at these road-blocks were reported to us by a probation officer in the Nottinghamshire area. Here is one of them:

> A man was stopped at a police road-block near to a local colliery. He was asked to produce identification as the police officer wished to check that

he was 'entitled' to picket or demonstrate near to that colliery. He was alleged to have said that he 'was not stopping' and attempted to drive on. A police officer standing in front of the car had to protect himself by placing his hands on the bonnet. . . . He was charged with assault on a police officer. He was already on bail, with the usual conditions. . . . The prosecution admitted that he was on route to [picket at] his usual workplace but [argued] that his actions were not peaceful and he was consequently in breach of his conditions.

The solicitor who defended the man gave an account of police procedures at this particular road-block. They had been provided with the identification numbers of all those who were employed at the local pit. Those who were stopped at the road-block were identified by their check number and allowed through if, in police terms, they were 'entitled' to picket. The accused in this case was accustomed to this procedure and accepted it. On this occasion the police refused to believe him and asked for further identification. He became irritated and made a gesture to exercise his right of free passage. This kind of uncertainty about liability to arrest was one of the principal grievances of those who encountered the police at road-blocks. The mildest of objections might be the occasion for arrest. But it might not. Thus the legitimate discretion of ordinary police constables to arrest or refrain from arresting was manifest for the first time to a large number of citizens.[2]

Other arrests, particularly after Orgreave, were made at heavily picketed coalfields or major demonstrations where the identification of particular offenders was by no means easy. The use of 'snatch' squads, brought to theoretical perfection in the manoeuvres outlined in the Tactical Options Manual, provided no guarantee that those who were arrested were stone-throwers, rather than simply less fleet of foot than their companions. There were, of course, methods of identification which could assist the arresting officers – hidden cameras, for example, or plain clothes police officers operating among the demonstrators. (Of the former there is some evidence. Cameras were clearly visible in some colliery buildings and the remains of secret equipment were found by striking miners at the end of the dispute.[3] The use of undercover police officers is entirely credible, perhaps not even discreditable from the point of view of police objectives. It remained a grievous affront to those who believed themselves to be acting within the bounds of the criminal law.)

THE CIRCUMSTANCES OF ARREST AND CHARGE

It was difficult for pickets to understand – and even for ordinary citizens it remains a puzzle – why the use of the word 'scab' should, in some cases, lead to arrest. The technical reason, from the police point of view, is that in the confrontation between striking and working miners a breach of the peace might occur if words like this were flung with real feeling from one side to the other.[4] But police language, not only to pickets but also to pickets' wives and families, was also on occasion contemptuous and provocative. We received a number of reports about such verbal abuse. Even members of

Sheffield Policewatch, who took great pains to respect the authority of police officers on duty, were treated once or twice with outrageous discourtesy. 'Bloody trio of fucking whores', said one officer (Brodsworth, 10 October 1984); 'Prostitutes', shouted another at the same place a week later; 'Commie bastards', said a third (Kiveton Park, 24 October 1984). We do not pretend that the use of this kind of vocabulary is not now fairly commonplace. But in normal exchanges and in conditions of freedom its meaning is blunted and the contempt in the words themselves obscured. That is not the case when insulting expressions are addressed by those in positions of power to others who cannot retaliate without unfortunate consequences. 'Because I say so' policing is occasionally taken one stage further by police officers who assume that their undoubted discretion allows them complete latitude in language and behaviour. Striking miners and those who supported them enjoyed no such liberty.

Individual instances of gratuitous violence towards those who were arrested were, as we have said, set in a context of reasonable picketing and policing. On a number of occasions, however, the treatment of arrested men and women showed a careless disregard, not only for good police practice but also for the law itself. We received many accounts of random arrests that made no sense to those who were arrested or to those who observed them. Here is one account, given by a constituent in a complaint to his MP, that is representative of many others of which we have evidence. At Barrow Colliery (South Yorkshire) on 28 November there was a relatively peaceful picket with a small amount of pushing by the striking miners. The picket who was later arrested was some distance from this shoving and took no part in it. The picketing ceased shortly after this and most of the men made their way to the miners' welfare. Finding it had not yet opened, some of the miners, including the narrator, sat on a wall outside. Suddenly six or seven transit vans arrived on the scene. The narrator goes on:

> The doors burst open and police wearing riot gear and waving truncheons jumped out. What followed was panic. Men trying to get out of the way of the rampaging police. In a split second I made my mind up to stand my ground as I had done nothing wrong. Immediately an officer grabbed me, swore at me several times and told me to lie down, face down.

He was then put in a police van along with another rather elderly miner. He asked what he had done. One officer replied that he would tell him when he was alone. The van was driven some distance, then stopped about a quarter of a mile from the original encounter. The narrator was taken out and photographed with the arresting officer. Again he asked what he had done. The officer replied, 'You pays your money and you takes your choice.' The narrator said he had done nothing. The officer replied, 'Hard luck'. Taken to Barnsley police station, he was again photographed, fingerprinted, and locked up. Subsequently he was taken to the arresting officer who cautioned him and read out a list of charges: threatening behaviour, breach of the peace, insulting language. Later in the day he was brought before the magistrates. He goes on:

In court, the prosecuting solicitor – to my utter horror and disbelief – told the bench that I had been seen leading a group of about forty men at the top of Wasborough Park. . . . My solicitor then pointed out that this was unbelievable as the charge sheet showed that I had been arrested some quarter mile away from the alleged incident. The magistrates then remanded me on bail and placed me on a curfew between midnight and 8 am.

After waiting twelve months on conditional bail the narrator was acquitted on all counts when his case came to court and the prosecution offered no evidence against him.

Another account comes from a collection of interviews with striking miners in the Durham area (Parker 1986: 25–7). It describes the random arrests of miners during the demonstration at Mansfield on 14 May. Police vehicles were said to travel round picking up demonstrators and hurling them into the back of transit vans. No words were spoken, no reasons for the detention given.

These disturbing incidents illustrate some of the reasons for disquiet about police practices in the matter of the arrest and charging of alleged offenders during the strike. It is well established that the reason for an arrest should be given at the time of arrest.[5] There is much evidence that this legal requirement was ignored and even, as in these cases, outrageously flouted, when demonstrators, or anyone else involved with the striking miners, were first arrested. Police officers might counter with the argument that in the press of events during a picket this requirement could not be met. Even if this were true, the alleged offender is entitled to a statement of the charges he is likely to face at the first possible opportunity after his detention. Otherwise, he is illegally detained and has a right to full redress. It is particularly necessary that reasons for detention should be given when the offender is subjected to humiliating physical conditions while he is detained. To be required to lie face downward on the ground demands an answer to the question 'What for?' To give a proper consent to being photographed and fingerprinted, the arrested person should know what charges are to be made, since he has a right of objection both to the taking of photographs and of fingerprints. In the latter case, at least as the law then stood, his case could be referred to the magistrates for an order compelling fingerprinting to be considered.[6] Most arrested miners and their supporters had, as we have said, little experience of the judicial process and practically no knowledge of their legal rights.

The photographing of an alleged offender with the arresting officer at the point of arrest was common practice during the strike. Police arguments in justification spoke of the need for the arresting officer to be identified in situations of great pressure and confusion. At this point, the arrested person was in no position to object. (He was usually in handcuffs by this time and may have spent an uncomfortable time in a police van.) Had he done so his objection would certainly have remained unheard. One firm of solicitors who sent evidence to the inquiry noted that consent to the photographing of prisoners when they reached the police station was not usually sought. Where arrested men and women 'expressed a reluctance to be photographed they were either informed that they were obliged to have their photographs taken or the photographs were taken by means of a trick or deceit'. In the one or two cases where force *was* used, the arrested persons were women.

The number of women arrested and charged for alleged offences during the coal dispute was small. Their contemptuous treatment when it did happen has been documented by a number of people. Probably the worst incident reported to us was the arrest of a London woman who was helping to raise money by sale of *The Miner* outside Collett's bookshop in London. A highly respected person, in her 70s, she had obtained full permission from the manager of the bookshop to stand on the entry to their premises, at a point within their jurisdiction. Police officers passing in a police van noticed her there, jumped out, arrested her, and bundled her face first into the van. Unable to move, she lay there with her clothing disarranged, her jacket over her head, her tights at her knees, and her head on the floor. She, too, could obtain, when she could speak, no reasonable answer to her questions about the reasons for this arrest. She was later charged with obstruction of the highway.

BAIL – REMAND IN CUSTODY

In the normal course of events, those who are arrested for all but the most serious offences (sexual offences, robbery, and burglary are high on this list) are charged by the police and released on bail to appear before a magistrates' court on a given day. The statutory provisions for such release have been enlarged and developed since 1879. The consolidating statute of 1980 sets out the duties of the police as they stood at the time of the strike – the law has since been changed in detail – in respect of alleged offenders who have been arrested and charged.[7] They are to be brought before a court as soon as possible. If, however, it is not practicable to produce a particular prisoner within twenty-four hours, a police officer not below the rank of inspector or the station officer to whom the prisoner is brought 'shall inquire into the case and, unless the offence appears to the officer to be a serious one, grant him bail in accordance with the Bail Act'. Police bail should, therefore, be refused in only two sets of circumstances: if the offence is serious or if the production of the offender within twenty-four hours cannot be effected. The legislation does not provide for the attachment of conditions to police bail, such as residence in a certain place or regular reporting. If the police wished bail to be subject to conditions of this nature it would be necessary for the prisoner to be brought in custody before the magistrates' court.[8]

Practically nothing was known about the use of these provisions until the first tentative statistics appeared in 1978.[9] Since then, records have been examined with increasing sophistication and the figures for 1984 include an analysis of practice in each police area. This shows that the general level of police bail is around 83 per cent but there are clear variations between police areas, reflecting perhaps the local pressure upon magistrates' courts or the management of their calendars. Returns from the Nottinghamshire police area show a more than average use of the provisions (95 per cent).[10] Those who were arrested and charged as a result of offences during the coal dispute, however, rarely enjoyed the benefit of immediate discharge on police bail, but were kept at various police stations until a court appearance could be arranged. Formally therefore one of the conditions for substituting magistrates' bail for the more usual discharge by the police was fulfilled. But this was not done without serious distortion of court timetables and practices. Defendants were produced in considerable numbers and at hours that were unreasonable for magistrates, for solicitors, for probation officers, and for defendants. Thus the processes of consultation and advice so necessary for all defendants, but particularly for those unused to court procedures, were made difficult if not impossible in many cases. The processing of Nottinghamshire defendants was concentrated in the Mansfield magistrates' court, which alone handled one-fifth of all the cases in England and Wales arising from the strike. The conditions which resulted were bitterly summarized by one accused miner as 'supermarket justice'.

The second condition for the granting of police bail, that the offence be not serious, was present in the majority of miners' cases. Offences of obstruction, breach of the peace, even assault upon the police, cannot be classed with the serious offences of robbery, sexual assault, and burglary, which the legislation and general police practice suggest are inappropriate for police bail. This particular injustice, which had its origins, it would seem, in the Nottinghamshire police area but soon spread to other forces, was general rather than particular. It could not be blamed on a few aggressive or devious officers. Indeed some of those who worked in the Nottinghamshire courts went out of their way to stress to us the genuine helpfulness of police officers who had to deal with the production of offenders and the arrangements for their well-being.

The advantage desired from, and obtained by, securing magistrates' rather than police bail was the possibility of imposing conditions upon the granting of bail that do not seem to have been fully envisaged by the Bail Act, 1976. Despite desperate attempts by solicitors acting for striking miners to prevent the imposition of punishing conditions, justices' clerks consistently assisted the courts to grant bail with requirements that closely resembled a civil injunction: no picketing at any pit save their own, no contact with or entry into pits in other areas, and so on. The process of attaching conditions became most routine in the Mansfield court, whose officers were subsequently admonished by the Lord Chief Justice over a practice of stapling conditions to bail forms before the magistrates had reached their decision. The conditions generally adopted became known as 'the usual conditions'.[11] These and other conditions were applied in all but a handful of cases in Nottinghamshire.[12] Elsewhere practice was less systematic but conditions restricting picketing, curfews, and requirements to live away from dispute-affected areas were regularly applied even to those accused of quite minor infractions.

We received evidence of many injustices caused by these conditions. Union officials were unable to travel to areas where they had legitimate concerns. In some extreme cases miners suffered the imposition of curfew restrictions that put even greater restraint upon their daily lives. An almost ludicrous example of magisterial unconcern was described to us by a solicitor who had made frequent unsuccessful attempts to prevent the imposition of bail conditions.

> One particularly striking example of the accumulation of burdens upon a miner was the miner who was a tenant of a council house very close to the entrance of a pit which was not his work-place. He was on bail to the courts with the 'usual conditions' and had been told by a local police sergeant that he would be arrested if he actually came to live in his house which he had recently been allocated. His liability for rent was accruing but Social Security officers would not make rental payment for him and his family because he was not able to live there.

Of course it could be argued that miners who appeared before the courts were probably guilty of some offence or another. Restrictions upon their liberty were therefore fair and prudent. Moreover the legality of the usual conditions under the Bail Act was affirmed by the High Court in the test case of *R* v *Mansfield Justices, ex parte Sharkey* (1984), brought as a specific challenge to the practices that had developed. But the bail legislation was designed to remove from minor offenders the more onerous burdens of the judicial system (and, of course, to ease the pressure on magistrates' courts). The majority of those who were arrested in connection with the coal dispute were charged with the kind of summary offences which were rarely expected to result in custodial sentences.[13] Some of them did not even carry the power of arrest. The bail conditions normally imposed in these cases were, therefore, an inappropriate response to the level of charges laid.

REMANDS IN CUSTODY

There are no figures available to show the general use of remands in custody for those who were arrested and charged in the twelve months of the strike. We have only the evidence of individual instances which were described to us by miners themselves and by the solicitors and probation officers who had knowledge of specific cases. No one would question the need for remand in custody where there is a substantial risk of further serious offences. There is therefore reasonable ground for arguing that miners charged with criminal damage of a significant kind should have been remanded in custody, certainly at the initial stages of the process of trial. This is what happened, and most of the miners charged with serious offences probably spent at least a week in custody. Those on more trivial charges also faced a remand in custody if their conditions of bail had been breached (or allegedly breached) by the commission of a further offence. The difficulty here was the haphazard nature of arrest and charge which we have described. Since bail conditions were usually constructed to allow picketing at the alleged offender's own pit, repeated picketing could not be construed as a breach of bail conditions. Police requests for remands in custody seemed to assume that it was.

CHARGES BROUGHT AGAINST THOSE ARRESTED[14]

It cannot be denied that the miners' strike occasionally generated the kind of violence that no society can tolerate. There were a number of savage attacks by striking miners upon their working colleagues and a few by working miners upon those who were on strike. These grave offences were fortunately in the minority, for they represented fewer than 0.5 per cent of all the offences charged during the strike and fewer than 6 per cent of all assaults which reached the stage of prosecution. They did, however, include the killing of a taxi-driver when a concrete block was launched on to a motorway by Welsh miners. It hit a hired car which was taking a working miner to a pit which had long been picketed out. The miner escaped but the taxi-driver was killed when his car veered off the road. Three men were charged with murder, an indictment probably pitched high to satisfy public feeling at the time, for the conviction was reduced to manslaughter on appeal.[15] One of the defendants had already been acquitted.

Other charges which were serious enough to involve trial at the Crown Court arose from the damage which was done to Coal Board property and to the property of those who helped to bring working miners to striking pits. Some of this damage was extremely serious – setting buses on fire and destroying conveyor belts, for example. It was for these kinds of offences, together with the serious assaults which we have described, that most of the custodial sentences were handed down. Generally speaking the criminal process in cases of assault and damage was less open to criticism than was the case with minor offences. Decisions about remand in custody, about full legal aid and, with the exception of charges of riot and unlawful assembly, the justification for the terms of the indictment seem to have been considered with some care.

The most visible evidence of a specific prosecution policy intended to have a deterrent effect even before charges were proved and sentence pronounced was the series of riot and unlawful assembly cases that were initiated by the Chief Constables of Nottinghamshire, South Yorkshire, and South Wales. Events at Barlborough motorway in March 1984 resulted in seven charges of unlawful assembly.[16] However, the use of riot charges began only in May after the disturbances in Mansfield on 14 May 1984.[17] It is admitted on all hands that charges for riot are difficult to sustain and few have been brought in recent years.[18] The decision of the Chief Constable of Nottinghamshire to institute the first of the riot prosecutions was made, he said, after careful consultation with his legal advisers. The Chief Constable of South Yorkshire also spoke out in defence of his decision to bring a similar indictment against fifty-five of the Orgreave pickets. The offence of unlawful assembly, which presents equal difficulties to the courts, was more frequently used in the autumn disturbance at colliery gates and at the Port Talbot steel plant in South Wales. An interesting ploy followed disturbances at Harworth Colliery in August. The Nottinghamshire police did not arrest the defendants at the time of the alleged offences. They were prosecuted after their car registration numbers had been checked. Fifty miners were charged with unlawful assembly but twenty-six were discharged at committal. A further ninety-two indictments were framed but eighty-four were dropped before the cases reached the first hearing. Not one single riot charge came up to proof in court. A few indictments for unlawful assembly resulted in conviction. Thirty-one defendants pleaded guilty in respect of disturbances in Wales in September 1984, and subsequently another ninety-nine pleaded guilty in respect of another incident, also in South Wales. They were given to understand that custodial sentences would not be imposed and accepted the suspended sentences which were handed down.[19] (Such guilty pleas avoided a long trial and the expense of legal fees.) In general, however, police policies in the use of the common law offences of riot and unlawful assembly were almost wholly frustrated and the judgement of the Law Commission vindicated.[20]

In lesser cases, destined to be heard in magistrates' courts, the position was less satisfactory. Here, where legal aid may have been thought to be unimportant, it was frequently refused. In addition the charge is made by a number of solicitors that particular benches, in cases arising out of the mining dispute, refused all legal aid on the assumption that legal costs would be paid by the National Union of Mineworkers. For some defendants, sensitive to their union's difficulties, this induced a plea of guilty that would not otherwise have been forthcoming. Refusal of aid meant too that some defendants were unable to trace witnesses to the action that resulted in their prosecution – a matter felt to be an injustice, whatever the truth of it may be. Conflicting attitudes to legal aid attracted particular attention in Scotland, where there were widespread complaints that particular Sheriffs (who are responsible for deciding legal aid, under Scottish legislation, in the light of relevant factors including the strength of the accused's likely defence) were refusing legal aid as a matter of policy, thereby implying a prejudgement of defence arguments. Matters came to a head after an indiscreet remark by the Sheriff of Kilmarnock at a social event led to fourteen defendants convicted before him raising a successful appeal to the High Court of Justiciary on the footing that justice had not been seen to be done.[21]

On the whole, however, the weaknesses in the process of summary prosecution were seen most clearly in the quality of the evidence against the accused. The witnesses were usually police officers heavily committed to the control of the very picketing and demonstrations which gave rise to the charges. Many defendants were unable to call witnesses in their support since the circumstances surrounding their arrest were confused and witnesses unidentifiable. Yet we have reports from solicitors and probation officers in some areas that give grounds for the belief of many miners that magistrates, particularly in areas where striking miners were outnumbered, preferred police evidence to any other. One report described a case where two Metropolitan police officers claimed that a miner had punched one of them in the chest. Two defence witnesses, one of them a working deputy, said that this was untrue. The miner was convicted. Again, a defendant faced a charge of criminal damage in that he had thrown a brick through the window of a lorry. The window had indeed been broken but the lorry driver did not see the brick thrown. The miner was a known trouble-maker, he said, 'and he looked as if he had just thrown a brick'.[22] The charge was found proved. There were of course a substantial number of cases which resulted in acquittal either in the absence of evidence or having heard all the evidence.[23] Few conclusions can be drawn from this, however, since we do not know the number of defendants who pleaded guilty to the charges that were brought against them. What is beyond doubt is that the overloading of magistrates' courts in the mining areas with avoidable remand hearings, the grouping of defendants in numbers that jeopardized a fair hearing, and day and night special sessions put such serious strains upon the system of summary justice that it is difficult to avoid the conclusion that standards, and indeed the system itself, were impaired.

THE CONSEQUENCES OF ARREST AND PROSECUTION

Since the majority of the criminal charges brought against striking miners were not grave, relatively few custodial sentences were given – probably some 200.[24] Even so, the hardship caused by fines was considerable. In many cases the local union saw that the fine was paid, but their funds for other necessary purposes – such as welfare payments to pensioners and miners' dependants – were already seriously depleted by the imposition of fines and costs that were quite beyond the means of individual miners. Union officials saw this as a deliberate attempt to weaken their capacity to give financial help to their members. This may not have been true but it was given colour by the consistency of the policy in some magistrates' courts and by the actions of one or two Crown Court judges. A young miner, towards the end of the strike on 17 December 1984, aimed a kick at a coach which was leaving Lea Hall pit after delivering working miners. He was charged with threatening behaviour and criminal damage to the coach. He was refused legal aid for his appearance at the magistrates' court on 22 February 1985, and was duly convicted. On appeal the Stafford Crown Court overturned the magistrates' verdict but refused an application that the costs incurred at the original hearing should be repaid – a judgement of Solomon, perhaps, but one that the defendant and his union could not be expected to accept as just.

The custodial sentences handed down in serious offences, of which the most severe were eight years for manslaughter, five and three years for inflicting grievous bodily harm, and two, two and a half, and three years for arson and criminal damage, were within the established 'tariff' applied by the courts in cases of their kind.[25] At a lower level, there were some inconsistencies which defendants felt to be less than fair. One man describes how he painted 'SCAB' on the wall of a working miner's house and blacked out the windows. The offence took place at night, a fact which the magistrate noted as particularly heinous. Explicitly for purposes of deterrence, a sentence of two months' imprisonment was given. The sentence itself was heavy enough for a man whose only contact with the law had been as a juvenile when he was fined £20 for assault; it was followed at the end of the strike by dismissal and, since then, continuous unemployment. He asked the local management of the Coal Board, who owned the house, if they would allow him to make good the damage so that he could return to work. They refused. Another miner, in the same area, who was charged with the grievous bodily harm of a lorry driver at an open-cast mine, received a suspended sentence of nine months and a fine of £200. From these two cases it would seem that damage to the Coal Board's property was thought to be more worthy of immediate imprisonment than a serious physical assault upon a lorry driver who was helping to execute Coal Board policy.

DISMISSALS

Apart from sentences of imprisonment, the most serious effect for miners of being caught up in the criminal process was the dismissal from Coal Board employment of many of those who were arrested during the strike. These effects were felt not only as an additional punishment for offences which were proved, but also as an unfair consequence of an unsubstantiated charge, for some miners were dismissed (or an earlier dismissal reaffirmed) even after they had been acquitted or the charges against them had been dropped. Of course some very serious offences had been committed, which no employer could condone. Some miners no doubt deserved their dismissal and would in any other employment have been equally liable to be sacked for serious misconduct. But the way in which 1,019 miners were selected for dismissal and the uneven, arbitrary way in which pleas for reinstatement were handled in different NCB areas give cause for concern.

It is difficult to link the dismissals to the seriousness of the actions of the individuals concerned. Only about one in ten of miners arrested were subsequently sacked, or about one in six of those convicted; but five times as many were dismissed as were sent to prison, and in a number of cases, as mentioned above, dismissal was not connected to conviction at all. One theory put forward by miners and supported indirectly by statements by Coal Board officials was that criminal damage to NCB property was the principal reason for dismissal. However in England and Wales a total of 1,038 charges of arson and criminal damage were brought (many not involving NCB property) and some 700 men lost their jobs by virtue of their arrest. In Scotland, only 30 charges of the equivalent offence of vandalism were laid but 200 men were sacked. It has also been suggested that sackings were used to weed out militants and union activists; certainly union officials figured prominently in the ranks of the dismissed but it cannot be said definitely how far this represents their more frequent subjection to arrest (and how far that reflects police choices).

What gives rise to most concern about the dismissals is the lack of any pattern, suggesting very substantial exercises in discretion by managers (sometimes in defiance of the verdict of the court, or the outcome of unfair dismissal claims). The discretion was even more marked in the process of reinstatement, which eventually extended to all but 357 of those dismissed. In some areas a relatively relaxed attitude was evident. In others this was far from the case. In Scotland, with a much higher rate of sackings relative to the incidence of serious offences, no reinstatements at all were conceded by the Area Director, Albert Wheeler, and only after his transfer did matters improve. In Kent miners at Betteshanger Colliery went on an unsuccessful strike in aid of their forty-seven sacked colleagues. At least one finding of unfair dismissal was affirmed by the Employment Appeal Tribunal when challenged by the Board. After the retirement of Sir Ian MacGregor, his successor, Sir Robert Haslam, sought to improve relationships by conciliatory gestures, but the issue remains, to the union leadership, and to many men besides the individuals concerned, a continuing open sore.[26]

Some of those who were dismissed were prepared to admit that what they had done was serious. But in one or two accounts of what happened the offences that resulted in dismissal are clearly seen as the intemperate violence of men caught up in situations where anger and frustration resulted in actions that were out of character.[27] Thus one miner, picketing an open-cast mine, joined in 'roughing up' a truck driver who came to collect coal and to taunt the striking miners in the process. The miner reflected on the incident nearly two years after it happened.

> I look back on it and I know we went too far. I'm not saying this to excuse us, but we'd been in a bit of a scrap already with the police that day and our tempers were up, and things did, things got out of hand. . . . I wasn't a bad man, at least I don't think of myself as a bad man. . . . It's a high price to pay, at my age, to think you can't see yourself being back in a job for the rest of your life.

Once again as in most other events in the lives of striking miners, it was the highly discretionary nature of the decisions which were made about dismissals that caused bewilderment and anger.

This demand for fair and equal treatment by striking miners was denied in many of the procedures which followed their arrest and charge. Yet there is a contradiction here. In the recognition that local communities have different styles of living, different ways of expressing themselves, and different responses to crime and its punishment, the support for local policing is strong. When it comes to the appearance of local or individual discretion in the operation of criminal procedures and their consequences, complaints about unfairness are widespread. It is a dilemma faced by local police forces and local magistrates pursuing local policies. In the circumstances of the coal strike, the demands for manifest fairness were, at times, irreconcilable with the acceptance of local practices. And it was this that added to the bewilderment of first-time offenders in their contact with the police, the courts, and the Coal Board.

NOTES

1. There were 9,808 arrests in England and Wales and 1,504 in Scotland. See Appendix 1 for a detailed analysis of arrests and charges.
2. See Appendix 2, p. 179 for an example.
3. Samuel, Bloomfield, and Boanas (1985: 228). Two of us observed a video camera at Bolsover Colliery mounted directly beside the main road past the colliery gate.
4. Those arrested were usually charged (if at all) with using threatening, abusive, or insulting language likely to cause a breach of the peace (Public Order Act, 1936, section 5). On many occasions the prevention of this particular safety valve must have been just as likely to create disorder.
5. *Christie* v *Leachinsky* (1947), now given statutory effect in section 28 of the Police and Criminal Evidence Act, 1984. See also Article 5(2) of the European Convention on Human Rights.
6. Magistrates' Courts Act, 1980, section 49; the law was changed, after the strike, by section

61 of the Police and Criminal Evidence Act, 1984, which exceptionally allows the police to approve compulsory fingerprinting.

7. Magistrates' Courts Act, 1980, section 43.
8. Section 3(6) of the Bail Act, 1976, which allows conditions to be attached to bail, stipulates that this may be done only by a court. The exception is that the police may require sureties (financial undertakings from third parties) as a condition of bail.
9. *Criminal Statistics England and Wales, 1977* (Cmnd 7289, 1978) Tables 8.1 and 8.2.
10. *Criminal Statistics England and Wales, 1984* (Cmnd 9621, 1985) Table 8.6. The figures are for indictable offences, which most of those in Nottinghamshire connected with the strike were not; but usually even less use is made of remands in custody for the less serious category of summary offences.
11. In their final form these read: 'not to visit any premises or place for the purpose of picketing or demonstrating in connection with the current trade dispute between the NUM and the NCB other than peacefully to picket or demonstrate at your usual place of employment'.
12. Of the 1,317 accused on bail in Nottinghamshire on 5 July 1984, 97 per cent were subject to bail conditions. See Appendix 1, p. 164 for further details.
13. The exact number of custodial sentences imposed in connection with the strike is not known. Our best estimate is a little over 200. See Appendix 1, p. 165. Of 10,372 charges recorded, 6,951 were for obstruction of one kind or another, or conduct likely to lead to a breach of the peace. See Appendix 1, pp. 161-3.
14. See Appendix 1 for a detailed analysis of the charges brought. The figures show that in England and Wales almost 20 per cent of those arrested were not charged at all, while in Scotland nearly one-third of those arrested were not proceeded against by the public prosecutors.
15. *R* v *Hancock and Shankland* (1986). The two were sentenced to eight years' imprisonment.
16. All those charged were subsequently acquitted.
17. See Chapter 6.
18. Thus the Attorney-General commented that 'the law of riot creates some grave evidential problems' (HC Debates, 9 July 1984, col. 691). There were however several government hints about the use of charges which would carry a sentence of life imprisonment (as riot then did). The Home Secretary (Leon Brittan) spoke in this vein in Worksop (September 1984), Brighton (October 1984), and Horwich (January 1985).
19. *Guardian*, 28 June 1985.
20. Law Commission (1983). For a full analysis of riot and unlawful assembly charges see *Legal Action*, September 1985. For statistics see Appendix 1.
21. *Bradford* v *McLeod* (1985).
22. This case was reported to us by a Staffordshire solicitor.
23. The percentage of acquittals was about 24. See Appendix 1 for details.
24. See Appendix 1.
25. See Appendix 1.
26. The dispute between the NUM and British Coal in the late summer of 1987 over a proposed new disciplinary code, which led to a successful ballot for industrial action and an overtime ban, was much more intense and difficult to resolve precisely because of the suspicion and bitter memories left by the actions of management in the matter of dismissals and reinstatement.
27. Parker (1986: 84).

PART III
Aftermath of the strike

8
The aftermath of the strike

Events subsequent to the ending of the strike in March 1985 are of concern in helping to clarify the events and processes involved in the strike itself, and more importantly to set the context of the trends in policing and the constitutional position of the police of which the strike was part. We consider the first of these perspectives in this chapter, the second in Chapter 9.

EFFECTS ON THE NUM

Whatever the formal status of a return to work without an agreed settlement of the closures dispute, the reality was a rapid implementation of closures and an equally rapid collapse of effective resistance to them. Within two years of the end of the strike 60 of the 170 collieries open at the start of the dispute had closed, and 78,000 of the work-force had left the industry.[1] Although privatization of the remaining pits was ruled out in the short term by Sir Robert Haslam, the incoming chairman of the renamed British Coal, in 1986, its presence on the political agenda was increasingly real.

Some voices were indeed raised against the closure policy. NACODS, which had secured what it thought was a satisfactory guarantee regarding closure procedures as part of the October 1984 settlement of its dispute, found the immediate closure proposals in the aftermath of the strike unacceptable, and attempted to mount a legal challenge to the closure of Bedwas Colliery in South Wales. The High Court's refusal of leave to bring proceedings for judicial review of the Coal Board's proposals swiftly ended this avenue of challenge.[2] The General Secretary of NACODS gave evidence before the House of Commons Energy Committee in March 1986 that the agreed closure procedures were being ignored. Pit managers giving evidence to the committee the same month said that the pit closure programme was a reckless drive towards economic success without regard to the future of coal as an energy source. But closures continued apace, and attempts within the NUM to generate opposition were consistently unsuccessful. Terms for redundancy remained (initially at least) relatively generous, the enormous pressures of debt created by the strike increased the readiness particularly of older men to accept them, and compulsory redundancy could in most cases be avoided by transfer of those who wished to stay to other pits.

The NUM itself, as became apparent in a number of ways, was greatly weakened and deeply riven by the strike. Its relationship with British Coal remained critically strained, even two years after the end of the strike. Not until November 1985 did an apology by the union to the High Court secure the release of the sequestrated funds and the lifting of the receivership. Membership of the union plummeted from around 180,000 at the end of the strike to little more than 100,000 by late 1986. As well as the major exodus from the industry, this decline owed much to the decision of some of the working miners to form their own union, which became the Union of Democratic Mineworkers (UDM). Mineworkers in Nottinghamshire, encouraged, it would seem, by the Chairman of the Coal Board, took the first steps towards the formation of a breakaway union after the NUM annual conference in July 1985.[3] The leaders of this movement hoped to recruit the miners of South Derbyshire and Leicestershire who had worked throughout the strike. In Leicestershire, where the local union leadership had skilfully managed relationships with members and police during the strike and the bitterness evident elsewhere towards the NUM was more muted, a ballot of the membership resulted in a clear decision to remain in the NUM. But the ballot arranged in Nottinghamshire in October 1985 yielded a three to one majority in favour of the creation of a separate union. The UDM attracted support from miners in a number of collieries and workshops in South Derbyshire, Warwickshire, Staffordshire, and Lancashire, and membership reached a peak of 40,000.

The NCB naturally welcomed the birth of the UDM; recognition and full negotiating rights were immediately forthcoming and talks on a new pay deal followed soon after. Although there was a slow return of UDM members to the NUM – members who had perhaps had unrealistic expectations of the immediate gains to be achieved from the new union – the bargaining position of the NUM was inevitably strained by the pressure of its rival.[4] Having reached a pay settlement with the UDM which the NUM refused to accept, the Coal Board implemented the agreed pay increase only at pits where the UDM had a majority of members. At one pit (Ellistown), where the UDM was in a minority, the increase was paid to the UDM members only, but this was successfully challenged by the NUM in the courts as anti-union discrimination.[5] Other outstanding issues on which the NUM made little progress in negotiations included pension contributions covering the period of the strike, and the particularly emotive issue of the fate of the dismissed strikers. By mid-1987 the NUM was split over proposals by British Coal to introduce six-day working and an extended working day to justify commercially the development of a major new pit in South Wales and the continuation of workings extending many miles under the sea in the north-east, while the UDM waited on the sidelines to step into the breach if the NUM refused to do so. Overall the NUM survived the strike with a weakened and demoralized membership, forced to acknowledge the authority of the courts and suffering revolt and secession within its ranks.

THE LAW OF INDUSTRIAL DISPUTES

Changes in the legal status of picketing and other aspects of industrial action brought about by litigation arising from the strike are of cardinal importance to the future of industrial relations and the distribution of rights between workers and employers. The clutch of civil actions brought against the NUM and area unions by those affected by the consequences of its decisions certainly played a large part in bringing the strike to an end. Most of the cases were of little more lasting importance than this, because they involved the interpretation of the NUM's own rules in relation to the failure to ballot, and the possibility of a repetition of the ballot policies seems unlikely.[6] The exception, which was of potentially wider importance and soon proved to be capable of even further development, was the South Wales case, *Thomas* v *NUM (South Wales Area)* (1985) where an injunction was obtained by working miners against their area union preventing the organizing of mass pickets, defined in the injunction as anything in excess of six.

The judgement itself, given only three weeks before the end of the strike, had no noticeable effect on its final stages. The reasoning of Mr Justice Scott, however, opened an important avenue for future challenges to picketing by those who wish to continue to work – the case itself being the first such action to be brought successfully. In a legally controversial judgement, the court ruled that picketing which amounted to harassment of those seeking to enter the picketed premises was an unlawful interference with their rights as users of the public highway. In seeking to indicate the scope of what was unlawful, Mr Justice Scott said:

> I think it plain from the evidence before me that the picketing at the colliery gates is of a nature and is carried out in a manner that represents an unreasonable harassment of the working miners. A daily congregation on average of fifty to seventy men hurling abuse and in circumstances that require a police presence and require the working miners to be conveyed in vehicles do not in my view leave any real room for argument.

The prominence given to the presence of the police in defining civil liability opens the disturbing possibility of the police having a role in creating such liability, as well as being open to the charge of circularity. In framing the injunction so as to limit picketing to six the court implicitly opened any picketing which goes beyond the 'statutory six' to civil action, and strongly reinforced the police practice of enforcing the figure of six derived from the Code of Practice.

The South Wales judgement was followed in 1986 by an even more important decision building on its principles. In the course of the Wapping dispute (discussed on pp. 110–13) an action was successfully brought by News Group Newspapers Ltd together with one of their employees working at Wapping for an injunction to restrain the picketing of News Group's plant.[7] The picketing was secondary picketing unprotected from civil action by the employers because of the 1980 Act, but the important point of the judgement was that an injunction was also awarded to the aggrieved employee, limiting pickets to a maximum of six. Mr Justice Stuart-Smith accepted that mass picketing amounted to the civil wrong of intimidation, and that, rather than the fact that the picketing was not at the pickets' place of work, was the justification for the injunction. How far this can be taken to confirm that mass picketing is necessarily intimidatory in any criminal sense is an open point not definitively resolved by this case. However the subtle distinctions between the definitions of intimidation in civil and criminal law are likely to be blurred on the street and the judgement taken as confirmation that mass picketing is a matter for the public order powers of the police – a point to which we return shortly.[8]

These two judgements have succeeded in doing what the then Employment Secretary, James Prior, did not wish to do when the Employment Act, 1980, was being drafted: they have put the Code of Practice, and in particular the limitation on numbers of pickets to six, in full legal dress. But they may have other, more far-reaching consequences which have to do with the kind of definitions made by senior police officers when they are involved in the control of picketing. We have already noted (p. 48) that the chief constables, in their evidence to the Select Committee on Employment in 1980, made a point of distinguishing between 'official' pickets, whose numbers and disposition they have always had power to control, and supporters or 'demonstrators', whose role was different but whose connection with the official pickets was nevertheless clear and whose presence and behaviour was not always intimidatory. Indeed it was, on most occasions, merely a means of giving visible support to their colleagues on the picket lines and a demonstration of the strength of the strike itself. The government, wishing to establish some legislative check on picketing, adopted the Code of Practice compromise which left the police free to interpret the law in the way in which they had indicated they wished to continue. The more complex question of defining and controlling secondary picketing was left to the civil courts. The subtlety, perhaps also the vagueness, of the relationship between civil and criminal liability was occasionally exploited by the police during the miners' strike but it left a basis for pragmatic policing which was operated successfully, for instance in West Yorkshire.

Picket organizers are now to a considerable extent boxed in by the two judgments, and mass picketing as an official tactic is almost bound to attract civil action from either employers or workers seeking to go to work. The court has also, perhaps inadvertently, given to the police a clear area of operations. Six pickets now have the sanction of case-law. Any number more than that may be regarded as intimidating and therefore a threat to the public peace. Senior police officers may be tempted to accept this definition in exercising their powers under the Public Order Act, 1986, at least for the larger picket gatherings.[9] Industrial disputes and demonstrations in support of them would then, contrary to long-held police beliefs, be on a par with other public order problems like inner city riots or ideological clashes between anti-racist groups and the National Front.

THE WAPPING DISPUTE 1986–7

The dispute between the print unions and the News International group of companies owned by Rupert Murdoch, which gave rise to the second of the cases considered above, was the first major and prolonged industrial dispute since the miners' strike.[10] It is worth considering in a little detail because it exemplifies many aspects of the issues under discussion, and although it differed crucially from the miners' dispute (it was, for instance, a lock-out not a strike) it suffered from its fall-out. Aspects of the policing of the picket lines at Wapping are also dealt with here, in order to maintain the coherence of the account.[11]

As with the miners, a major dispute between employers and print unions had been anticipated for some time. Newspaper proprietors in general and the major London proprietors in particular were anxious to adopt fully the new technologies of production, which would reduce labour costs and in the process weaken the power of the print unions – traditionally regarded as among the strongest groups of organized labour. The issue had led to a confrontation in the provinces between Eddie Shah's *Stockport Messenger* group and the unions in 1983, in the course of which the first use of the new legislation removing immunities from trade unions nearly bankrupted the NGA. London printers seemed to be a tougher proposition but Rupert Murdoch prepared the ground well for a fierce but unequal battle.

A site at Wapping, just east of the City, had been in Mr Murdoch's possession for some years. Talks with the print unions about the terms for using new printing processes broke down in 1984. News International then began to prepare the plant which had by then been completed at Wapping for operation, and the premises for possible siege, with barbed wire around the perimeter and elaborate internal and gate security systems. Mr Murdoch then put final terms to the unions, including flexible working, an end to the closed shop, and a no-strike agreement incorporated in a binding five-year contract. Talks continued for a few weeks but towards the end of December 1985 Mr Murdoch announced that work at Wapping would start early in January whether or not the terms were accepted by the unions. This was possible because agreement had been reached with the electricians' union, the EEPTU, for the recruitment of 500 people to operate the plant, while journalists were offered financial inducements to move location. Arrangements had also been made to switch distribution of the newspapers away from British Rail to a road haulage company (TNT Roadfreight (UK)) whose drivers could be expected to cross picket lines if so instructed.

The print unions, unable to accept the terms offered, successfully balloted their members for strike action. A strike was called for 24 January 1986. The 5,500 union members who obeyed the strike call were immediately dismissed; work, and subsequently picketing, then began at the Wapping plant.

The printing unions appealed for support to obtain the reinstatement of their members to the EEPTU, to the National Union of Journalists, asking them not to cross the picket lines, and to the TUC, all with little success. The EEPTU remained defiant, the NUJ ambivalent (its disciplinary powers soon came under legal challenge), and the TUC hesitant to act against a powerful member. Road access through the picket lines was maintained, and the pickets had little impact on the stream of lorry traffic. The police tactics effectively denied any contact between the pickets and TNT drivers, who routinely sped in and out past police cordons. The pickets' weakness was underlined by one tragedy in January 1987 in which a picket was crushed to death under the rear wheels of a lorry leaving the plant, which a coroner's jury found to be an 'unlawful killing'.

As well as routine picketing, with numbers swelled on Saturday nights, demonstrations in support of the sacked print workers were regularly held at Wapping. Since no work remained for them at News International's old premises, they could only claim the right to work at Wapping.

The early stages of the dispute brought some limited success in restricting output of News International titles not printed at Wapping, and disrupting distribution in some areas. The company soon sought the protection of the courts and obtained injunctions against these interferences which were served on both the major print unions, the NGA and SOGAT'82. The injunctions had little effect and both unions were brought back to court for alleged contempt. SOGAT'82 was fined £25,000 and its funds were sequestrated. The NGA, whose response to the court action had been more sure-footed, avoided the sequestration but not the fine.

This early phase of the dispute demonstrates well the interplay between civil and criminal jurisdiction in the policing of industrial disputes since the process of reform began in 1980. The methods adopted by the strike organizers greatly influence the balance between civil and criminal law in the enforcement of whatever restraints there may be on the strikers' conduct. However the alternatives, for the strike organizers, may be a Hobson's choice. Thus although there were considerable numbers of demonstrators outside the Wapping gates, they were, certainly in the early days, efficiently marshalled and controlled by union officials.[12] The police policy was to clear the way for incoming and outgoing lorries by restricting the access and movement of residents and others, and blocking off particular streets. It was this policy which generated early complaints about police action, primarily from local residents rather than the unions. An investigation of the restriction of movement by an NCCL inquiry revealed that the 3,500 residents of Wapping were subjected to restrictions on movement and identity checks on a scale at least equal to that experienced in the critical centres of the mining dispute, but over a much extended period.[13]

The sequestration of SOGAT funds in April 1986 led to the ending of the strike pay which had hitherto sustained those of its dismissed members who remained without work – at that stage a considerable majority – and that decision led in turn to a large and angry demonstration on 3 May. The police responded with a full-scale resort to riot-control tactics; there were many arrests, and complaints from union members and local residents. In mid-June the action against the picketing of the Wapping plant which we have already discussed was brought to court; the court issued an injunction in July. This prevented the unions from organizing demonstrations in the immediate vicinity of the plant; the limit of six pickets laid down by the court was reinforced by the police. Demonstrations took place, but they were essentially demonstrations of solidarity from those who supported the sacked workers. The latter were present too, but unauthorized, disowned almost, by their unions.

Various attempts at the settlement of the dispute included the offering of different forms of enhanced redundancy compensation to those dismissed;

these were rejected because the print workers wanted reinstatement, not compensation. On the first anniversary of the strike, 24 January 1987, there was a very large protest march culminating in a mass demonstration at the Wapping plant.[14] It was carefully arranged as a public meeting, with a stage prepared for speakers, public address systems, and the paraphernalia of a rally. At the fringes of the crowd a small group of men began throwing stones at police waiting in a side street. The police response was a full-scale sweep of mounted and riot-equipped officers moving towards the platform and the main demonstration. In the panic which followed many were caught in the line of advancing police horses or fell victim to the stampede away from the riot police. Over 300 injuries were recorded, including 167 police officers, and there were 67 arrests.[15] The Home Secretary rejected demands for a public inquiry into this, the single most violent incident in the dispute.

Meanwhile the print unions continued without visible success to press the plight of their members and to seek other unions' support. As the will of the dismissed workers slowly ebbed and more found alternative work, the final pressure which brought the strike to an end came from the legal straitjacket in which the unions had been placed. Threats by News International to seek further penalties for contempt by breaches of the picketing injunctions finally forced the unions, first SOGAT then the NGA, to withdraw their support and recommend members (some of whom had already done so) to accept the compensation terms on offer and end their fight. With some brief, ragged resistance from the ranks of the strikers the dispute ended in April 1987.

Some of the parallels with the miners' strike will be obvious: the fatal weakness of a lack of effective union solidarity; the ineffectiveness of the picketing in the face of efficient policing techniques; the surprising tenacity of the strikers against overwhelming odds; the critical role of the law in forcibly curtailing the unions' leadership, organizationally and financially. It was the last of these elements that was markedly stronger in the Wapping dispute, altering the tactical options of the unions from an early stage, crippling their finances, and ultimately forcing surrender. The web of law had been ingeniously exploited by Mr Murdoch.[16] However, it was also clear that the impact of both civil law and police enforcement of public order greatly restrict the possible actions which a union can undertake in defence of its members' interests.

It is important to recognize that some industrial disputes can be conducted without police intervention and with the minimum of public disruption beyond that resulting from the fact of a strike, and without contravention of the civil law. Apart from the statutory requirements as to strike ballots, three conditions are necessary. First, there must be sufficient unanimity in the work-force, with no possibility of a breach in the ranks of the strikers; second, no other (union or non-union) work-force should be available to substitute for the strikers; third, the work itself must be sufficiently important to the public and the state that the strikers cannot simply be ignored by their employers or the authorities. These conditions were present in the two-week strike by British Telecom engineers during the early part of 1987. Official pickets were posted outside work-places, with minimal police attention and no disorder; workers did not cross the picket lines when asked not to do so; and apart from authorized emergency work the strike was complete. The result was a settlement of the dispute conceding some success to the union.

Unfortunately for the smooth resolution of industrial disputes these conditions are by no means universal in times of high unemployment, rapid technological change, and the relative weakness, economically as well as legally, of trade unions. Old loyalties are hard to maintain if the price of their maintenance is unemployment, and new aspirations may appear easier to achieve by renouncing union membership. For those who are forced to strike, by conviction, fear, or despair, but without the preconditions for success, there are strict limits on the public ventilation of their cause which are now more likely to be enforced by the police than by the civil courts.

For the police until relatively recently the policing of industrial disputes presented few problems. Some picketing could be ignored, some given passing attention, and only a very small number of episodes necessitated the full-scale response of a permanent and sizeable police presence. Many rank-and-file police officers have viewed with dismay the change in the police function over the last decade which they observed in full effect during the miners' strike.[17] The weakening of trade union cohesion has made far more common the 'some in, some out' type of dispute most likely to necessitate full-scale police attention. At the same time the emphasis in many judicial decisions during and since the strike on the denial of any possibility of peaceable intent to those picketing in numbers in excess of six, or excessive numbers of supporters, in many cases explicitly derived from the accounts of violence in newspapers and scenes viewed on television, may well, as we have noted above, force a change in the view taken by the police of the rights and wrongs of picketing.[18] Police officers know that these are not and were not a fully realistic account of events. But case law has now strengthened the innuendo of the Code of Practice that there might be violence in numbers. The evils of secondary picketing which were the focus of the Employment Act, 1980, have become the dangers of mass picketing which are to be countered by the laws, policies, and practices of public order policing. To see how this has developed we must look at the developments in policing and public order law in the period following the miners' strike.

NOTES

1. Figures given by Sir Robert Haslam, quoted in the *Guardian*, 3 March 1987.
2. *The Times*, 29 March 1985, briefly reports the application to Mr Justice Woolf for leave to take proceedings. The background is more fully discussed in W.M. Rees (1985).
3. MacGregor (1986: 338).
4. At the time of its first annual conference, UDM membership had fallen to under 30,000.
5. *NCB* v *Ridgway* (1987); the case, which was finally decided in the Court of Appeal, was based on section 23 of the Employment Protection (Consolidation) Act, 1978, which prohibits action short of dismissal against an employee because of his membership of a particular trade union.
6. The NUM rules on the calling of industrial action were subsequently changed. The Trade Union Act, 1984, gives clear rights to employees to obtain injunctions where strikes are called without a ballot, and a somewhat greater readiness to use this law has been shown since the strike ended; proposals in the Conservative Party's 1987 election manifesto would

give a statutory right to union members to challenge a strike called without a ballot on a basis that would not, as in the miners' case, depend on the construction to be given to the union rule-book. (Since our report was completed these proposals have been presented to Parliament in the Employment Bill, 1987. See also above, p. 17, note 11, for another aspect of the Bill.)

7. *News Group Newspapers Ltd* v *SOGAT'82* (1986).
8. In its civil sense intimidation extends to any threat to act unlawfully, including threats to interfere with contractual rights, whereas criminal intimidation requires threats of at least the use of physical force against person or property. In this case the basis of the finding of intimidation was the threats made by pickets to those entering the premises, which were interpreted as threats of violence.
9. Particularly the new powers under section 14 to restrict demonstrations on the ground that the organizers' intentions are intimidatory – see Chapter 9 for this.
10. The long-running teachers' dispute has been, to date, the other, but although it has raised occasional issues of civil liability, the conduct of the dispute has not created policing or public order issues nor been affected in any significant way by the legal developments under discussion.
11. See, for an account of the legal issues arising from the earlier part of the dispute, Ewing and Napier (1986), and for the impact on the local community of the policing NCCL (1986).
12. One effect of the subsequent injunctions against picketing was to make it more difficult for the union to provide this restraining influence.
13. NCCL (1986).
14. A very full account of events that day is given in the *Guardian*, 26 January 1987.
15. The total of arrests throughout the dispute was 1,337.
16. Particularly by setting up separate companies for different parts of the group's production and distribution, to maximize the effect of the legal restrictions on secondary action, and by dismissing all the strikers – or locking them out – at a time when their remedy for unfair dismissal was excluded by law. See Ewing and Napier (1986) for discussion of these points.
17. These concerns were aired, for instance, at the Police Federation Conference in May 1985.
18. A strong example is the material used in evidence in the case of *R* v *Mansfield Justices, ex parte Sharkey* (1984) which prompted the Lord Chief Justice to describe the notion of peaceful picketing in Nottinghamshire as a 'colourful pretence'. Some of the evidence included opinions formed by police officers derived explicitly from newspapers and television.

9
Policing after the strike

NEW LEGISLATION AFFECTING POLICE POWERS

The context in which police decisions are made and police action taken is determined partly by legislation and partly by developing expectations and modes of thought which, in the long term, legislative changes create. Thus one of the effects of the 1964 legislation was, as we have seen, to produce an independent, well-organized, and confident police establishment which was able to give effective public expression to what it saw as the needs of the police service. Recent legislative changes owe something to this pressure; the way in which the separate interests of police and government have been integrated shows how deeply involved in the political process the bodies representing all ranks in the police have become.

Like changes in police organization, the development of recent legislation was slow, its tone and colour affected by varying political priorities and by the evidence of deep fissures in the social structure of the country. This can be seen most clearly in relation to the first two of the four statutory reforms we discuss here.

PUBLIC ORDER LEGISLATION

A discussion paper on proposals for public order legislation published in 1980 included a statement of the police belief that in situations where disorder might be expected, their current methods of control by superior numbers and the minimum of physical force would continue, with little change in the legal framework, to be sufficient to keep the peace.[1] In the six years between the publication of this discussion paper and the passage of the Public Order Act, 1986, several events altered the attitude of government – and of the police – to the scope of the legal changes necessary. The inner city riots of 1981 and 1985 persuaded police chiefs that more efficient organization, new strategies for riot control, and a new range of armoury were necessary. Much of this need had been satisfied, following the 1981 riots, by the changes which were put to the test during the miners' strike. Ministerial and legal thinking inclined to the belief that new definitions of riot and disorder, together with further legal control over demonstrations, processions, and marches, might be effective in preventing the assembly of those whose common purpose might end in violence. New offences and penalties were also thought necessary for lesser disorders, the harassment of citizens in the streets, and the alleged nuisance of trespasses by 'travelling people'.

The result was an Act which extensively (but far from systematically) reviewed the legal structure of public order offences and the mechanisms of control open to the police.[2] Thus the Act creates new statutory offences of riot, affray, and violent disorder, replacing the older offences of equivalent name (violent disorder replaces the former unlawful assembly), and two offences of a narrower and wider scope respectively to cover the ground previously occupied by the much-employed 'conduct likely to lead to a breach of the peace' under section 5 of the Public Order Act, 1936. The wider new offence, covering threatening, abusive, or insulting words or behaviour which the perpetrator can reasonably foresee will lead to harassment, alarm, or distress, gives a much enhanced discretionary power to the police on the street.[3] The original, at least ostensible, reason for including the new offence was to deal with young gangs of hooligans, but its potential for reinforcing the 'do as I say' style of policing, whether of political demonstrations or picketing, is clear.

The Act also creates an extended framework of powers for the police to prohibit or regulate processions, for advance notice of processions to be given, and – for the first time in statutory form – to control the location, duration, and size of stationary assemblies of more than twenty people. These powers to some extent codify existing powers at common law to preserve order; even so their importance and the potential readiness of the police on the spot to resort to them will be enhanced by this declaration of parliamentary approval. The powers to control processions and assemblies go significantly further, however, in that they may be called upon whenever the senior officer present deems it necessary to prevent serious interference with the life of the community or the carrying out by the organizers of an intention to intimidate.[4] It is at this point that the importance of judicial readiness to find intimidation in numbers becomes of especial significance in equipping the police to control mass picketing. More generally a higher political profile is assured to the police by their newly imposed task of judging the intent of demonstrators on potentially emotive criteria in politically tense circumstances. The 1986 Act is perhaps as symbolic as it is practical. The symbolism – which, unchecked, may generate changes in the police role well beyond the scale of the formal legislative amendments – is heavily slanted towards an endorsement of the drift of changes in policing exemplified in the strike and the subsequent events examined later in this chapter.

Many of the legal measures which the Act attests to be acceptable would, before the 1985 riots and the disturbances in 1985 and 1986 at and near Stonehenge, have been called illiberal. Without viable provision for redress of injustice or the prevention of abuse, that is what they are. The control by a senior police officer of the size, location, and duration of a public demonstration is a form of Riot Act which does not require any judicial imprimatur in the shape of a magistrate's presence or the order of a judge.[5] For those subject to the new forms of control there is no immediate alternative but submission or defiance followed by arrest – there are no means by which the annulment of a police decision given on the spot may be effected. And for demonstrations held in urgent protest against injustice, cruelty, or discrimination, *ex post facto* remedies are useless.

That such provisions have the effect that the legislation intended was demonstrated by the events of the 1987 journey to Stonehenge by groups of people wishing to celebrate the summer solstice there. (Events over the two previous summers will be considered shortly.) The police had acquired in addition to the powers described above a new power added specifically in response to the events of midsummer 1985 and 1986 to evict and arrest trespassers on open land or national monuments whose intent to reside was evidenced by their bringing on to the land twelve or more vehicles or threatening the occupiers.[6] One group of 'travellers', stopped on their way by the police, were addressed through a loud-hailer by a senior officer, who pointed out that the new provisions prevented them from assembling at or near the stone circle without police permission or the permission of the owners of the land.[7] This would not be given and the group must disperse. They did disperse, although a few were later allowed nearer to the site to observe the sunrise. There was no trouble for the police. Public tranquillity was bought at the price of individual freedom; for the 'travelling people', like many others whose life is spent in public rather than private places, lack the resources to contest the imposition of police restrictions on them.

REFORMS IN CRIMINAL LAW ENFORCEMENT

In another area of police work, the detection of crime and the prosecution of offenders, a powerful police lobby had kept up continuing pressure for particular reforms in the criminal process – the abolition of suspects' right to silence, restrictions on the selection of jurors and indeed on the right to trial by jury itself.[8] One of the arguments put forward in support of such changes was that if the police were not given effective backing in their efforts to catch criminals, they would be compelled to use unorthodox, even unlawful, methods to do so. From time to time there was disturbing evidence that this was the case.

An example of serious failure by the police to adhere to prescribed legal safeguards was the conduct leading to the obtaining of confessions from three vulnerable suspects in the Confait case.[9] An inquiry by Sir Henry Fisher revealed serious procedural inadequacies and misdemeanours which suggested that a full-scale investigation of police methods at every stage in the investigation of crime was overdue. Once again it was the abuse of the criminal process rather than problems of public order which provided the impetus for the appointment of a Royal Commission. Its report, published in 1981, was based on formidable amounts of evidence submitted by various interest groups together with the results of up-to-date research.[10] The Commissioners sought (as required by their terms of reference) to balance the demands of fairness to the accused with the realities of the police task. But the establishment of priorities in this area is also a political question, which can be determined only by legislation.

The Police and Criminal Evidence Act, which finally reached the statute book at the second attempt in 1984, implicitly acknowledged the police case by giving statutory recognition to some of the practices widely used in criminal investigation but not always capable of justification under the previous law. Powers to stop and search allegedly suspect persons, together with the setting up of road-blocks, were to be governed by a 'reasonable suspicion' test, together with procedures for establishing the identity of the officer responsible for the action. Extensions of powers in such matters as arrest and subsequent detention, fingerprinting, taking samples, and search and seizure of evidence, were to be balanced by detailed new procedures and some specific rights for suspects. Codes of Practice were written into the legal framework, thus affording some further protection to the citizens against arbitrary police action.[11]

A specific power of detention for ninety-six hours gave legal recognition to a practice widely used in serious matters, and usually referred to as 'helping the police with their enquiries'. Judicial intervention in the process of detention after thirty-six hours, with an associated right to legal representation, makes *incommunicado* detention for an extended period almost impossible, but the oppressive effects of long interrogation upon citizens in any circumstances is a serious matter.[12] The most effective sanction against improper use of such powers to detain and interrogate is to deny the prosecution the use of confessions or incriminating evidence procured improperly. The former test for the admission of confessions, that they must be proved to have been obtained voluntarily and without oppression, has been replaced by a test likely to prove less restrictive to the police, that confessions obtained by oppression or in circumstances liable to make them unreliable, may not be used as evidence.[13] The Act also confers a general power on the courts to exclude prosecution evidence on grounds of fairness, expressed in more narrow terms than originally proposed by Lord Scarman, its progenitor; the disciplinary influence of this power also is likely to be of modest effect.[14]

Commentators on the Act suggested when it was passed that it had altered in favour of the police the balance struck by the Royal Commission between greater flexibility for the police and more protection against misuse of enhanced powers for suspects.[15] The balance has tilted still further since lack of money has prevented the full implementation of a duty solicitor scheme, which was intended to ensure that suspects' rights to legal advice were not just theoretical. It is also already evident that the combination of pressures on police manpower and resources is being increasingly focused on the 'burdensome' procedures created by the Act to ensure the fair treatment of suspects.

THE CREATION OF THE POLICE COMPLAINTS AUTHORITY

A vital ingredient in the acceptability of the criminal process is public confidence that individuals are protected against abuse of the system. That confidence could not be obtained under the 1984 legislation without some change in the system for hearing complaints against police behaviour. In his report on the Brixton riots of 1981, Lord Scarman spoke of a public lack of confidence in the police which could be overcome only by the establishment of clearly independent methods of investigating and adjudicating citizens' grievances against the police. The battle for such an independent system had been bitterly opposed by senior police officers, one of whom, Sir Robert Mark, stood down when the Police Complaints Board was established in 1976.[16] The Board had little independent power, and established little confidence or respect. The 1984 Act therefore attempted to make some advance in providing for an independent body to oversee the investigation of matters referred to them. This rather faint-hearted response to the concerns articulated by Scarman may however turn out to be more effective than it looks.

One particular case illustrates both the limits and the potential role of the Police Complaints Authority (PCA). In 1983 a group of innocent teenagers was attacked in Holloway Road by police officers who arrived in an unidentifiable police transit van. Investigations following their complaint showed that the officers could have been from any one of a small number of serials. A four-year obstruction of all attempts to identify the culprits so disturbed the Authority that in their Annual Report for 1986 they gave publicity to their inability to resolve the genuine complaints of assault, and appealed for public assistance.[17] Information obtained shortly afterwards from one of the officers involved led to the identification, prosecution, and conviction (in July 1987) of those responsible. This incident shows clearly a major defect in the present complaints system, that police officers are under no obligation to co-operate with investigators (an omission easier to understand where criminal behaviour is in issue than for merely disciplinary matters). The publicization of the initial failure also shows a readiness to redouble efforts to overcome structural and procedural problems that is encouraging.

The control of the Authority (as of its predecessors) does not, as we have already noted, extend to supervision of the policies and operational decisions of chief constables. Yet more than twenty years ago, the control of chief constables was acknowledged to be the essence of control of the police as a whole. Today high-level decisions on police operations arouse the greatest public anxiety when they concern control of the streets, the management of demonstrations, and other matters which have to do with public order rather than the prevention and detection of crime. The paradox – and perhaps the explanation of the exclusion of operational policies from the new complaints procedure – is that the creation of the PCA was part of the 1984 legislation whose principal purpose was to regulate police practices in the investigation of crime rather than in the maintenance of public order.

If the PCA could take on responsibility for the oversight of police power in the streets – including the review of decisions to deploy police officers and equipment in a particular way, and leading inevitably to review of policy decisions of chief constables and their deputies in this area – a major gap in the accountability of the police could begin to be bridged. There is a hint of this idea in the PCA's Annual Report for 1986:

> We take the view that ordinary citizens will not be familiar with the details of the Codes of Practice or indeed with Force Orders and *therefore all matters revealed in an investigation which adversely affected the complainant should come within our jurisdiction unless the complainant specifically states otherwise.*   (Police Complaints Authority 1987: para 2.9; italics added)

THE CROWN PROSECUTION SERVICE

The major legal change arising from the second half of the Royal Commission's report was the creation of the Crown Prosecution Service in 1986.[18] This new independent service now undertakes the prosecution of nearly all offenders (aside from those processed by other statutory enforcement agencies and private prosecutions) after the first steps in the process have been undertaken by the police.[19] This latter restriction in the functioning of the service, framed, no doubt, to allay the fears of the police establishment, has weakened the impact of the reform by excluding from full scrutiny the early stages of the criminal process. Recent experience of the established public prosecution system in Scotland, reinforced by the chronic staffing problems endured by the Service at its outset, suggests that problems of time, caseload, and lack of information seriously hamper later scrutiny of initial police decisions to charge.[20] Nevertheless the disturbing link between investigation and control of prosecution has now been broken. Had the new service been in operation at the time of the miners' strike, there is at least a possibility that the grievous mishandling of riot and unlawful assembly charges would not have occurred.

Looking at these developments in the criminal law, it is clear that the miners' strike had little influence on the process. It delayed, through a wholesale disruption of training schedules, the implementation of the Police and Criminal Evidence Act. It was at least influential, but far from the only influence, in shaping the reforms of police powers contained in the Public Order Act, 1986. But its real, and much greater, significance was to demonstrate the effectiveness of newly developed police organization, training, and equipment that owed nothing to law at all.

POLICING IN RELATION TO THE NEW LEGISLATION[21]

Important policing incidents accompanied the progress of legislation in the period after the strike. They did not, save in one case, determine or influence the course of the changes being enacted. On the other hand, it is possible to see in the behaviour of some police officers and their superiors the subtle consequences of what some of them had experienced themselves and – more importantly – what the police culture had come to regard as the experience of most police officers during their tours of duty in the strike, namely that any large assembly of protestors was to be regarded as a threat to the peace and to the authority of the police.[22] It is also possible to see the reception into police practice of a sense of vindication of the new methods of riot control proved during the strike and accredited by Parliament in the Public Order Act.

THE MANCHESTER UNIVERSITY PROTEST

Just before the strike ended, on 1 March 1985, there was a confrontation between police and students at Manchester University arising from a protest at the visit to the university of the then Home Secretary, Leon Brittan.

There was a savage attack by police on protestors standing on the steps of the Union before the Home Secretary arrived. Thirty-three people were arrested and many subsequently convicted. But the students themselves and a number of their relatives and supporters, all articulate and resourceful citizens, registered seventy-one complaints about the conduct of the police. The investigation of these complaints led to a full-scale inquiry by the Police Complaints Authority, extending beyond specific misconduct to policing arrangements and allegations of subsequent police harassment of students who had played a prominent part in the incident and the making of complaints. As a result of the inquiry (which took fifteen months to complete), three officers were prosecuted and a few others 'advised' about their behaviour; two students (one of whom had apparently fled the country) were recommended for prosecution in connection with their statements to the police. The PCA came under strong criticism over its report, particularly from within the university, not least because under pressure from the Director of Public Prosecutions it declined to publish the full report of the inquiry while criminal cases were pending.[23] Nevertheless, there was a small move towards oversight of operational policing in that the PCA discussed its concern about the incident with senior officers responsible for the planning and execution of the operation.[24]

THE PROTECTION OF STONEHENGE

In 1985 and 1986 the police became involved in controversy as a result of the attempts to reach the stone circle at Stonehenge by what was called, with varying degrees of accuracy, the 'peace convoy', 'the hippies', or the 'travelling people'. The purpose of these attempts was to celebrate at sunrise on the summer solstice a renewal of the values which these groups, by their abandonment of generally accepted modern life-styles, wished to demonstrate. But it was just this abandonment, this failure to conform, that moved the authorities to impose control on them in ways which in some sections of the public aroused grave disquiet.

The first episode was at the time of the 1985 summer solstice. One large group with its tents and vehicles settled at and around Stonehenge. Alarmed at what might prove to be a continuing threat to the site and to its importance for other groups in the community, the owners and guardians of Stonehenge, English Heritage and the National Trust, asked for the convoy's removal. The Wiltshire police ejected those who had settled at Stonehenge with considerable force, and drove them away from the site and out of the county.

Prior to the 1986 solstice the owners and guardians of the site had armed themselves with an injunction against trespassing and erected barriers around the site. A large police presence ensured that the disturbing convoys were kept away; the latter, prevented from camping at Stonehenge, settled on neighbouring farmland. The owner was unable to obtain a sufficiently swift legal order for their eviction, and suffered much damage; this in turn focused much media hostility on the errant convoy, to which government spokesmen lent weight. Deriving confidence from this, the Chief Constable of Hampshire (in whose area the encampment had occurred) gathered a force of 400 police officers, including reinforcements from three neighbouring forces, to enter the land before dawn and remove all the occupants.

The public portrayal of these events was of a sad, straggling group of people, protected against the rain by their blankets and bedding, walking between lines of police officers and police vehicles; a tiny body of citizens, awkward, untidy but single-minded, deprived of their vehicles by the police, and forced to move to a designated reception centre for subsistence and travel warrants to wherever was to be their official, legal place of abode.[25] Despite understandable prejudices fanned in some parts of the press, many people must have been disturbed by the nature and purposes of this exercise of police power. The ironic consequence of this episode was the inclusion in the Public Order Bill of powers to enable the police to evict such trespassers in future without the need to resort to the courts.

The events of 1987 have been briefly described on p. 118. Again, protective barriers were erected round the site and admission was limited to 500 ticket-holders – how tickets were issued is unclear but they were not issued to travellers.[26] Travellers who tried to reach the site submitted to police instructions about where and how long they could stay. On this occasion there was no use of force or aggressive confrontation.

On the face of it, the events indicate that the new statutory power was successful. Yet the increment of police power it embodies is disturbing. Granting the need for protecting individuals from an invasion of private property, the use of force against those who do not act forcibly themselves should not be undertaken lightly. The use of police in numbers well in excess of those of the travellers, the gratuitous additional sanctions exacted by the authorities,[27] the hostile image presented by the police,[28] all display an authoritarian attitude to the definition of deviance, and the proper response of authority to its emergence, that is deeply worrying.

THE INNER CITY RIOTS

Neither of the matters we have discussed could compare with the riots in September and October 1985 in Handsworth, Brixton, and Tottenham, involving violent clashes between the police and the mainly black populations of the fairly small areas affected.

Events at Tottenham, the last of the three outbreaks of disorder, were the most serious and tragic, encompassing the murder of PC Blakelock.[29] The riots followed defensive and insensitive police responses to the death of Mrs Cynthia Jarrett at her home on 5 October 1985 in the course of a police search of the house for stolen goods suspected to have been stored there. The circumstances of this highly speculative search of the Jarrett household have been painstakingly described in the report of Lord Gifford's inquiry, and we need not therefore go into details here.[30] What is important to consider is the sequence of events which were the occasion for the riots and the explanations put forward for their occurrence.

In each case, in Handsworth, Brixton, and Tottenham, there was a well-publicized police policy of co-operation with the local community designed to be carried out by men and women on the beat.[31] In each case this policy was undermined, not only by the attitudes of particular senior officers, unfamiliar with the needs and prospects of certain key areas in their command, but also, and more immediately, by the practices of officers involved in the investigation of crime in the areas concerned. The heavy-handed approach of an officer in Handsworth who sought to interrogate and arrest a suspected car-thief in a public place where support for the suspect among onlookers was clear; the armed search of a house in Brixton which resulted in the accidental shooting of the householder, Mrs Cherry Groce; and finally the death of Mrs Jarrett in Tottenham, suggest that the detection of crime took precedence over conforming to the needs of policies of co-operation and consultation with the community to maintain effective policing. Vigorous programmes of community experiment and well-based research in Handsworth failed to prevent the burning and looting that caused the death of two innocent shopkeepers, many injuries and arrests, and great economic damage. The benign mantle of Scarman in Brixton, which might have preserved the area from future trouble, could not stop the violent protests against police behaviour that followed the shooting of Mrs Groce in late September. The death of Mrs Jarrett in Tottenham a few days later was the final event which demonstrated the grave dangers inherent in the policing of areas which were cautiously beginning to overcome the barriers of alienation from the police.

There can be no doubt that police concern with the detection and prevention of crime permits and even encourages suspicions and beliefs about inner city areas which are incompatible with a sympathetic co-operation with their communities. These beliefs have the further effect that confrontations between the police and residents in these areas are put down to the existence of powerful 'criminal' elements within the community rather than to the effects of social deprivation and a well-founded distrust of police behaviour. This creates a conflict of interest between the criminal side of police work and the maintenance of order and harmony in the community. On occasion the consequence of the disjunction between the two functions is violent disorder, leading to the third and most powerful police function, the suppression of riot.

There is a sense of history repeating itself here. During the early years of the provincial police forces in the 1840s, the riots that occurred in many towns and cities were often occasioned by attempts to arrest thieves or assailants in the face of opposition by a local populace suspicious of attempts to control their lives by police officers often recruited from outside the area. The hostility and suspicion of local communities to the presence of a crime prevention force which might interfere with settled habits of working life and leisure made vigorous and sometimes violent protest a fact of life for police and people in the working-class areas of industrial towns.[32] The strike-breaking function often assumed by the police was also resisted, as was the political surveillance they were thought by some to exercise.

In modern times the *embourgeoisement* of many sections of the working population has brought about a general acceptance of police practices which do not normally bear heavily on them. The major exception is in the course of industrial conflict. That apart, the day-to-day control of life by constant observation, however benevolent, is felt principally by diminishing but still significant groups of people who live in areas of multiple deprivation which attract intensive police attention.

THE MINERS' STRIKE AND PUBLIC ORDER

Consideration of the disorders which occurred in the immediate aftermath of the strike leads to the conclusion that there was little similarity between the causes and consequences of the violence on picket lines, and the circumstances of the outbursts of rage that characterized the inner city riots. In the first place, picket-line violence was exceptional, its duration brief, and its incidence infrequent. In the intervals between conflicts with the police the normal pattern of noisy but peaceful picketing reasserted itself. This was true also of the events at Wapping, where protests against the dismissal of print workers extending for more than a year led to a relatively small number of arrests in infrequent incidents of violence – though media coverage might suggest otherwise.[33]

The singularity of industrial confrontation, and its remoteness from the normal concerns of law enforcement, had been accepted in police thinking for many years. Its absorption into the general category of public order for policing purposes occurred primarily during the 1970s. The separation of industrial conflict from riot control may however have re-emerged in police thinking over the two years following the strike; the criticisms of the police role in the strike articulated within the Police Federation lend support to this perception. It is important that this differentiation of police functions, temporarily lost in the early 1980s, be re-established; this is perhaps one of the key lessons of the experience of the strike.

NOTES

1. Home Office (1980: para 15) quoted p. 50.
2. For a more detailed analysis of the Act in this context see Wallington (1987); more generally see A.T.H. Smith (1987); Williams (1987). Most of the relevant provisions came into force on 1 April 1987.
3. Section 5. The police may arrest suspected offenders who repeat their conduct after a warning, or where it is necessary to prevent a breach of the peace, or the police officer cannot establish the identity or address of the culprit.
4. Sections 12 and 14.
5. The original Riot Act was dependent on the reading of a formal proclamation by a magistrate. One argument for the reintroduction of the Riot Act in a modern form is that it would preserve some element of independent judgement about the necessity to restrict or disperse a demonstration – though we do not regard this as a sufficient gain to outweigh the relatively draconian powers such a measure would be likely to confer on the police.
6. Public Order Act, 1986, section 39.
7. Stonehenge and the immediately surrounding land is owned by English Heritage and administered by the National Trust. The decision of these two bodies to exclude people whose mores and life-styles were deemed anti-social from the area of the stone circle, by legal means and physical barriers (including barbed wire), attracted substantial criticism.
8. A persuasive voice in the early 1970s was the then Metropolitan Police Commissioner, Sir Robert Mark, notably in his famous Dimbleby Lecture, 'Minority Verdict', which argued amongst other things that acquittal rates in contested jury trials were too high. The question of jury selection is, as we write, again before Parliament in the Criminal Justice Bill reintroduced after the 1987 general election.
9. Maxwell Confait was murdered in 1971. Three teenage boys (one of whom was mentally retarded) were charged with and convicted of his murder principally on the evidence of their confessions and despite contradictory forensic evidence. One of the boys' parents managed to interest the local MP, Christopher Price, in the case and after intensive lobbying the case

was referred to the Court of Appeal, which quashed their convictions. Subsequently (after the Fisher Report) another man confessed to the murder. See generally Fisher (1977).

10. Royal Commission (1981) (Chairman Sir Cyril Phillips).

11. Codes of Practice are not in themselves legally enforceable, though they may be taken into account in legal proceedings, and breaches of them by the police are disciplinary offences. Their real importance perhaps lies in their contribution to police training and to the bureaucratic side of police practices.

12. Sections 43 and 44: the matter is referred to a private sitting of a magistrates' court, but the suspect must be present and has a right to legal representation.

13. Section 76. The first case under this section to reach the Court of Appeal (*R* v *Fulling*, 1987) produced the ruling that 'oppression' requires something over and above the inherently oppressive relationship between police interviewer and detained suspect.

14. Section 78. In *R* v *Mason* (1987) the Court of Appeal used this section to exclude evidence of a confession obtained by deception of both the suspect and his solicitor by the investigating officers.

15. This is best illustrated by the history of the legislation itself. Thus, one Introduction to the Statute (*Current Statutes Annotated*, 1984, vol. 4, c 60–4, Sweet & Maxwell) comments: 'The Police and Criminal Evidence Act 1984 is one of the most controversial pieces of legislation in recent years. . . . Opposition to the Act, or parts of it, came from the professions (the British Medical Association, the Law Society), from the Church, from journalists, even from the police.' A special edition of the *Criminal Law Review* (September 1985), is devoted to critical comments on various sections of the Act (pp. 553–88).

16. However the Police Federation, representing all ranks of police officers up to chief inspector, came to support a fully independent complaints system, provided it was coupled with legal representation for their members when complained against.

17. Police Complaints Authority (1987: para 3.2.3.).

18. Prosecution of Offences Act, 1985.

19. The Service is independent of the police; it is under the Director of Public Prosecutions, who is answerable to the Attorney-General.

20. Moody and Toombs (1982).

21. For the Wapping dispute see Chapter 8.

22. Press and television reporting was, as so often, a primary source of 'information'. It is the nature of the media that they find no news in peace, only in conflict. In terms of publicity the largely peaceful picketing over the whole course of the miners' strike was completely overshadowed by the less frequent events of violent and tragic confrontation.

23. See also the trenchant critique by Professor John Griffith, Chancellor of the University: the *Guardian*, 3 April 1987.

24. Police Complaints Authority (1987: para 3.10).

25. Their vehicles had been declared unroadworthy. The police said they could be reclaimed on being made roadworthy and subject to proof of ownership, but to those being forcibly shipped from the area this must have seemed a cruel joke to compound effectively permanent confiscation.

26. Druids, apparently less dangerous in their eccentricities than the travellers, were much in evidence at the solstice ceremonies.

27. The opportunity was taken to scrutinize social security status, as well as to impound vehicles.

28. The Chief Constable of Hampshire was reported as describing the travellers as 'anarchists', with the implication that this somehow legitimized the police action.

29. The course of the riot and events leading up to it are briefly summarized in a report by Assistant Commissioner Richards to Haringey Police/Community Consultative Council (Metropolitan Police 1986). Haringey Borough Council commissioned an independent inquiry into the events, chaired by Lord Gifford QC, whose report (Gifford 1986) contains a rather fuller analysis than the police summary.

30. Gifford 1986. We also refrain from reviewing the claims that the riots were planned in advance by criminal elements. Even if and to the extent that this did happen, it would scarcely remove the real concerns over the spread of violence, the hostility shown to police, or the inherently explosive potential of inept handling of police responsibilities in sensitive situations.

31. Handsworth was the subject of a report by the chief constable to the Home Secretary which deals fully with the course of the riots and more briefly with background issues and local policing initiatives (West Midlands Police 1985).

32. For an excellent account see Storch (1975).

33. See Chapter 8.

PART IV
Conclusions and recommendations

10
Conclusions and recommendations

Having now outlined the background to the strike and its policing, the policing of the strike itself, and important subsequent developments, our conclusions must be stated. In this chapter we first set out those conclusions,
covering police objectives and priorities, the constitutional issues of accountability, more detailed questions of police conduct, and the impact of the
strike on the workings of the criminal justice system. We then extend our
conclusions to embrace the effects of subsequent developments and current
trends in policing. Finally we put forward recommendations for action to
correct the defects identified in the conclusions. Of these the first and most
important is for a Royal Commission on the police and policing. Most of our
recommendations are in the form of an agenda for a Royal Commission; we
also make specific recommendations on points beyond the remit of such a
Commission, principally in the area of the enforcement of the criminal law.

The context of our conclusions is not just the strike itself but the very
significant and longer-term changes in policing and institutions which it
brought to light and which have been built on since. Some of our conclusions
derive from points discussed fully in the text or in this chapter, but others
are more broadly based assessments based on an overall view of the materials
available to us, not all of which can be fully reflected in the text of the report.

CONCLUSIONS: THE ROLE OF THE POLICE

The first of the central questions raised by the strike is what was the role and
what were the objectives of the police, how were they determined, and were
they proper, and properly determined?

Critics accused the police of acting as agents of the government and the
NCB to break the strike, and argued that they had been improperly used in
substitution for the NCB's civil law remedies to procure a return to work and
continued supplies of coal regardless of the cost. These criticisms came not
only from striking miners and their leaders and supporters, but also from
within the police and their representatives in the Police Federation.

The opposing view, urged by chief constables and government spokesmen, was that the police carried out the duties which the circumstances necessitated, of keeping the peace, preventing crime, and securing that individual miners were not prevented from exercising their lawful freedom to return to work.

We believe that the critics were basically right. This, in our view, was in part the fault of the government, for exposing the police to pressure to undertake the responsibilities they did, by discouraging resort to civil law remedies, and offering incentives to the police to fill the breach thus created. It was also in part the fault of the chief constables for their acquiescence in undertaking a role which became partisan, with inadequate awareness of or sensitivity to the repercussions this would have. Beyond both, much of the blame lies in the constitutional weaknesses of the systems of police accountability which facilitated the conscription of police resources to assist the defeat of one party to an industrial dispute.

These conclusions are not as obvious as they may have appeared to some critics of the police, and it is necessary to explain at a little length how we arrive at them. The first two are the subject of this section, the third of the next section (p. 135).

The miners' strike, if it were to be resolved by policing and the criminal courts, demanded extraordinary police responses and a substantial diversion of resources from other police work. This was most clearly so where miners and their families were in need of protection from violence and intimidation in their homes and communities. It was also clearly the case where, as in Nottinghamshire and Derbyshire in particular, significant numbers of working and striking miners would otherwise have met at pit gates in circumstances indicating a real risk of serious disturbances. With hindsight the numbers of police deployed were sometimes excessive, but hindsight is a much easier basis for judgement than the circumstances under which deployment decisions had to be taken, and we wish to avoid generalized criticisms of over-reaction.

Notwithstanding the clear need for large-scale policing, the police were widely regarded as having been diverted to serve the government's purposes of defeating the strike. The police resources provided to enable individual miners to return to work gave the clearest ground for this belief. For instance, several hundred police were deployed to escort Paul Wilkinson into Easington Colliery over an extended period when he was the only miner working at the pit, while in a particularly significant episode at Cortonwood (the pit whose proposed closure triggered the strike) the first miner to return to work was escorted by over 1,000 police on 9 November 1984. Whether the police acted properly in ensuring, regardless of manpower consequences, that those who wished to do so got to work (a few isolated instances early in the strike apart) depends to a considerable degree on the priority that should be accorded to the symbolic exercise of a fundamental freedom and its protection.

There are several powerful arguments for the view that it was proper for the police to act as they did. The working miners sought to exercise a fundamental freedom to go to their place of work, and because of the risk of their being prevented from doing so by violence and intimidation, police protection was needed to enable them to do so. It was strenuously urged on us by a group of Conservative MPs with whom we discussed our interim report that the alternative was to concede the pass to the forces of lawlessness and anarchy, and that if we criticized the police response, it was incumbent on us to suggest a viable alternative course of action. Without necessarily accepting the implied characterization of the miners' pickets, we fully accept the thrust of these points. We also accept that it may be important, indeed crucial, to the protection of civil liberties to protect the symbolic exercise of a right; the cases of symbolic acts of desegregation in the early years of the US Civil Rights movement are a cogent instance. The symbolism is important because it asserts the importance of the right and opens the door to others who wish to exercise it, and because it is impossible to fix any other threshold which is not arbitrary or open to the inference that the right concerned is only available to groups.

These are powerful arguments, which if they stood alone would compel the conclusion that the priority treatment of returning miners' freedoms was correct. Nevertheless we feel that this priority should not have been accorded, and that the analogies drawn to support it are misleading. In the first place, normal police practice is quite different. Resources are finite, indeed severely stretched, so that a variety of essential calls on the police cannot be catered for, such as the protection of ethnic minorities from racial harassment, securing the safety of inner city streets, and the investigation of burglary in metropolitan areas.

The police have a duty to prevent disorder but a discretion as to the methods chosen. Indeed, they have powers to prevent even lawful activities where they reasonably anticipate that the pursuit of the activity in question will result in a breach of the peace.[1] It is not a condition for the exercise of these restraining powers that those stopped would have *caused* the disorder. The police freely and regularly used these powers to stop striking miners from getting to picket lines throughout the strike. Indeed, in the very first days of the strike they did stop a small number of intending returnees from going through picket lines in order to preserve the peace.

Our point is not that the police should have used their powers to interfere more extensively with other people's liberties. That would be the antithesis of our general argument, and in due course we comment critically on the use of preventive powers against picketing and the subsequent statutory extension of those powers. The point is simply that the police dealt with the question of returning miners in a different way from their normal operational approach to the conflict between preserving order and protecting and enforcing rights. That they were able to do so at all was the result of government undertakings that chief constables could use whatever resources they felt necessary, regardless of pre-existing budgets. This however did not and could not prevent the use of police in this way from severely depleting policing elsewhere in the country. Either the chief constables made use of their blank cheques because they accorded an exceptionally high priority to the rights of miners wishing to return to work, or they were influenced by government pressure into taking an operational decision they would not have chosen independently (or both).

Sir Ian MacGregor, in his account of the strike, makes it clear that the NCB sought government assistance at the highest levels to put pressure on those chief constables who initially declined to secure a passage to work for miners who wanted to go through the picket lines. Thereafter all miners who wished to do so were escorted through the colliery gates by however many police were felt to be required.[2] The 'return to work' movement was organized with great skill by NCB managers and became the principal plank of the NCB's strategy to defeat the strike.[3] There was thus a real question how far the true symbolism of lone returnees was of individuals exercising their civil liberties or of the Coal Board overcoming the strike. In the early stages those who did return to work could rarely be given anything productive to do, but the Coal Board could and did publicize the fact that they were at work and that the police would safeguard anyone else who wished to follow them.

Our conclusion therefore is that the issue of protecting the symbolic exercise of fundamental freedoms was not the real point. The police gave systematic priority to achieving the objectives of one party to an industrial dispute, to the detriment of normal police services, through a mistaken assessment of their priorities or in response to pressure, or both.

The consequences of this choice of priorities were severe. Immense ill-will was generated, especially in those closely knit mining communities where feelings of solidarity were outraged by the return of individual miners often not themselves resident in the immediate community. The consequent influx of pickets and police was a high price, paid by the community, for the individual's exercise of his freedom to go to work. The ill-will against the police was unfortunately compounded by inexcusable conduct by some police officers, but the very exercise of providing police protection was enough. Away from the mining areas, the policing supplied for returning miners simply aggravated the denudation of police resources. It is impossible to say how much of the mutual aid requirement would have been avoided had the police adopted different priorities, but it cannot have been insignificant. In Greater Manchester, police availability fell on occasion to as low as two-thirds of normal strength, while in London, Metropolitan police officers were sent out of the capital in considerable numbers at a time when in East London the incidence of racial violence and harassment of the Asian communities, and the lack of an adequate police response to it, was a matter of pressing concern.[4] Even in areas to which thousands of additional police were sent, ordinary police services declined in effectiveness.[5]

What alternatives were open to the police? We believe that the following actions could and should have been taken.

I. REFUSAL TO PROVIDE SPECIAL ASSISTANCE TO THE NCB OR OTHER
EMPLOYERS UNLESS AND UNTIL THEY MADE USE OF THEIR CIVIL LAW
REMEDIES, AND THEN ONLY IF THE CIVIL LAW DID NOT SUCCEED

In particular, the NCB could have pursued the injunction it did obtain to restrain Yorkshire NUM from sending pickets into Nottinghamshire, and taken action to prevent the organization or payment of pickets sent by Yorkshire or other areas. Other nationalized industries, particularly British Steel, could have obtained injunctions against interference by secondary picketing with their essential supplies. That they chose not to do so was a matter either of industrial relations (the view publicly argued by Sir Ian MacGregor)[6] or government pressure (as most commentators suggest).[7] Whichever it was, the chief constables could collectively have made it clear to the Home Secretary and to the Coal Board and British Steel that they could not divert scarce resources to deal with *civil* matters.[8] (In saying this we accept that policing could not have been withdrawn where it was necessary to preserve the peace, but there is a great deal of difference between protecting the individual safety of a man who wishes to go to work and co-operating in the planning of a sophisticated operation publicized by the employers to attract miners to break the strike.)

II. TAKING OPERATIONAL DECISIONS IN THE LIGHT OF COMPETING DEMANDS FOR RESOURCES AND THE NEED TO BALANCE CONFLICTING FREEDOMS

We do not believe that chief constables considered whether getting one man back to work was really an objective which overrode the priorities that had to be relegated in order to furnish the required police manpower. Had they done so, and concluded (as on occasion they inevitably would have done) that there were other competing priorities and that they could offer only a modest police presence, then the preservation of the peace would have required them to balance the liberties of all parties, some of which would have to be sacrificed. Ways in which they might have done so include the following:

1. Negotiating with strike leaders for reductions in numbers of pickets and for assistance in minimizing disorder, obstruction, or intimidation in return for an agreement to ensure that official pickets were assisted to speak to the returnees so as to persuade them to turn back. This was the basis of the most successful policing undertaken, in West Yorkshire, South Wales, and Gwent, and could have worked elsewhere.
2. Arranging with the employers for those who wished to return to work to be temporarily transferred to locations already working. In pits where only a handful of men had returned they could do almost no useful work, and the importance of their returning to a particular pit was almost exclusively in terms of the propaganda opportunities which it gave to the employers. It was no part of the function of the police to abet these, still less to lay on a large force for the purpose, when the employees' wish to return to work could be sufficiently met in other ways.
3. Instructing intending returnees that they could not return to work, and would be arrested if they attempted to do so, in any case where the decision to return to work could properly be regarded as provocative in the community concerned, or where this was the only way, with resources available, of preventing serious disorder. We do not like the erosions of freedom either ground implies, but they are part of normal police practice and it is a distortion of the even-handed balancing of liberties, which is a primary police duty, to exempt working miners from this process.

Similarly in relation to supplies of coke and coal to British Steel, we cannot accept that there was no latitude as to the timing of movements, and the police could have taken much more control over movements in the interests of preserving order and avoiding violence. The two days of really serious conflict at Orgreave need not, in our view, have happened if the police had used their common law powers to prevent the movement of lorries on the days concerned. All too clearly, however, the political implications of doing so would have been a sufficient deterrent for any but the most courageous or foolhardy chief constable. In effect, the memories of Saltley demanded a return match and the question of policing priorities did not arise.

III. WORKING OUT PRIORITIES, RESOURCES, AND GENERAL STRATEGIES IN CONSULTATION WITH THE RELEVANT POLICE AUTHORITIES

The police authorities were shabbily treated both by the government and by many chief constables. Major issues of priority in the sensitive use of limited resources, and the acceptable methods of maintaining so far as possible the support of the local communities, were not discussed; police authorities appeared not to be trusted. To some extent this was a failure of institutions; we examine this shortly. Within the areas being policed, the consultations we envisage could have taken place. In some areas, such as Nottinghamshire, they would probably have shown clear support for police objectives. Elsewhere, especially in South Yorkshire and Derbyshire, they might have led to a clearer understanding by police 'management' of the alternatives open to them and their implications. They might well have led to different policies being pursued, but even if not, the task of maintaining local confidence in the police would have been less daunting if the confidence of community representatives had not been diminished by insensitivity and professional arrogance.

The blame for these very serious errors and their consequences lies in considerable part with chief constables. Collectively and individually they pride themselves on their independence, particularly from 'sectional interests'. In the miners' strike they made no attempt to defend that independence against the demands made of them by the results of government policy (if not demands implicitly made of them directly by government). Many defended their actions with a conviction that bordered on zeal. 'We are driven to the view that some of the latter group in particular did not see the contradictions or dangers in their policies or the possibility of other views. This alarms us precisely because of the high degree of operational autonomy the present system accords to chief constables. Ordinarily the kind of policing we enjoy is determined by this small group of men whose personal attitudes are a major factor in the creation of policing styles. *Some* attitudes were all too clearly displayed during the strike.

However, much more blame must be attached to the government. It was responsible (*pace* Sir Ian MacGregor's rather unconvincing explanation) for discouraging the use of civil law. The Home Secretary gave out the clearest indications of what he wanted from the police by releasing all financial constraints on policing the strike, by belittling and humiliating the police authorities, and by hawkish speeches about offences carrying life imprisonment (as to which Mr Brittan must carry some personal blame for the disastrous riot prosecutions). The Attorney-General, by his March 1984 Commons statement, encouraged some of the most serious overreaching of the limits of police power in relation to road-blocks. The government as a whole willingly encouraged (not least by the Prime Minister's notorious remarks about the 'enemy within') the creation of a political climate in which it became impossible for the police as a whole to avoid a distortion of priorities and for individual police officers it became more and more difficult to disentangle fact from prejudice in assessing those whom they were sent to police. Above all it is the government which must take responsibility for a situation in which the police collectively were cast in a pivotal role in the defeat of a strike.

CONCLUSIONS: THE CONTROL AND ACCOUNTABILITY OF THE POLICE

Our conclusions in this section are concerned with the general constitutional position of the police which allowed and facilitated the misapplication of resources during the strike, and with more specific questions concerning ACPO, the NRC, and the investigation of complaints. On the constitutional question matters can be more briefly discussed because the major failures of the system were seen to be so serious as to be self-evident.

The tripartite system of police accountability created in 1964 embodied four ultimately fatal flaws. It made no provision for the constitutional repercussions of really major calls on the mutual aid system, which in 1964 was still seen as a minor administrative exercise. It failed to resolve the longstanding issue of the system of accountability needed for the Metropolitan police. It gave to local police authorities outside London extensive responsibilities without corresponding powers. Most seriously, it left unresolved the boundary between chief constables' autonomy and police authorities' supervisory powers.

These weaknesses were not immediately apparent, and it was possible for the police service to function effectively without undue strain on relationships so long as there was sufficient consensus about objectives and methods, absence of abnormal strains on policing, financial flexibility, and a readiness on the part of police authorities to accept a very subsidiary role. None of these preconditions remained by the early 1980s.[9] Indeed the problem had developed more serious dimensions because the temporary palliative of passive and quiescent police authorities had created a power vacuum into which the Home Office and chief constables had managed to slide. When in the early 1980s some police authorities sought to enforce powers commensurate with their duties and representative roles, they found that even the exiguous accountability afforded by the tripartite system as originally enacted had been seriously eroded.

In the situation prevailing at the start of the strike the local authorities had almost no effective power left. Their weakness was compounded by the availability to government of a simple way round their one remaining effective control, that of the purse strings. It was compounded further by the ready support given by the government to chief constables in dispute with their police committees over the ambit of their autonomy. In these circumstances the system itself left the door wide open to government to finance and procure a police-led strategy to defeat the striking miners, and subsequently to control inner city discontent.

Such a situation is in our view wholly unacceptable and in need of urgent reappraisal and reform. Not only did the strike expose the vulnerability of the police to excessive influence by government, it also laid bare the extent of the collapse of any credible system of local accountability or influence over choices and priorities in policing. It showed moreover that a whole range of fundamental policing issues had been effectively removed altogether from local accountability through the centralization process of the previous decade or so. It is important to stress that only in a narrow sense is the problem a legacy or consequence of the strike – it brought matters temporarily into the public domain. The visible problems of 1984–5 remain, if less visible, every bit as acute.

The components of the present system-failure can be briefly summarized.

1. The concept of chief constables' operational autonomy has expanded so much that no duty is recognized to account for strategy or policy, still less its detailed implementation. Any dialogue between chief constables and police committees is a matter of concession.
2. Police committees have stringent financial responsibilities, but no say in the incurring of substantial extra expenses by their chief constable calling in mutual aid, for which the police authority must pay.
3. Conversely police committees (in England and Wales) have the legal duty to secure efficient and adequate policing but they cannot prevent either the inefficient use of resources within their area or the loss of resources to other parts of the country under mutual aid.
4. It has been shown that it is possible for national initiatives in riot training to be taken by the Home Office and ACPO, which have radically altered the methods of policing a major and sensitive aspect of public protest, without *any* involvement or consultation of local representatives. Presumably this exercise can be repeated in other areas of policing.
5. The NRC was set up, and operates when required, with no consultation with, still less accountability to, the police authorities.
6. Increasing emphasis on the power of the Home Secretary to override police committees has further diminished their powers: for instance over the suspension of senior officers, or the stocking of plastic bullets.[10]
7. The introduction of local consultative committees in 1985 has had only a marginal effect owing to the lack of any obligation on chief constables in such matters as providing information or responding to suggestions.[11]
8. At the same time the formal responsibility of the Home Secretary – and therefore any system of effective parliamentary accountability – has been limited in two ways: by the existence of the local police authorities, on whose shoulders the Home Secretary can dump unwanted responsibility, and by the use of guidance and informal collaboration with ACPO, rather than formal powers of direction.

There is a superficial contradiction in presenting all these points together as matters of criticism, since they contain an element of increasing account-ability – to government – as well as the loss of local powers. The point needs to be met, but it has several answers. First, we accept that there *are* arguments for a national police force. If those arguments prevail, however, the proper response would be the setting up of such a force by Act of Parlia-ment, after proper public debate, and with proper constitutional procedures to ensure accountability. Instead what we have experienced is a considerable degree of nationalization of the police by stealth. There has been no real opportunity for public debate and the machinery of democratic accountability which a national force would require has not been considered.

Second, however, we regard the balance between local and central accountability as the key to effective control, and it has been so tilted as to have all but disappeared. Local accountability is preferable to national in part precisely because experience suggests that it can be subjected more effectively to safeguards against abuse than can national control. The balance of the Home Secretary's residual powers and responsibilities, and those of the Inspectorate of Constabulary, can provide a check, which is not present where the power is in the hands of central government. The courts' role is more active and effective in controlling local authorities than Ministers of the Crown, because the courts are hesitant to take on what should be Parliament's role; but Parliament as it is currently conducted falls far short of the task implicitly allotted to it. In short, central control of the police is not, in our view, productive of the degree of democratic accountability which local police authorities with effective powers and influence over general policy and methods of implementation, and with residual checks through central government and the courts, can and should provide.

There are, too, other reasons for the police, as for other public services which need to be responsive to the local communities they serve, to be subject to local accountability. Services which are responsive to community needs are likely to be better services, and if they are seen to be responsive the community is more able to accept the legitimacy of the constraints policing necessarily imposes. (Put the other way, we accept the view urged, for instance, by Margaret Simey, that without an element of democratic control the consent necessary for 'policing by consent' cannot be required or obtained.)[12] Therefore we regard machinery for the democratic accountability of the police for decisions about the way the community is policed and for the allocation of police resources, through representatives of the local communities concerned, as an essential component of a democratic society, and a necessary precondition of the preservation of civil liberties.[13] To all intents and purposes it no longer exists. We outline in our recommendations some of the ways in which the system might be reconstructed.

The more basic objection to our concern is the view, held by many senior police officers and some politicians, that the independence of the police from 'political interference' is essential to the protection of democratic values and the rule of law. This is in part the argument for autonomy advanced by all professional groups, which in other areas of public service such as education or the health service is reconciled more or less satisfactorily with the demands for lay representatives to be involved in policy. This view sometimes goes further in perceiving a danger that local control of the process of law enforcement might involve oppression or discrimination. We readily acknowledge that the danger exists, and must be safeguarded against. But we regard democratic accountability for policy not only as being an essential prerequisite of maintaining the consent and active support of the community; it also removes from the police the liability to be directly criticized which the lack of any other responsible agency necessarily produces.

Some more detailed points about the constitutional position must be added. First, the position of ACPO. Formally, ACPO is merely simply the professional association of the most senior police officers. It has no statutory basis, nor legal accountability beyond that of any other private, voluntary body. We are gravely concerned at the extent to which this body has assumed such a key role in modern policing without any steps being taken to establish the responsibilities we believe to be concomitant. The president *pro tem* of ACPO automatically commands the National Reporting Centre. It was ACPO which produced and issued the controversial Tactical Options Manual. ACPO has been the major conduit for Home Office influence on policing, particularly in recent years in public order training; and in the policy of policing the miners' strike. It represents a major alternative source of policy for individual chief constables as well as a shield against pressure from each police committee; as a result it has aided the abstraction of the latters' influence on policing. It is no exaggeration to describe it as the chief constables' (and to some extent the Home Secretary's) private power base.

Much the same can be said of the NRC; like ACPO it has no statutory basis or constitution, and its operation excludes local police committees from any effective say over the diversion of their resources. Again the beneficiaries are the chief constables collectively (though not necessarily individual chief constables, who may effectively be overruled by the NRC as to manpower priorities) and the Home Secretary.

The system of mutual aid laid down in the Police Act, 1964, was hardly designed to cope with the scale of aid engaged in the miners' strike. The Act fails in particular to lay down clear financial rules for the reimbursement of salaries and expenses between police authorities or by the Home Secretary. The result was that it was possible for the then Home Secretary to categorize the mutual aid as 'larger scale' rather then 'major' in an ill-advised attempt to spread the burden for extra policing costs across all police authorities. The Home Secretary's attitude to the financial plight of police authorities' receiving mutual aid or being forced to pay out open-endedly for overtime was inexcusable, and contributed greatly to the weakening of the authorities' position and their status in the eyes of their chief constables. A system which permits such consequences (albeit the heaviest of the financial burdens were eventually and grudgingly met by central government) cannot be retained unreformed.

The last particular matter for comment is the handling of complaints against the police. We have already noted in some detail the limitations of the police complaints system as exposed during the strike.[14] Its key weaknesses are twofold: first that matters of general policy, as distinguished from individual acts of impropriety, are outside the complaints system laid down in the reform of 1976, and remain outside the revised system introduced in 1985. At the same time such matters – for instance the use of a turn-back policy or of mounted police during the strike, or policy decisions as to the numbers of official pickets to be permitted or the facilities they would be allowed – are not adequately controllable, even by subsequent report and review, by the police committees. All too often the same decision is 'policy' when put into effect to the detriment of an individual and 'operational' when its rationale is raised at the police committee. So long as it is a lawful exercise of discretion it is beyond external scrutiny.

The second key weakness is that the system lacks public confidence and credibility. This was acknowledged by Lord Scarman in 1981; it was demonstrated clearly by the negligible number of formal complaints laid during the strike, in comparison to the numbers undoubtedly aggrieved by their treatment by the police; and it has not been allayed by the reform of the system in 1985. The most remarkable single statistic of the miners' strike is that *no* police officer was officially prosecuted or formally disciplined as a result of the policing of the strike. The Police Complaints Authority, to its credit, has acknowledged the serious difficulty it faces in supervising investigations that police officers are not obliged to co-operate with investigators, and as a result the identity of culprits may be extremely difficult to establish.[15] We believe however that this is only part of a more basic problem of approach to complaints: an inbuilt assumption that most complaints are false and some are malicious, and therefore the safeguards afforded to a suspected criminal should be given to officers under investigation, but no effective acknowledgement of the implicit consequences for the conduct of investigations of complaints (especially against unidentified officers). These problems were exacerbated, not created, by the particular circumstances of the strike. The division between operational control and disciplinary authority for visiting forces created delays which formed a further ground for dissatisfaction with the complaints system. The whole question of complaints is one to which we return in our recommendations.[16]

CONCLUSIONS: THE CONDUCT OF THE POLICING – GENERAL STRATEGIES

We stress at the outset that there was a great deal of routine, ordinary policing of relatively routine situations during the strike, of the kind characteristic of almost all industrial disputes, uneventful and boring but a necessary part of ensuring that nothing untoward occurs. Over and above this there was a great deal of good policing: resourceful, sensitive, and on occasions courageous. Many pickets freely acknowledged and appreciated this, or at least had a grudging respect for the professionalism that the police brought to their task. There were, however, many criticisms. Some of these followed from the observation that police organizations were, for the first time, clearly seen to be beyond the control of the democratic institutions to which they were formally subject. Others had to do with the oppressive behaviour of police officers, singly or in formations, as they exercised their power over striking miners, their families, and supporters.

It is, of course, acknowledged that the circumstances giving rise to the criticisms we adopt were exceptional both in terms of the strains imposed on the police system and on individual officers by the duration of the strike and the scale of the policing, and because the police were significantly less free agents in determining priorities and methods than is usual. Moreover the policing was, within the objectives set by (or for) the police, a signal success. It was a proving ground for new techniques and tactics that clearly produced their intended effects. But in saying this we choose our words carefully, because we take a different, wider, view of success and failure, derived from our philosophy of civil liberties, and by these criteria the policing is open to serious criticism in a number of respects. We deal with those criticisms in this and the following section, first in general terms of the direction and styles of policing at a policy or strategic level, then in terms of the actual conduct of the police.

STYLES OF APPROACH

Different police forces adopted widely differing general approaches to their task, in part of course in response to circumstances but in part also reflecting different perceptions of good policing. The Chief Constable of West Yorkshire, in his Annual Report for 1984, described his approach thus:

> Central to the strategy adopted in policing the miners' dispute has been an acute awareness that we were policing part of our own community with whom 'normal' working relationships need to be maintained during and subsequent to the strike. It was also recognised that the large majority of striking miners are honest, decent, law-abiding members of the community with only a small minority ignoring their legal responsibilities and seeking to achieve their aims with unnecessary violence. Our attitude, therefore, could properly be summarised as policing with reasonable firmness but with maximum tolerance. In pursuing this strategy, the policing of picket lines has generally been undertaken by our own officers and, to avoid giving a militaristic appearance their duty has, whenever possible, been performed in normal uniform.

We endorse and commend these sentiments, and are glad to record that, so far as we can judge, the approach indicated was in fact maintained in West Yorkshire – with fewer injuries, arrests, and complaints being the result as much as the precondition (as exponents of the 'heavier' styles of policing would say they were) of this style of policing. Similar standards were generally maintained in a number of other areas, particularly in South Wales (where riot equipment was not used at all during the strike) and Gwent.

Elsewhere policing was, regrettably, too often lacking in this sensitivity and flexibility. 'Heavy' policing, authoritarian approaches to the control of picketing, over-use of riot equipment, and over-reaction to minor deviance were witnessed by observers from Chesterfield NCCL and Sheffield Policewatch.[17] Much heavy policing was necessitated by the violence offered to police or working miners; but by no means all. It is an open question how much of the violence would not have occurred had more subtle approaches been adopted initially. Certainly we feel bound to agree with observers that minor initial violence was greatly exacerbated on occasions – Orgreave being one – by premature and excessive police responses. Such policing is misguided in its failure to focus on the central objective of policing – the preservation of order – as a broad goal, and in its disregard for the civil liberties of all concerned (not just those being escorted to work).

We consider that the factors likely to influence policing for the worse during the dispute included the strategy advocated by the Tactical Options Manual, and the deployment of police officers from outside the area, particularly from inner urban areas. The latter, as well as having experience of a very different kind of environment and much more aggressive policing styles, were operating in geographically and culturally unfamiliar territory towards which few can have felt the same loyalty as local officers. These factors were liable to be magnified by the de-individualizing effect of training and working together in PSUs. The result was a style of policing almost bound to forfeit the respect of miners' pickets and easy to caricature as a colonial militia.[18] Sadly the reality was sometimes not far removed from the caricature. Apart from the use of officers imported from inner city areas, these factors are not peculiar to the miners' strike. They rather represent the nature of the new approach to policing public disorder. This approach, understandably given its origins, is riot-control led. Nevertheless the use of techniques developed to control urban riots in the altogether different context of an industrial dispute has shown that whatever their justification in the control of riots they are not an effective substitute for the appropriate style of policing the participants in an industrial dispute.

ROAD-BLOCKS AND TURN-BACK POLICY

The miners' strike saw the most massive exercise in policing by exclusion from potential areas of conflict ever experienced; and it is clear that that experience has led to the incorporation of the strategy into the catalogue of recognized responses to potential disorder. It has been quite commonly used since 1984. The legal status of road-blocks has been confirmed by legislation.[19] Within limits of temporal and geographical proximity the turning-back of suspected demonstrators has been sanctioned by the High Court.[20] However we do not accept that the policy was proper, and are concerned that it was exercised in an almost indiscriminate and certainly arbitrary way. Too little attention was paid to the civil liberties of those prevented, on pain of arrest, from proceeding about their lawful business. In the name of preserving freedom to travel to work, the freedom of many others to travel, officially only to picket but in practice for many other purposes also, was barred. The inference that miners bound for Nottinghamshire were intent on violence, or even likely to become involved in it, was not borne out by the normality of peaceful and non-violent picketing elsewhere. The strategy must undoubtedly have contributed to the tension between police and pickets and the difficulty of the police task in adjoining areas such as Yorkshire, if not actually increasing the violence later experienced there.[21] It was also a clear example of using a criminal law power in default of the enforcement of the civil remedy already in the hands of the NCB.[22]

CONCLUSIONS: THE CONDUCT OF THE POLICE IN ACTION

In dealing with aspects of individual police conduct we must first make clear the basis of the criticisms we endorse. We are not attempting to pass judgements on individual incidents: those referred to here and earlier are essentially illustrative. What has most influenced our view is the weight of the reports, both published and first hand, coming from ordinary citizens of integrity who were plainly shocked and dismayed by police behaviour at odds with the standards they expected and assumed. Our sources have included clergymen, magistrates, probation officers, trade union officials, councillors, and MPs, as well as the observers from Chesterfield NCCL and Sheffield Policewatch. We are disposed to take such reports seriously – a view reinforced by their pattern and consistency and the impressive genuineness of those informants we met personally.

But we feel it is important to go further than this. When allegations against the police are made and denied, it is a common response to assume they are false – and indeed some complaints against the police may well be false, some maliciously so. It by no means follows that a police denial is a sufficient answer to every complaint by members of the public, regardless of the nature of the allegation or supporting evidence. We do not accept that allegations made by striking miners were invalidated by their source. Most miners who went picketing were ordinary, honest citizens with little previous contact with the police. Their complaints, as well as police accounts and explanations in reply (when given) are entitled to full weight, and we have endeavoured to give this to both. In our opinion the police evidence does not negative the general thrust of many of the criticisms, even acknowledging, as we do, the very difficult circumstances, extending occasionally to physical attack, under which the police acted. Violence against the police certainly occurred, but not as a norm, and much of the police action complained of was not perpetrated in response to or in fear of attack.[23]

EXCESSIVE RESTRICTIONS ON PICKETING

Generally the police allowed and recognized a small number of 'official pickets' at colliery gates. Usually no more than six were allowed, sometimes fewer and occasionally none. The reasons for restricting numbers seemed to be more a matter of the attitude of the senior officer present than the nature of the picket, and there was rarely consultation on numbers to be allowed. The latitude given to official pickets varied more than was justified by the differing circumstances of the picket lines. Where (as in West Yorkshire) the police allowed pickets to speak to drivers, relationships were less strained and nobody was forcibly prevented from crossing the picket line. Where the pickets were held back while vehicles were waved through, often at speed and sometimes dangerously so, frustration and tension inevitably mounted. In our view the containment of pickets in this way, when it was avoidable, and restriction of numbers to fewer than six, was a narrow and short-sighted policy.

Police responses to those attending the picket lines not recognized as official pickets – invariably classed as 'demonstrators' – also differed widely, but common characteristics were that they were contained behind cordons, often moved in a seemingly arbitrary way, and not infrequently kept excessively confined or at an unreasonable distance from the pit gate.[24] Arbitrary dispersal, or prevention from dispersal, was a further frequent cause of complaint. Some containment and direction was necessary and proper, but the general attitude displayed by the police seems to us to have given insufficient weight to the fact that while not within the statutory definition of official pickets, the 'demonstrators' were exercising the equally important freedom to protest. Police restrictions on their exercise of this freedom should have been more clearly confined to what was *necessary* to preserve the freedom of others.

POLICE VIOLENCE

We have already made clear, and repeat here, our rejection of violence in the dispute from whatever quarter. That includes violence by the police beyond the limits necessary for the proper discharge of their duties. We have accordingly been very troubled by clear evidence of acts of unnecessary and indeed gratuitous violence by some individual police officers, occasionally on the picket line, more often while pickets were assembling or dispersing, or at road-blocks, and occasionally against those taken into custody. These were isolated instances but the volume of reports raises doubts about the adequacy of supervision by senior police officers, and responses to complaints have been far from satisfactory.[25] Most serious is the series of incidents in villages in South Yorkshire in August and September 1984 where violent and indiscriminate attacks on innocent bystanders and forcible invasions of private homes were reported. The most worrying aspect of this is that a full investigation under the Police Complaints Authority of the incident at Stain-forth in September led to the conclusion that acts of violence had indeed taken place, but no action was taken because the officers concerned had not been identified.[26] This reinforces the concerns we have already expressed about the effectiveness of the complaints machinery.

PROVOCATIVE BEHAVIOUR

Complaints under this category, which again we find cogently supported, include instances of the waving of payslips or flinging of coins at pickets, taunting, obscenities (often addressed to miners' wives), taking advantage of close proximity in cordons to inflict surreptitious assaults, rhythmic drumming on riot shields (a practice swiftly forbidden when it received national publicity), and applauding as injured pickets were carried away. The range and volume of complaints again points towards a lack of effective managerial control by senior officers, but equally worrying is the way in which antipathy towards the strikers and their families was openly displayed by some groups of officers – to the dismay of some of their colleagues – almost as a matter of police culture.

Some aspects of the police operation were inherently provocative: for instance the basing of police operations, contrary to past practice, within NCB premises,[27] and in particular the appearance of police with riot equipment at the outset of picketing and before any signs of imminent violence. We regard this as more than simply an operational decision taken to safeguard the officers concerned, since even the use of purely defensive equipment such as shields and helmets can have the quality of a self-fulfilling prophecy, inviting attack.

OVER-REACTION

Here we are concerned with three matters briefly referred to above: numbers of police deployed, the use of snatch-squads to arrest isolated stone-throwers, and the forcible break-up of groups of pickets. These have in common that they were as likely to worsen as to contain difficult situations, and examples can be found in our narrative and the observers' reports quoted in Appendices II and III where precisely this happened. Excessive numbers of police at a particular location were difficult to avoid given the uncertainty of knowing in advance the numbers and mood of the pickets, but since the general practice was to deploy officers only as required and to maintain reserves in coaches in the vicinity, there was no obvious need to have excessive numbers of police actually deployed. That police on many occasions outnumbered pickets indicates a misuse of trained men and a potentially self-defeating display of force.

The use of snatch-squads is a prominent feature of the Tactical Options Manual; this fails to stress the inherent dangers of premature action which may turn a restless crowd into a violent one. It also overlooks the problems of accurately identifying culprits to be arrested and avoiding the impression of arbitrary arrests. Less use of this technique might have lessened general levels of violence. A similar criticism can be made of the dispersal of pickets using mounted or riot-clad officers, after relatively minor disorder.[28] In many respects these points are as much matters of general policing style or strategy as of individual policing responses. All of this smacks of unprofessionalism in policing, and reinforces our criticism of the training philosophy from which much of it was derived.

CONCEALED IDENTITY

On many occasions, pickets and observers complained that the police had removed or obliterated their identifying numerals. This is far from the first time such complaints have been raised. Official police policy is that numerals should always be displayed when on duty in uniform. We regard this as an important principle which senior officers have a paramount responsibility to enforce, however irksome it may be to a constable in the front rank of a cordon that he can be identified by the demonstrators facing him. The identifying mark is simply one of the conditions for the grant of extensive coercive powers over fellow citizens and extensive legal privileges, and it is one of the conditions for the effective accountability of the police as a whole that individual officers can be identified and made individually responsible for any misuse of powers.

SURVEILLANCE, TELEPHONE TAPPING, AND AGENTS PROVOCATEURS

All major confrontations with the authorities bring claims of the use of a variety of legitimate and illegitimate methods of surveillance. The miners' strike was no exception. It was officially admitted that the registration numbers of some picketing miners' vehicles were put on the Police National Computer (as having been observed in 'noteworthy circumstances'). This may have had operational advantages but these must in our view have been outweighed by the suspicion and antagonism aroused by the disclosure, and the innuendoes about picketing miners the practice conveyed. Allegations of the infiltration of strike meetings by police, and of strike and picket organizers' telephones having been tapped were also conveyed to us. These allegations are inherently difficult to prove or disprove, although the circumstantial evidence of some episodes of telephone tapping is strong.[29] The practice itself is less objectionable than the absence of any effective remedy however improper or abusive of privacy the action may have been. Recent changes in the law to meet the requirements of the European Court of Human Rights have not cured this serious defect in the law.[30] A recent test case involving the admitted tapping of the phones of senior officers of CND fell foul of the courts' inability to probe effectively where issues of national security are asserted by government.[31] Only parliamentary scrutiny can overcome this problem.

The use of agents provocateurs would if established merit the strongest condemnation. Again, any evidence of this was anecdotal or circumstantial, and often blended into examples of particularly inept policing. We can do no more than record the firm belief of many pickets that the police did resort to these tactics.[32]

CONCLUSIONS: THE ADMINISTRATION OF CRIMINAL JUSTICE

TREATMENT ON ARREST

The fact that the great majority of those arrested in connection with the strike had no previous experience of arrest or police detention gives us an opportunity to see through their eyes the reality of this part of the law enforcement process. There is no reason to suppose that those arrested were accorded treatment any different from normal police practice save in two respects: there could not be the kind of interaction that exists between officers and their 'regular' or known customers, and on occasions of multiple arrests the facilities of time and space were insufficient for normal, orderly processing of cases. Therefore the shock with which so may recounted their experiences should alert us to the degree of brutality inherent in the processing of suspects and the severity of the psychological impact on law-abiding citizens who fall foul of the system. This is not only a matter of the police beating people up (though no doubt this happened on occasion) or even handling suspects roughly, but also a matter of the loss to the latter of dignity, individual identity, and a sense of possession of rights. The demeanour of police officers in this situation is of the highest importance, and training should emphasize the importance of not belittling or intimidating prisoners in the routine way in which too many police officers readily do.

BAIL AND BAIL CONDITIONS

The police in most areas adopted an unprecedented routine of refusal of police bail in even the most minor of cases, with one purpose in mind. This was to ensure that bail conditions which directly or indirectly restricted picketing activities could be imposed by the magistrates. The lack of any power for the police, even temporarily, to impose such conditions on bail is arguably an anomaly. Even so its systematic avoidance in this way, at the cost of a major disruption of magisterial business, was an abuse of power. We regret that magistrates and their clerks showed little inclination to resist the will of the police, and indeed routinely acceded to police requests for conditions.

The conditions themselves were onerous and in a number of cases productive of real hardship or loss of freedom. Yet a quarter of all those charged, and probably a similar proportion of those given conditional bail, were not convicted. In many cases this was because the prosecution, months later, simply offered no evidence. A great many other cases were of offences not involving violence, and offenders of previous good character, who would not normally have been subjected to special restrictions before trial, because it would not have been thought necessary. The bail conditions most commonly imposed were worded in almost exactly the terms that a civil injunction against secondary picketing would have employed. Their imposition reflected an assumption by prosecutors and benches alike that picketing was an illicit act tending to crime and violence; it was on this footing that the Lord Chief Justice upheld the general practice. We have already indicated that this was not the reality of the strike.

We accept that as the law stands the handling of bail in the strike was lawful; nevertheless it produced much injustice and in our view it was inherently objectionable for all the reasons we have given and, in particular, because it encroached on the freedom of individuals entitled to the presumption of innocence, and afforded the police a new instrument of social control whose use exceeded any rational basis of necessity.

CHOICE OF CHARGES

Most charges were minor and of the kind normally seen in industrial conflict that spills over into disorder. Where more serious charges were brought generally this reflected the gravity of the situation. The conspicuous exception was the extensive use of charges of riot, none of which resulted in conviction, and unlawful assembly, which produced guilty pleas in a quarter of the cases and acquittals for the rest. This disastrous track record of cases collapsing, prosecutors withdrawing, and juries acquitting should not have occurred. The outcome could and should have been foreseen, and prosecutions confined to such charges, if any, as could be proved on the evidence. We accept that there are particular problems in proving an individual's participation in a riot, of which the greatest is often the confusions of the disorders themselves. This does not mean that the law is necessarily inadequate, still less that the acquittals were wrong. It does place a high premium on careful judgement. Although it may seem easy to say this with hindsight we are bound to comment that judgement was not sufficiently carefully exercised in these cases.

The police asserted that they acted on legal advice. Nevertheless at that time the relationship between the police and their lawyers was that of ordinary clients – the *decision* is the client's. Either the police acted uncritically on bad advice (in which case they must take the responsibility but little opprobrium) or, as has been suggested to us, they deliberately used riot charges *in terrorem* to raise the stakes and frighten off would-be pickets. We are not in a position to say whether this was so – if so it would be a very serious misuse of police power – but in the result several hundred miners spent many months, sometimes more than a year, facing the risk of imprisonment on severely restrictive bail conditions. Whether or not intentionally, a degree of duress and intimidation was achieved.

LEGAL AID

Variations in the pattern of granting legal aid from court to court have been a blot on the criminal justice system for many years. The pattern during the strike showed the worst features of the problem, but it is the general problem rather than its particular manifestations in one episode that concerns us. This problem is of different and unstated criteria and approaches being used to decide the same question simply because of attitudes of individual magistrates and clerks.

SENTENCING

Most of the sentencing, especially for more serious offences, was not out of line with established judicial conventions. That is not to say it was right, but it *was* normal. We share the concern at the number of sentences of imprisonment handed down but acknowledge that this is a much wider issue than the enforcement of the law during the strike.

At the lower end of the tariff, fines in most cases were of quite small amounts, but a significant number were clearly beyond the means of striking miners with no incomes. They may well have been imposed on a tacit assumption that the NUM would pay. If so, the assumption was not a proper one. There can hardly have been evidence of the union's willingness, or ability, to pay. An agreement before the event to pay all the fines would in all probability have been illegal, and in any case the union no longer had the power to pay after its assets were sequestrated. Any departure from the principle that a fine should be within the means of the defendant was therefore inept.

One form of sentence in particular which was imposed very frequently was a binding-over order. The use of a contingent sanction against future disorderly conduct or violence is in principle a proper sentence for a court to impose following conviction of an offence in one of these categories. We cannot judge whether the frequency of its use was excessive in the circumstances, but we do note that it was unusually widely used. Much more disturbing is the use of binding-over orders against 'offenders' whose cases had not been proved, often as a trade-off with the prosecution for not pursuing the case. This occurred particularly frequently in the riot and unlawful assembly prosecutions; those accused who refused the prosecution offer were subsequently acquitted. This suggests that binding over was used to justify retrospectively charges that should not have been brought, and as a result innocent individuals 'consented' effectively under duress to a curtailment of their liberty, social stigma, and the probability of close attention from the police. This outcome is not unique to the strike and reinforces the need for this highly unsatisfactory area of the law to be reformed.

CONCLUSIONS: TRENDS AND DEVELOPMENTS IN POLICING

Most of what can usefully be said here has been developed in Chapter 9. Here we can be relatively brief. The policing which was observed during the strike reflected changes in the organization and perceptions of the police service which had come about in the decade or so prior to 1984, but were more visibly displayed in the strike than hitherto. The changes have not in general been desirable developments in the policing of industrial disputes. In particular the riot-control approach to policing has both evolved in sophistication and taken over a discrete part of policing for which it was not previously seen as the appropriate response. The policing of the strike and of subsequent events show the importance of that take-over. The interplay of various aspects of policing, and between the police and their clientele, necessitates a sensitivity to the nature of the situation, and the attitudes and expectations of individuals, by the police. This was lost in the tension between police and strikers, often avoidably so, not only because of the government's misuse of the police collectively but also because of the loss of a separate method of policing an uncommon and distinctive aspect of community life.

The change to a riot-control philosophy of policing strikes to some extent reflects the changes in society generally and the ending of the process of apparent integration of social strata and divergent economic interests witnessed in the first two or three decades after 1945. The police inevitably hold a mirror, however cracked and distorting, to the society they police, and it is as much a symptom as a cause of a more authoritarian and divided society, as Britain now is, that we experience a more authoritarian and divisive philosophy of policing. At the same time it is also a reflection of the internalization of police thinking that a lack of effective external influence on policy permits to take place. The police are not forced to confront the problems of their chosen methods of acting until things go wrong, and can then often do so, within their own terms of debate, in such a way as to make the failure justify a reinforcement of the original error. The lack of a free dialogue between the providers and users of this public service results too easily in introspective and myopic planning. All this has happened to the police. The full extent of some aspects of the problem became apparent to some police officers as well as to a wider audience during the strike. The need for a reassessment of methods, objectives, and accountability, as interlinked issues, is overdue.

I. RECOMMENDATION: THERE SHOULD BE A ROYAL COMMISSION ON THE POLICE

The terms of reference of any Royal Commission are crucial. The issues which most urgently need to be reviewed are the constitutional governance of the police at national and local level throughout Great Britain and the policing of public disorder and industrial disputes.[33] The enforcement of the ordinary criminal law has recently been substantially reformed and although there are serious issues of difficulty within this area it would divert attention from much more pressing concerns if these matters were included in the Commission's terms of reference.

It will be clear from our conclusions on policing and accountability, and from our analysis of civil liberty principles in Chapter 2, what general approach we would wish the Commission to adopt. Recommendations at a detailed level will emerge from the full interplay of competing evidence and the commissioners' deliberations. We cannot pre-script this process. However we do indicate what we regard as the key issues and the broad approach to them that the Commission should adopt.

SHOULD THERE BE A NATIONAL POLICE FORCE?

The Commission will have to address this question in view of the extent to which we have experienced a drift in this direction. We believe the answer should be no, but with the firm corollary that the institutions for local accountability must be reformed and reactivated.

TO WHAT BODIES SHOULD THE POLICE BE ACCOUNTABLE?

The primary purpose of accountability is to ensure that representative views influence or determine policy. Therefore institutions which are representative of the local community should be the primary basis of accountability.[34] This means – despite well-known police misgivings about 'sectional interests' – elected bodies. Whether the police authorities should be composed of people directly elected to the Authority (as with the Inner London Education Authority) or from appointed members of other elected local authorities is a question for careful consideration, complicated as it is by the abolition of the Greater London Council and Metropolitan Counties. Whichever arrangement is preferred, the inclusion of magistrates as voting members of police authorities is incompatible with the representative purpose of the Authorities, as well as dangerously confusing law enforcement and judicial responsibility, and should cease.

WHAT ARRANGEMENTS SHOULD BE MADE FOR NATIONAL POLICE SERVICES?

One barrier to the effective accountability of the Metropolitan police has been its provision or oversight of 'national' activities such as the Diplomatic Protection Group and the Police National Computer. Unless there are insuperable logistical problems these services should be formally separated from the normal patterns of finance and accountability, nationally funded and answerable to a national body representative of local police authorities as well as central government.

WHAT SHOULD BE THE ROLE OF CENTRAL GOVERNMENT?

To prevent the recent incremental erosion of local accountability from being repeated, central government powers and responsibilities should in future be viewed rather differently, not as checks on local authorities but as national responsibility for relevant aspects of policing, with appropriate accountability of the police to the Home Secretary and thence to Parliament. To achieve this in practice clearer duties could be given to local police authorities, enforceable in the courts, and the restraining influence of the Home Office (for example over appointments and dismissals) removed.[35] Where national responsibility remained the Home Secretary should answer to a Parliamentary Select Committee on the police; accountability to Parliament now exists only in name.

HOW SHOULD THE POLICING OF MAJOR DISORDER BE SUPERVISED?

The present system of mutual aid works (just) for small-scale problems. It was not designed for larger-scale, extended demands on the police, and should not be used for such situations. Instead, if a strike or disorder (or some major calamity) necessitates police action on a major scale or over a long period the Home Secretary, on the application of the chief constables concerned, should initiate a special procedure effectively placing the disposition of the police in the hands of a standing emergency committee, composed of representatives of local police authorities, the Home Office, and the Select Committee, which would control the work of whatever body held the responsibilities of the present National Reporting Centre. This latter body would determine the needs and priorities for the use of police resources and be accountable to the emergency committee for the use of resources diverted from regular police duties. The cost of these resources – including normal salaries – should fall on national funds. We believe that a structure of this kind is necessary to ensure that policy decisions of the kind taken about the policing of the miners' strike are openly reached and capable of being brought to account.

A subsidiary question is whether we should have a separate riot police. This has been seriously argued as a less damaging alternative to the present contagion of riot-control tactics affecting other policing activities. However we would view it as a counsel of despair; the control of the contagion is far more important, and the preferable route forward.

WHAT SHOULD 'ACCOUNTABILITY' MEAN?

The idea that the police might be ordered, for partisan reasons, to enforce specific laws in a partial fashion, dies hard. Accountability is or should be about control, but that does not mean manipulation; control of general policy is what is in issue. The traditional idea of a line between policy and operational matters has been effectively discredited by Lustgarten and following the lead of his analysis we suggest that a more systematic approach is needed, identifying what are the chief constable's accountabilities and how they are to be discharged.[36] We tentatively suggest that accountability should operate at two levels. The first would be the annual submission of proposals for force policy for approval by the relevant authority. This might encompass policy on methods and criteria of recruitment, training programmes, policy on promotions and deployment of personnel, the allocation of resources as between different categories of policing, equipment plans, and statements of policy as to potentially controversial questions such as cautioning instead of reporting for prosecution or the priority to be given to preventing drug abuse, as well as matters of more direct relevance to this report such as the policing of industrial disputes. Policy statements would necessarily be liable to rejection or amendment by the police authority, but that would not imply any interference with the actual implementation of policy – the chief constable would be responsible for ensuring its proper implementation once it was finally agreed.

The second form of accountability would be for the discretionary decisions taken within the approved policy guidelines. Here there is accountability to the law, which suffers from the twin limitations of practical difficulties for aggrieved individuals to obtain redress in law, and the broad range of discretion which the law confers on police officers. Actions taken by individual officers in the exercise of a discretion, which might be classed as improper but not illegal, should as now be subject to the twin safeguards of the complaints and disciplinary machinery. The former needs to be reformed, as we indicate shortly. But more serious is the gap between the upper limits of individual actions and the lower limits of policy formulation, where there is no form of accountability at all – such as the decision by the chief constable (or a senior officer on the spot) to use road-blocks to deter pickets, or to issue riot equipment before a demonstration.[37] We suggest two possible (perhaps parallel) avenues. One is a duty to account to the police authority after the event for any operational decision above a certain level of seniority or involving more than a stated deployment of police resources. The other is to extend the right of individual complaint in such cases. The former raises fears of interference which, however justified, are not easy to dispel. The latter, building on a reformed and extended Police Complaints Authority, has the clear attraction of independent and quasi-judicial redress against oppressive consequences of police action within the limits of law but outside the parameters of reasonableness. We have indicated some hints of a move in this direction in the thinking of the Police Complaints Authority. We offer this possibility as a way of resolving the most critical gap in the present structure of safeguards for the citizen.

CONSULTATIVE MACHINERY

An analogous but distinct issue is the role of consultative committees. The statutory machinery set up in 1985 is weak but potentially important. It provides a way in which community needs at a lower level can be articulated both to the local police and to the police authority (which may represent a very diverse range of communities). As a source of contact and dialogue between the police and those they serve, the concept is invaluable. However to work effectively consultative committees must be, and be felt by the police to be, representative of a wide range of community groups; they must have a right to relevant information from the police; and the police must have a duty to consult them about relevant policing proposals. Within a general framework of accountability such structures would assist in developing police perspectives, and we support them. They should not preclude concerned groups mounting police monitoring programmes any more than consultative committees in the educational field remove the need for parents to monitor the standards of their local schools.

HOW SHOULD THE POLICE APPROACH THE POLICING OF PUBLIC DISORDER AND INDUSTRIAL DISPUTES?

Our recommendations here are embodied in Section III, following.

II. RECOMMENDATION: BRITAIN SHOULD ADOPT A BILL OF RIGHTS

The creation of a democratic structure of police accountability will not of itself ensure that police practices are better. Democracy is an essential value but so, in our view, is a proper respect for the maximization of human rights. We believe that the time has come for a formal constitutional embodiment of human rights through a Bill of Rights incorporating the European Convention on Human Rights and its Protocols into domestic law. The duties of those having oversight of the police should extend to ensuring that the police act within the Convention and discharge their duties in such a way that so far as practicable the liberties of individuals and groups are not overridden. Only in this way can we hope to attain a system of policing that is not only responsive to the wishes of local communities but also resistant to those pressures which tend towards authoritarian and over-restrictive styles of policing and illiberal strategies.

There are many disadvantages to a Bill of Rights, in particular its tendency to substitute government by judges for government by Parliament, and the limiting effect of a code of rights drawn to meet the needs of a wide range of political and social cultures several decades ago.[38] These however are outweighed by the prospects for the education of public attitudes, increased awareness of rights, and changed perceptions of public servants which a Bill of Rights can offer. Building on this foundation we believe that in relation to the police the following actions are needed:

1. A statutory duty for all police officers and all police authorities to comply with the Convention in the discharge of their powers.
2. In particular, police authorities should have a duty in approving policy proposals to ensure that they are not unnecessarily restrictive of the liberties of any section of the community and that they will maintain compliance with the Convention.
3. Disciplinary and complaints procedures should cover police action in

breach of the Convention or unnecessarily restrictive of citizens' rights not specifically protected by the Convention.

4. Police training should be revised, in the light of the Council of Europe's recommendations, to include training in human rights and policing methods compatible with their protection.[39]

III. RECOMMENDATION: THE POLICING OF INDUSTRIAL DISPUTES SHOULD BE SYSTEMATICALLY REVIEWED

This falls within the proposed brief of the Royal Commission which should be guided in its deliberations by the approach we advocate above. Within that framework, the objective should be to re-establish the conventions of policing which operated, generally successfully, in the 1950s and 1960s and were employed in some areas, such as West Yorkshire, through much of the strike. In particular the Royal Commission should aim to separate clearly the tasks of suppressing disorder and riot from the maintenance of the rights of parties involved in industrial conflict, and within the latter restore the distinctions between civil and criminal law in the definition of police functions. Some practical points we commend to the Commission are as follows.

1. There should be a duty on the police to consult all parties to any industrial dispute which appears likely to necessitate significant police presence. The object of the consultation should be to establish and maintain links and negotiate working agreements for the conduct of picketing and the passage of goods or people across picket lines.

2. The attitude towards picket supporters other than the 'statutory' pickets should reflect the existence in the European Convention of a right of peaceful assembly; the exercise of this right should be accorded full protection in the same way as other civil liberties. Road-blocks and similar restrictions should not be used simply to prevent people assembling to protest.

3. The Code of Practice on Picketing should be revised. It is a one-sided document devoted almost entirely to the duties and responsibilities of pickets and the rights of others. It should acknowledge that all concerned have rights and responsibilities and that the police have a duty to protect both (or all) sides' rights. It should require the police to assist official pickets in exercising their rights of peaceful communication by stopping vehicles on their behalf (using existing statutory powers) for long enough to establish whether the occupants wish to be spoken to by the pickets; the only exception should be where this would endanger the peace.

4. The need for the police to be seen to be impartial should be reinforced by ending the practice developed during the strike of police operations being conducted from within the employer's premises.

5. When restrictions on pickets or demonstrators become necessary, the police should explain what is happening, and why (using loud hailers if necessary).

IV. OTHER RECOMMENDATIONS CONCERNING THE POLICE

1. The present complaints system still, despite recent reforms, lacks public credibility and fails to ensure that disciplinary action is taken when necessary. Partly the problems are institutional, but no real change will occur without changes in attitude. In street confrontations, alleged assailants of police are arrested and processed as suspects; the converse does not happen. Senior officers on the spot should bear a personal responsibility for violence by their officers, as a failure of managerial command, and should have power at least to suspend on the spot any officer reasonably suspected of violence. Whether or not a completely independent system of investigating complaints is adopted (we think it should be) the absence of a duty to co-operate with investigations is wrong and should be ended.[40] It is difficult to justify the police alone among employees being immune from dismissal for misconduct simply because it cannot be proved beyond reasonable doubt. The objective must not be to turn the police into second-class citizens, but the possession of unique coercive powers requires correspondingly high standards of discipline and a readiness to enforce them vigilantly. When the police use video-tapes of disturbances to identify police misconduct as well as criminal acts by civilians, then the public credibility of the system will be assured.

2. A specific associated point is the display of identifying numerals. The problem has persisted too long, and firm measures to ensure the ready identification of officers in uniform are vital. In particular the non-display of numerals should be a disciplinary offence not only for the officer concerned but also for any superior officer shown to have permitted it; the former sanction alone would self-evidently be ineffective to deal with subsequent public complaints.

3. As well as the specific new subjects for police training we have recommended above, a general review of the concept of police training is needed. The police have a strong internal and self-reinforcing culture, passed on to new entrants through extended on-the-job induction processes, which makes attitudes and philosophies much more difficult to change. In particular authoritarian categorizations and stereotypes of disadvantaged or unconventional groups, well documented in the Policy Studies Institute (1983) Report on the Metropolitan Police, and applied to striking miners and their families by too many officers brought into the coalfields on mutual aid, are powerful obstacles to even-handed policing based on the affirmation of fundamental rights. Training at present is also internalized – organized and conducted largely within the police service – and only at more senior levels are non-police trainers used to a significant extent to introduce a broader perspective. Thus training provides little counterbalance to prevalent cultures. We believe it can and should. Professional training for most other professions is conducted at least in part in public colleges where students mix more widely with their peers and are presented with a less introspective introduction to their profession. Most police skills are not a trade secret and we see no reason in principle why (as in the USA) they cannot be taught by civilian teachers in civilian institutions.[41]

V. RECOMMENDATIONS ON THE ENFORCEMENT OF THE CRIMINAL LAW

BAIL CONDITIONS

The law on bail conditions should be reviewed. In principle bail should be unconditional, or subject only to reasonable financial sureties, unless more serious restrictions on the defendant's liberty are necessary to ensure his or her attendance at trial. To this principle the only exception we would make would be where imposition of further conditions allows the court to grant bail which it would otherwise have had to refuse. Bail conditions should not be used as an alternative to civil injunctions.

BINDING OVER

The power to bind over should be confined to its use as a penalty imposed following conviction of a criminal offence, and cases where there has been a threat of personal violence not amounting to an offence. Nobody should be bound over as an alternative to being prosecuted.

LEGAL AID

The procedure for granting legal aid in criminal cases should be reviewed again to seek ways of ensuring greater consistency between courts, and in particular legal aid should not be refused on assumptions about financial support being given by trade unions or other organizations.

VI. RECOMMENDATION: A NEW APPROACH TO KEEPING THE PEACE

We have stressed the role of the police in keeping the peace. In reality it is a role which should involve all sections of the community, not in the suppression of riot but its prevention. As well as legal responsibilities there are moral obligations to avoid unnecessary conflict-provoking actions. No agency other than the police has specific functions here, and in particular the restraint of powerful groups' behaviour which may provoke disorder is not catered for. We commend for consideration as a way of filling this gap the suggestion put forward by one of our number, John Alderson, for the creation of a Peace Commission, modelled in structure and responsibilities on ACAS.[42] This body would be charged with conciliation of potential conflict, initiating dialogues, and restraining inflammatory actions. Its remit would cover industrial disputes but not be confined to them; it would need to be able to defuse potentially ugly situations in inner cities, or to mediate where conflict had occurred. Like ACAS its formal powers would come to be less important than its public reputation. It would need to be able to deal on equal terms with the police, and be able to stop the police as well as local authorities, employers, or the organizers of racialist demonstrations taking unjustifiable action of a kind likely to provoke disorder. The Royal Commission we propose should include this idea within its remit, if only because the suppression of riot, however skilfully achieved, is a police function that inevitably damages its capacity to meet other pressing social demands.

Our recommendations are aimed at the creation of a better and more professional police service meeting the requirements of the community it serves. We believe these requirements must include the protection and promotion of basic civil liberties. Policing has an influence on the state of a society, and for this reason the issues of policing policy and accountability are fundamental. But the influence of the state of society on the police is far greater. A deeply divided society cannot be policed by consent; a society whose laws unfairly restrict access to economic power will face social pressures which strain the limits of police resourcefulness. The problems of an inner city underclass, of a legally crippled trade union movement, of groups pinned down by institutionalized racism, confront the police now, and will continue to do so, just as surely as they confront society as a whole. A society which is not vigilant in recognizing these problems, but simply leaves it to the police to maintain tranquillity through forcible control, will indeed have the police it deserves.

NOTES

1. See Chapter 3.
2. MacGregor (1986: 181, 192–5).
3. See the accounts in MacGregor (1986: 200–4, 319–32) and Adeney and Lloyd (1986: 184–7).
4. The Metropolitan police supplied 213,000 man-days of mutual aid during the strike – see Appendix 1 for more details. The level of racial attacks has been rising steadily, and it had been brought to police attention at least by a Home Office Report in 1981 (Home Office 1981). The Home Affairs Committee (1986) records that 1,877 racial attacks were recorded in the Metropolitan district in 1985.
5. For figures on this see Appendix 1 and on the general question Waddington (1985).
6. MacGregor (1986: 216–18).
7. cf. Adeney and Lloyd (1986: 158–9).
8. In arguing this we do not necessarily adopt the view that the civil law would have provided a just or effective resolution of the dispute. The point is that it is the law, and it is not for the police to act in substitution for it. Rightly or wrongly this approach is adopted in other areas such as landlord and tenant disputes and domestic assaults, and the inadequacy of the civil law in these cases does not necessarily indicate that the police should interpose equally inappropriate enforcement measures.
9. On the 'consensus' question see the very cogent analysis by Reiner (1985: 61–82) of the factors leading to the creation of a period of 'consensus policing' and the reversal of all of them over the period 1959–81.
10. The former was made subject to the Home Secretary's consent in 1985 after the suspension of the Chief Constable of Derbyshire for alleged financial irregularities. The Home Secretary issued a Circular (40/86) offering chief constables stocks of plastic baton rounds on loan if the police committee refused to sanction their purchase; this Circular was upheld by the High Court in *R* v *Home Secretary, ex parte Northumbria Police Authority* (1987). (After our report had been completed this decision was affirmed by the Court of Appeal on even wider grounds including his statutory powers under section 41 of the Police Act, 1964: *The Times*, 19 November 1987.)
11. Under the Police and Criminal Evidence Act, 1984, section 106, following the recommendation in the Scarman Report (1981).
12. Simey (1984).

13. Not, of course, a sufficient precondition. Much more is needed, as we explain in our recommendations.
14. Chapter 6; and see the statistics in Appendix 1.
15. Police Complaints Authority (1987).
16. Remedies for surveillance and telephone tapping raise separate questions which we also touch on below.
17. See their detailed accounts in Appendices 2 and 3.
18. The mythology surrounding Winston Churchill's dispatch of Metropolitan police officers to Tonypandy in 1911 is still strong in mining circles.
19. Police and Criminal Evidence Act, 1984, section 4 (which came into force after the strike was over).
20. *Moss* v *McLachlan* (1985).
21. This was a clear view of two clergymen from mining villages in West Yorkshire with whom we discussed the point.
22. The injunction obtained by the NCB on 14 March 1984 was to restrain the Yorkshire area NUM from sending pickets into Nottinghamshire – the very process that road-blocks were most often used to prevent.
23. See Appendix 1 for statistics of police injuries; these should be viewed in the context of a year-long strike involving picketing at over 200 locations.
24. The most extreme example we encountered, in South Yorkshire, was of demonstrators being kept at the far end of a mile-long access lane (immediately outside a primary school, in apparent disregard of complaints by the local vicar).
25. The immediate response to the much publicized truncheon-wielding episode at Orgreave (see Chapter 6) is an exception which tends to reinforce rather than refute the point.
26. Police Complaints Authority (1987).
27. cf. South Yorkshire Police (1985: 70) where this is acknowledged to have been the norm in South Yorkshire.
28. Especially at Orgreave on 18 June 1984: see Chapter 6 and Appendix 3.
29. Left-wing activists tend to assume that their telephones will be tapped, and act accordingly. Occasionally this enabled incidents to be 'set up' and police reactions observed.
30. Interception of Communications Act, 1985.
31. *R* v *Home Secretary, ex parte Ruddock* (1987). The case was brought as a test case under the common law prior to the 1985 Act, but the substantive point would be dealt with similarly by the new tribunal set up under the Act. The case was unusual in that telephone tapping was not denied, following the disclosures of Ms Cathy Massiter, formerly of MI5, on a television programme.
32. Allegations were also repeatedly made that members of the armed forces disguised as police officers appeared on picket lines. This is inherently implausible, not least because of the political risks of such a practice. We have seen no credible evidence that it happened and do not believe that it did.
33. The Commission's remit should in our view include Scotland as well as England and Wales. Although there has been less difficulty over the constitutional arrangements north of the border the issues of principle are the same, and each country's system could benefit from the transplantation of some features of the other's. The unique problems of policing Northern Ireland should not be included; to do so would unnecessarily complicate and prolong the Commission's work. A separate study of policing in Northern Ireland would however be worthwhile.
34. 'Local' here being equivalent to the area covered by each police force; for London the Commission would need to consider carefully how a devolution to smaller population groups might be achieved.
35. Thus officers appealing against internal discipline could be given access to the ordinary remedies of other employees or there could be a right of appeal to the police authority; the Home Office need not and should not be involved.
36. Lustgarten (1986: ch. 10).
37. Or, perhaps of increasing importance, to exercise the powers of control over demonstrations in Part II of the Public Order Act, 1986.
38. But only the European Convention is likely to command sufficiently wide agreement as a code of fundamental rights, so whatever its defects we are committed to it.
39. See Alderson (1984) for a full exposition of how this might work in practice. See also our recommendations on the organization of training, p. 154.

40. Not of course in relation to criminal proceedings, where police officers should have the same legal protection as any citizen. In most companies, employees who refused to co-operate with a disciplinary investigation would be liable to be dismissed.
41. See Ennals (1984) for a development of this argument.
42. See Alderson (1986).

Appendices

Appendix 1
Statistics of the strike

One major incidental advantage of the activation of the National Reporting Centre was the central compilation (for England and Wales) of statistics of the policing of the strike. These were not published systematically, but much information *was* published, principally in Parliamentary Answers. Since the statistics are a useful source of understanding the strike, we have assembled and reproduced some of the most important in this Appendix. However two notes of caution are needed. First, because the statistics published depended on what questions were asked, they are not necessarily complete – MPs did not always ask the right questions. In particular figures ceased to be available once the NRC closed down, and matters (especially court actions and complaints) which were still in train then ceased to be subject to statistical reporting. Other sources fill in some gaps, but not all. Second, like all statistics, those relating to the strike need to be read with care and subject to a variety of qualifications. Some of these are spelled out in each section, together with some non-statistical supplementary information.

ARRESTS AND CHARGES: ENGLAND AND WALES

Arrests. Table 1 gives arrests by police area, that is the area in which the arrest took place, for four periods during the strike and for the strike as a whole; these figures may give a limited picture of the shifting patterns of action during the strike but the primary significance of the figures is in the totals for the strike as a whole. Table 2 gives running totals of arrests at various dates during the strike for England and Wales as a whole.

Occupations of those arrested. Of those 9,808 persons arrested, 8,788 (89.7 per cent) were miners; the percentage of non-miners arrested was markedly higher later in the dispute – thus of 3,444 arrests to 19 June, 96.5 per cent of those with a known occupation were miners, and of 7,930 arrested to 13 November, the equivalent percentage was 93.5 per cent. The percentage of non-miners among those arrested after 13 November was about 24 per cent.

Table 1   *Arrests by area*

Police Area	13 March–16 May	17 May–17 July	18 July–13 Nov.	14 Nov.–5 March	13 March–5 March
Cleveland	—	22	36	—	58
Cumbria	—	—	25	—	25
Derbyshire	189	409	514	80	1,192
Durham	90	86	220	91	487
Dyfed–Powys	—	—	2	14	16
Essex	157	51	4	—	212
Greater Manchester	17	155	62	40	274
Gwent	—	85	82	69	236
Hampshire	—	8	3	—	11
Humberside	1	45	48	27	121
Kent	47	27	137	100	311
Lancashire	2	23	1	—	26
Leicestershire	15	14	25	—	54
Merseyside	21	37	124	13	195
Metropolitan	—	126	—	129	255
Northumbria	33	42	383	179	637
North Wales	14	7	10	—	31
North Yorkshire	—	93	46	24	163
Nottinghamshire	1,077	623	629	88	2,417
South Wales	58	54	218	179	509
South Yorkshire	185	316	506	526	1,533[a]
Staffordshire	177	60	148	32	417
Sussex	—	—	—	5	5
Thames Valley	—	—	3	—	3
Warwickshire	78	55	61	3	197
West Yorkshire	3	11	130	279	423
Totals	2,164	2,349	3,417	1,878	9,808

Sources: HC Debates, 18 May 1984, col. *274*; 8 June 1984, cols *288–9*; 21 June 1984, col. *214*; 19 July 1984, col. *290*; 19 November 1984, cols *11–12*; 26 March 1985, cols *129–30*.
Note: [a] This is the Home Office figure, derived from NRC records. The Chief Constable of South Yorkshire's report on the dispute gives a figure of 1,701 (p. 46).

Charges. Of those arrested, 7,917 (80.7 per cent) were charged with one or more offences. The rest – almost 2,000 – were released without charge. Figures for charges need to be treated with caution; they relate only to *initial* charges, and the police subsequently charged additional offences in many cases. Thus the official figures record 275 charges of watching and besetting, but a detailed Parliamentary Answer on this offence (HC Debates, 31 January 1985, cols *232–3*) records a total of 643 charges for this offence. Similarly 137 riot charges are listed, but at least 158 of the people charged with unlawful assembly were also charged with riot (all were acquitted or had the charges dropped subsequently), giving a total of 295 riot charges (*Legal*

Table 2   *Arrests at various stages of the strike*

Date	Arrests during period	Cumulative total	Source[a]
12 March–11 April	910	910	HC Debates, 13 April 1984, col. *418*
12 April–16 May	1,254	2,164	HC Debates, 18 May 1984, col. *274*
17 May–19 June	1,280	3,444	HC Debates, 21 June 1984, col. *214*
20 June–17 July	1,069	4,513	HC Debates, 19 July 1984, col. *290*
18 July–11 Sept.	2,080	6,593	*New Statesman*, 14 Sept. 1984
12 Sept.–16 Oct.	725	7,318	HC Debates, 22 Oct. 1984, col. *432*
17 Oct.–27 Nov.	1,076	8,394	HC Debates, 29 Nov. 1984, col. *594*

Note: [a] Sources from HC Debates frequently give more detailed breakdowns by area, and are also available for some intermediate periods. Figures in column 1 are simply extrapolations from column 2.

Table 3   *Breakdown of offences charged*

Offence	Number	Offence	Number
Conduct likely to cause a breach of the peace	4,107	Breach of the peace	207
		Riot	137
Obstructing a constable	1,682	Drunkenness	66
Criminal damage	1,019	Offensive weapon	49
Obstructing the highway	640	Grievous bodily harm	39
Unlawful assembly	509	Breach of bail conditions	32
Actual bodily harm	429	Burglary	31
Assaulting police	360	Affray	21
Theft	352	Railway offences	20
Watching and besetting/ intimidation	275	Other	397[a]
Total			10,372

Source: The Times, 6 April 1985.
Note: [a] 'Other' includes 296 offences described as 'miscellaneous and minor', but also some serious offences: murder (3), criminal damage with intent to endanger life (4), arson (15), threats to kill (5), and explosives offences (3).

Action, September 1985, p. 7). With these major reservations Table 3 gives a breakdown of charges.

ARRESTS AND CHARGES: SCOTLAND

Figures for Scotland are less detailed (the NRC covered only England and Wales). However the following information is available.

Total arrests.

To 15 May: 513 (HC Debates, 16 May 1984, col. *358*)
To 26 October: 1,320 (HC Debate, 31 October 1984, cols *1,294–5*)
To 5 March: 1,504 (HC Debates, 13 March 1985, cols *299–300*)

Of those arrested, 1,483 were charged, but proceedings were instituted by the Procurator-Fiscal in only 1,046 (70.5 per cent) of these cases. Half of all arrests and charges (745) were made in Strathclyde, but *all but one* of the cases not proceeded with were in that region, giving a remarkable 59 per cent of cases dropped; 474 arrests were in Lothian, 225 in Fife.

Charges in Scotland in cases proceeded with included:

Breach of the peace	678
Obstructing the police	249
Breach of bail conditions	53
Vandalism	30
Others	36
Total	1,046

(See HC Debates, 13 March 1985, col. *299*; 4 April 1985, col. *718*; and Wallington (1985: 150) for details.)

DISPOSAL OF THOSE CHARGED: ENGLAND AND WALES

The figures here are particularly fragmentary. They give *some* indication of what took place but only a limited one.

Remands and bail conditions. It seems that relatively few people were remanded in custody. Thus at 13 November 1984 only eleven persons were currently remanded in custody (HC Debates, 20 November 1984, col. *106*). Where bail was granted it was frequently conditional, but national figures on this are not available and were refused in answer to a Parliamentary Question (HC Debates, 14 December 1984, col. *635*). However figures were given for the Nottinghamshire area: on 5 July 1984 there were 1,317 accused persons on bail, and of these 1,278 (97 per cent) were on conditional bail (HC Debates, 5 July 1984, col. *225*; by 23 July the figure on conditional bail had risen to 1,415; HC Debates, 27 July 1984, col. *832*; this compares with a total of 1,685 arrests in Nottinghamshire by mid-July).

Acquittal rates. Acquittal rates can be calculated only for those cases (5,653) concluded before the NRC closed down. These resulted in 4,318 convictions and 1,335 acquittals (23.6 per cent) (M. Rees and Brown 1985). There was a marked rise in acquittals from the first few months, where it was only 10 per cent (60 out of 656 as at 10 July: HC Debates, 16 July 1984, col. *21*). This is to be expected since contested cases take longer to come to a hearing. For the same reason, and in the light of the substantial numbers of acquittals or abandoned cases occurring later in 1985 (in the riot trials in particular) the overall acquittal rate was probably around 25 per cent. This is much higher than normal, but there are so many variables (nature of offences, percentage of guilty pleas, mode of trial) that no firm conclusions can be drawn from this.

Sentences. The total numbers sentenced to imprisonment in connection with the strike have not been given, but it almost certainly exceeded 200. By 26 February 1985, 182 sentences of imprisonment had been imposed (HC Debates, 28 February 1985, col. *250*). A detailed breakdown of cases heard in the Crown Court up to 25 January 1985 revealed one sentence each of five years and three years for grievous bodily harm, one of three years and nine of two and a half years for criminal damage, and six of two years for arson and conspiracy. Apart from the two men convicted of murder (later reduced to manslaughter) who received eight years each, these are, so far as we know, the most severe penalties imposed by the courts. (See HC Debates, 31 January 1985, cols *232–4*.)

A range of other penalties was imposed, as would be expected. Only two merit particular mention: fines and binding-over orders. The latter were widely used but the only figure we have seen is of the early period to 10 July; 237 out of 596 people convicted during this period were bound over (several being fined also) (HC Debates, 16 July 1984, col. *21*). Binding over was also extensively used as a trade-off for not proceeding with cases, especially in the riot and unlawful assembly trials. (Where it was not accepted, the prosecution sometimes simply offered no evidence instead.) Binding over was almost certainly much more widely used during the strike than is usual; of all non-motoring offenders in 1984 and 1985, only 1 per cent were dealt with in this way (and not also fined) (Criminal Statistics 1985, Cm 10, 1987, Table 7.1). A breakdown of fines imposed up to 13 December (HC Debates, 14 December 1984, cols *637–8*) shows that out of 3,040 convictions, 1,937 people were fined. The median fine was in the £75–£99 band (that is half of those fined were fined this amount or less), but in 166 cases the fine was £200 or more, which for a striking miner was clearly exceptional. This lends some support to the view that striking miners were dealt with more harshly than usual by the courts, but it does not reveal the nature of the offences for which large fines were imposed or the regional variations which almost certainly occurred in sentencing policy (and acquittal rates).

DISPOSAL OF THOSE CHARGED: SCOTLAND

Although proportionately more people were arrested and proceeded against in Scotland, the offences were much more minor, and so far as we know nobody was sentenced to imprisonment. (This is significant in relation to the NCB policy on dismissals of convicted miners, which was much harsher in Scotland than elsewhere.) The acquittal rate in Scotland was also 24 per cent, rising after an early 19 per cent shown on the basis of about 70 per cent of the prosecutions having been concluded (see HC Debates, 4 April 1985, col. *714*). Final published figures, with 64 cases outstanding, were 721 convicted, 227 acquitted (HC Debates, 17 July 1985, col. *312*). No information is available on levels of fines.

POLICE INJURIES

A total of 1,392 police officers were injured in England and Wales, 85 seriously. In Scotland 94 were injured, only 1 seriously. The definition of 'serious' appears to have been that the officer concerned required hospital treatment (cf. South Yorkshire Police 1985: 84).

Table 4 lists the injuries sustained by police forces, for those forces suffering the bulk of the casualties. However its value is limited by the fact that the locations of the incidents causing injury were not given. The bulk of the injuries actually occurred in South Yorkshire (880 on Home Office figures, 859 according to the chief constable's report), but only 12 of these were classed as serious. (A further 213 required outpatient treatment at hospital.)

Table 5 lists the cumulative totals of injuries sustained at various stages of the strike; as with arrests, it can be seen that the injury rate tailed off markedly towards the end.

Table 4　*Police injuries by force*

Force	Number	Force	Number
Nottinghamshire	317	North Yorkshire	104
South Yorkshire	301	West Midlands	93
Derbyshire	239	Merseyside	49
South Wales	142	All others	147

Source: The Times, 6 March 1985.

Table 5　*Police injuries – chronology*

Date	Total injuries	Cumulative total	Source
13 March–5 July	465	465	HC Debates, 9 July, col. *360*
6 July–22 Oct.	486	951	HC Debates, 24 Oct., col. *587*
23 Oct.–7 Dec.	321	1,272	HC Debates, 10 Dec., col. *332*
8 Dec.–5 March	120	1,392	*The Times*, 6 March 1985

COMPLAINTS

There were 551 complaints lodged against the police in England and Wales (of which 111 were withdrawn) and 13 in Scotland. This figure includes only those formally recorded – see the comments in Chapter 6 on the exclusion of complaints about matters of policy; 257 of the complaints were of assault.

Most of the complaints were made early on in the dispute: 516 were recorded by 11 December (HC Debates, 21 December 1984, col. *371*). However the rate of resolution was slow. By 19 June 1985 only 135 investigations were complete. These had resulted in no prosecutions, no disciplinary action, and the giving of 'advice' to officers concerned in four cases (HC Debates, 24 June 1985, col. *280*). (See also Police Complaints Board 1985: paras 6.2 and 6.3.)

The Annual Report of the Police Complaints Authority for 1986 gives a final 'tally'. Only 150 complaints were dealt with through the formal machinery, relating to 35 incidents, none emanating from Wales but no fewer than 102 relating to South Yorkshire. Remaining complaints (a total of 290) were presumably either withdrawn after the strike had ended or settled by informal conciliation. The PCA confirms that no formal disciplinary action was taken against any officers 'due to lack of positive identification' but 'various officers were admonished and advised about their behaviour' (Police Complaints Authority 1987: para 3.7).

MUTUAL AID

A total of 1.4 million officer-days of mutual aid were worked during the dispute (HC Debates, 12 November 1985, col. *121*). Details of numbers of officers deployed on mutual aid for the first eight months of the dispute have been given and are set out in Table 6. These figures relate to the maximum number of uniformed officers deployed on any one day during the week in question, although the text of the Answer announcing the figures suggests this is the weekly total. In fact more police may have been deployed during a week than the figure for the highest day.

Table 6   *Weekly totals of mutual aid*

Week	Maximum number of officers on mutual aid	Week	Maximum number of officers on mutual aid
14–18 March	6,900	9–15 July	5,300
19–25 March	7,500	16–22 July	5,200
26 March–1 April	5,800	23–29 July	4,600
2–8 April	5,500	30 July–5 Aug.	4,500
9–15 April	5,600	6–12 August	4,600
16–22 April	4,800	13–19 August	5,400
23–29 April	3,700	20–26 August	5,600
30 April–6 May	4,500	27 Aug.–2 Sept.	6,100
7–13 May	4,800	3–9 September	6,800
14–20 May	4,300	10–16 September	5,900
21–27 May	5,100	17–23 September	6,300
28 May–3 June	4,800	24–30 September	6,600
4–10 June	5,800	1–7 October	6,600
11–17 June	5,500	8–14 October	6,600
18–24 June	8,100	15–21 October	5,300
25 June–1 July	4,900	22–28 October	5,500
2–8 July	4,800	29 Oct.–4 Nov.	5,500
		5–11 November	5,400

Source: HC Debates, 19 November 1984, cols *12–13* (later figures not published).

Figures are also available for the Metropolitan police showing a total of 40,733 individual tours of duty, with sub-totals for each month of the strike; the largest number (7,695) was for September. A tour of duty could cover from one to eight days. (See M. Rees and Brown (1985: 10) for the details.) The total number of man-days served amounted to 213,000 by 9 February 1985 (HC Debates, 15 February 1985, col. *295*). This represents about eight days for every police officer in the Metropolitan police.

In Scotland there was a total of 2,383 police tours of duty outwith their police areas under mutual aid during the strike, drawn from the Central, Fife and Lothian, and Borders forces (HC Debates, 4 April 1985, col. *732*).

COSTS OF THE POLICING

No definite overall figure for the costs of the policing can be given: only one for additional costs. These covered the payments made for mutual aid, and additional overtime for local officers covering for those on picket lines, as well as the costs of transporting, housing, and feeding officers; 90 per cent of these sums were reimbursed by the Home Office, together with any excess over a 0.75p rate. M. Rees and Brown (1985) estimate these costs to be £225 million, of which Home Office payments would be £205 million. By May 1985 the total paid out by the Home Office was £193.2 million (HC Debates, 14 May 1985, col. *90*) so this figure is unlikely to be an overestimate.

Some indication of total costs can be derived from the Chief Constable of South Yorkshire's report on the dispute, and the Annual Report for 1984 of the Chief Constable of Derbyshire. The latter (for the first ten months of the dispute) estimates total costs at £23.2 million, of which £17.4 million was the cost of mutual aid and £5.8 million for Derbyshire officers. It is not clear whether the latter figure covers *all* or (more probably) only *additional* costs incurred.

The South Yorkshire report gives total *additional* costs of £27.95 million, consisting of £5.38 million in overtime payments to local police, £20 million for mutual aid, and £2.57 million costs of accommodation, feeding, and transport. But in addition the chief constable estimates that the basic salary costs of the South Yorkshire police on strike duty amounted to some £7.7 million while those of officers on mutual aid were a further £16.2 million, giving a grand total of nearly £51.9 million; this, he points out, is the amount that would have been recoverable from central funds if the Home Secretary had designated the aid as 'major' rather than 'larger scale'. South Yorkshire's police budget for 1984 was £56 million (South Yorkshire Police 1985: 99–103). Extrapolating from this information the cost of police resources devoted to the strike might be thought to be some £400 million.

In Scotland the additional costs of policing (excluding basic salary costs) amounted to £5,052,000 (HC Debates, 30 October 1985, col. *537*).

EFFECTS ON OTHER POLICE WORK

Extreme caution is needed in interpreting the effects of the strike on normal policing. It is unlikely that the offences reported and detected in respect of the strike itself had more than a marginal effect on overall totals even in the most heavily affected areas. In any event a national trend of increases in recorded crime continued in 1984 (and 1985) and no significance can be attached to particular figures. Slightly more significance can be attached to clear-up rates; so far as they are relevant they show a distinct pattern.

Nationally outside the Metropolitan area, the clear-up rate dropped between 1983 and 1984 by 3 per cent from 42 per cent to 39 per cent (Annual Report of HM Chief Inspector of Constabulary 1984: Table 4.3). The rate has been slowly declining for a number of years but it dropped by a total of only 3 per cent in the preceding three years combined. In 1985 the rate recovered slightly to 40 per cent (Annual Report of HM Chief Inspector of Constabulary 1985: Table 4.3).

Chief constables' annual reports show that the fall was unevenly spread. A number of areas away from the main coalfields showed improvements or marginal declines, while those most affected (and some Metropolitan Counties particularly involved in mutual aid) showed sharp drops. These are set out in Table 7.

Table 7 *Selected clear-up rates*

Area	% crimes cleared up 1983	1984	Percentage change
Greater Manchester	36.4	27.3	−9.1
Nottinghamshire	38.2	29.9	−8.3
South Wales	46.5	43.1	−3.4
South Yorkshire	49.7	40.1	−9.6
West Midlands	35.8	30.2	−5.6
West Yorkshire	46.0	42.0	−4.0

DISMISSALS OF STRIKING MINERS

During the strike 1,019 miners were dismissed for alleged or proven offences, including 203 in Scotland. By June 1985, 414 had been reinstated (none in Scotland) (HC Debates, 24 June 1985, col. 622). By the end of 1985 the first 63 had been reinstated in Scotland. Eventually an initiative by Sir Robert Haslam, the new Chairman of British Coal, in early 1987 led to the reinstatement figure rising to 662. It is not known how many of the other 357 are still actively seeking reinstatement.

Appendix 2
Observing the picket line: experiences of Chesterfield NCCL group

INTRODUCTION

The materials in this Appendix have been selected from the mass of original data collected by observers from Chesterfield and North-east Derbyshire NCCL who also produced monthly reports (part of the first of which is reprinted here) and a final analysis which we reprint in full. All materials are reproduced by kind permission of the group through its then secretary, Arnold Wynne. As well as the synopses, the reports of daily observations reprinted are selected to give a flavour of events which can reasonably be described as 'typical' police–picket encounters: usually relatively uneventful but, we hope, conveying some of the character of what happened.

MONDAY 13 AUGUST: JOAN, STEPHEN, AND ARNOLD AT
WARSOP COLLIERY

4.30 *am*	Left Chesterfield by Mansfield Road, followed by police car to Hassocky Lane; police presence, with cones on the roads, at Heath roundabout; stopped by 2 constables, one says 'You are not unruly pickets, are you?'; allowed to go on. Proceeded to Pleasley roundabout and via Shirebrook to Warsop Vale. Saw parked coach on the road side before reaching Warsop, with hazard lights flashing; bale of straw scattered across the road, some burning; further on quite a lot of broken glass on the road.
5.00	Parked in side road, between main road and colliery entrance. Walked up to colliery entrance, noting an overturned telephone kiosk, a broken shop window, and a street lamp standard at an unsafe angle. Introduced ourselves to police Inspector (Met.) and 6 official pickets. Inspector said, as far as he was concerned, only two categories of people present that morning, pickets and demonstrators, so we would have to stand with the demonstrators. After some insistence on our part, however, we were allowed to stand on the pavement, on the other side of road and

immediately opposite main body of picket supporters.

5.12   2 police buses enter;

5.15   2 cars enter; cry of 'bounder! – get off home'; 2 more cars enter – signalled in by official pickets; 2 police vans enter, police inside wearing riot gear; Superintendent asks us to move off the pavement to adjacent scrub land; estimate about 20 police present and 30–40 picket supporters;

5.22   2 police vans leave; 2 cars enter; the official pickets are moved off the road by the Superintendent, so they are not able to speak to drivers of vehicles.

5.25   About 25 more police deployed in front of the picket supporters.

5.27   1 car (driver only) leaves and 1 enters; about 20 more police deployed; 1 car (2 occupants) leaves; police van enters with about 12 police; 2 cars (each with 2 occupants) enter; Notts police van with 15 police enters; 3 cars enter (with total of 5 occupants).

5.30   Police prevent some picket supporters from crossing the road;

5.32   Fairly relaxed atmosphere; 3 police coaches, 3 vans and car parked in pit yard. 2 more picket supporters not allowed to cross the road; 2nd police Supt arrives.

5.37   Notts Co-op van enters with 6 police; police van enters with riot shields in the back; 2 cars enter; 2 coaches (?50 police), 1 van (?12 police) enter. About 12 more Met. police deployed (E Div. – at other times also noted Met. police from D, T and N Divisions); 1 car (driver only) enters.

5.44   Pedestrian enters to various shouts from picket supporters; – spoke to official pickets, whom he obviously knew personally.

5.46   1 car (driver only) enters.

5.47   Noted 3 policemen (?with binoculars and/or camera) standing behind parapet on top of the colliery winding gear.

5.48   1 car (driver only) enters, rather fast.

5.53   Estimate 70–80 police deployed and 120–150 picket supporters; police van and red bus (?30 occupants) enter, followed by 6 police vans, some of the police inside wearing riot gear; car (2 occupants) enters; official pickets moved to pavement; not allowed to speak to drivers.

5.56   2 green coaches with protected windows (?30 occupants, in all) enter with police van following.

6.00   A few picket supporters leaving; some prevented from crossing the road.

6.01   1 car (driver only) enters.

6.05   1 car (driver only) enters; 1 empty police van leaves.

6.07   1 police van followed by 3 vans, with protected and obscured windows, enter, then 2 police vans with riot gear enter. 2 cars enter; do not stop for picket. 5 police coaches and 9 police vans in pit yard, at this time.

6.12   A few picket supporters leaving, sent to end of police line, to cross road.

6.14   Some police being withdrawn from 'our' side of the road; hire van leaves. A more relaxed atmosphere; picket supporters now crossing the road.

WEDNESDAY 19 SEPTEMBER: DAVID AND LESLEY AT WHITWELL COLLIERY

4.40	Picked up Lillian Dawson;
4.50	Picked up Lesley Shooter;
5.05	Met striking miners at Doe Lea [*strike centre – where NCCL observers established daily picketing locations*]; followed their cars up Glapwell Hill, then through Bolsover and Clowne.
5.30	As we approached Barlborough roundabout the police set up a quick road-block, but allowed us through; police bus turned round and followed us.
5.50	Noted 5 'official' pickets, by the entrance into the pit yard; picket supporters were massing, about 300–400 being confined in one area by a double line of police, standing shoulder to shoulder. We saw one police bus and 14 minibuses/vans in the car park. Newly arriving picket supporters were sent down to the far end of the line. The atmosphere was like that of a football ground before a 'needle' match; – quite a lot of remarks being shouted by individuals and groups, leading into a spontaneous sing-song – 'We'll never walk alone . . .'.
5.53	The police officer in charge came over to us to make polite conversation, and comments were exchanged about carols at Christmas. He then moved away and we heard him saying into his radio that the pickets (estimated at 800) were quiet now, and the buses could come in. Some police reinforcements were taken across the road, and then brought back again. The picket supporters changed their song to 'Arthur Scargill' – and the police in reserve suddenly ran across the road, as the double/treble ranks of police started to push against the picket supporters; the combined weight and force knocked about 150 picket supporters backwards, like skittles, and took 30–40 feet of wall and railing with them. We could see the pavement, now behind the police ranks – since the police had pushed the picket supporters so far back.
6.11	Whilst all was chaos two buses came in, each with heavily protected windows and carrying 6 and 8 passengers. Shouts of 'Scab' and 'Scabby' from the picket supporters. The picket supporters picked themselves up and, surprisingly, no one appeared to be seriously hurt, although they were obviously shaken. They were then confined to the inside of the flattened wall (they had previously been inside, on top of, and outside the wall, on the pavement – as far as we could see, and the police were on the road; now the police were on the pavement). There was no immediate reaction from the picket supporters to the police attack.

6.22   15 Deputies crossed the road from the pit yard to the changing rooms and a particularly forceful surge developed between picket supporters and police; one man, more or less on all fours, appeared to emerge from the police lines; he was pulled out and pushed back further down the line.

6.30   A much weaker thrust developed when the Deputies returned across the road, from the changing rooms to the pit yard.
          At some stage during all this, a Ford Cortina (red), driven by a woman, came very quickly down the road, towards Whitwell, and several picket supporters narrowly escaped being mown down by her car. She was not stopped by the police.

6.35   Picket supporters drift away; we inspect the 12 yards of broken wall.

FRIDAY 5 OCTOBER: KEVIN AND ARNOLD AT BOLSOVER AND MARKHAM COLLIERIES

5.00   Left Chesterfield by the A632 road; noted 2 police vans parked
am   adjacent to bridge over M1 motorway, 2 more in entrance road to Markham Colliery and 2 more in the entrance road to NCB Derbyshire Area HQ;

5.15   Arrived at entrance to Bolsover Colliery; van, with protected windows, enters; noted about 12 picket supporters present, 3 'official' pickets, 12 constables here and there, in small groups; 2 police transit vans parked in pit yard;

5.20   Another police van arrives and is parked in the pit yard.

5.31   Motor cyclist enters, followed by single pedestrian;

5.32   Van, marked with protected and obscured windows, enters; no shouts from NUM supporters.

5.33   There are now 5 'official' pickets present; 6 police in the vicinity of the picket supporters, 6 in the bus shelter (opposite side of the road) and 6 in the adjoining car park; picket supporters still arriving;

5.34   1 car (driver only) enters; working miners' van departs;

5.40   A police sergeant (Metropolitan, Q Division) approaches and asks who we are; he tells us to stand with 'the other observers' – indicating the group of picket supporters; police Superintendent comes up – and allows us to remain on our chosen 'neutral territory'; about 20 picket supporters present now; motor cyclist enters; 1 car (driver only) leaves colliery;

5.42   Bus with protected windows and with 15 working miners inside, enters with police van escort, to shouts of 'Scab', 'Scabby bastard', 'Get off home';

5.43   Motor cyclist enters, rather fast; 1 car enters and another one leaves;

5.45   Police van enters; pedestrian walks in;

5.46   Another bus with protected windows and a further 15 working miners enters, with police motor cyclist escort, to renewed shouting;

5.50	2 vans, with protected windows, each containing 5 or 6 working miners, enter with police van escort; more shouts from picket supporters; 1 car enters; Superintendent and 2 constables stand chatting, nearby;
5.54	1 motor cyclist enters – more shouts;
5.55	1 car (driver only) enters; minibus with protected and obscured windows enters; more shouts from picket supporters; 4 constables change over duties;
6.00	1 motor cyclist and one pedestrian enter; 1 car (2 inside) leaves;
6.01	Police van enters – and leaves again, almost immediately;
6.05	Some picket supporters leaving; 2 police minibuses leave car park (opposite).
COMMENT:	Atmosphere has been generally calm; no 'heavy policing'; a few of the police seen chatting with picket supporters.
6.15	Arrive at entrance road to Markham Colliery; note 9 police minibuses and vans parked nearby; introduce ourselves to 'official' pickets and Superintendent; explain where we shall be standing: Super. responds: 'stand where you like';
6.20	Estimate about 100 picket supporters present; note quite a large convoy of cars arriving; presently discover they are picket supporters who have been at Shirebrook Colliery; numbers now estimated to be about 200;
6.25	4 picket supporters, standing near us, are 'moved on', seeing our tabards, constable says 'Oh; you're observers; O.K.'
6.30	More picket supporters arriving; 2 cars enter; police (mostly Devon and Cornwall) standing shoulder to shoulder around the picket supporters; Inspector says 'push them in';
6.34	3 cars stop and drivers talk to 'official' pickets, before entering;
6.40	3 more police vans enter; estimate 250–300 picket supporters at this time;
6.44	Metropolitan police coach arrives – to some jeers from picket supporters; 10 more Devon and Cornwall police deployed – now solid double lines, on corner; atmosphere still quite calm;
6.55	Van with protected and obscured windows enters to shouts of 'Scab' from the picket supporters; pushing starts; those at the front are forced up against the police. Police link arms and push back; Inspector is heard to say 'Calm it down'; pushing persists for 20–30 seconds; a gap is re-established between the police and the picket supporters;
7.00	Police suddenly link arms once more, as van containing working miners approaches and enters pit; there is no reaction from the picket supporters, apart from a few jeers at the police, who had braced themselves for another push.
7.04	A few picket supporters are leaving;
7.07	Only about 30–40 picket supporters and 11 police remain; a white van, with heavily protected windows, arrives to shouts of 'Scabby'.
COMMENT:	Police obviously prepared themselves for the arrival of the working

miners – surrounding the picket supporters more closely and herding them closer together. Whether there would have been a 'push' if the police had not prepared themselves in this way is a matter for conjecture.

GENERAL OBSERVATIONS BASED ON REPORTS OF OBSERVERS IN THE PERIOD 9 JULY – 10 AUGUST

The present NUM strike has seen nationally co-ordinated police action on an unprecedented scale. This has manifested itself locally in the apparently routine deployment of police at all the local motorway intersections and a massive police presence to surround and contain the NUM picket supporters at collieries in Derbyshire and Nottinghamshire. Despite this, on those occasions when Chesterfield NCCL observers have been present there has, more often than not, been a relaxed atmosphere, with picket supporters and police chatting here and there.

Tension increases noticeably when picket supporters are more closely contained by the police, who frequently stand shoulder to shoulder, sometimes two and three deep, immediately in front of and facing the striking miners. The numbers of police deployed is generally increased shortly before working miners are due to enter the colliery. This increase in tension occasionally leads to concerted pushing between police and picket supporters. Whether this is the result of animosity towards the strike-breakers, or is a reaction against the increasingly menacing stance of the police, who surround them on all sides, it is difficult to assess; possibly both considerations apply . . . .

It has been noticeable that the attitude of the Superintendent, or senior officer present, seems to have a considerable influence on the course of events. Some officers clearly do their utmost to 'cool' the situation; under these circumstances any feelings of animosity are largely contained, and arrests are quite unusual. It would appear that others feel it necessary to rely upon a show of force to contain the situation; in this case animosity between police and picket supporters inevitably increases, and arrests occur more frequently.

It appears that, at some collieries, sophisticated methods of surveillance are being used (certainly at Bolsover and, possibly, at Arkwright Colliery). This seems certain to increase feelings of frustration and animosity on the part of NUM supporters, unless the use of these methods is openly acknowledged and their use is justified. . . .

The use of road-blocks appears to be increasing and the decision of the police 'on the spot' regarding which vehicles shall be diverted and which shall be allowed to proceed, often appears to be quite arbitrary. . . .

Chesterfield NCCL observers have been interfered with in this way to a lesser extent. Although our cars have been stopped on a number of occasions, only in two cases were we not permitted to proceed along our chosen route, after having identified ourselves and shown photostat copies of letters sent to the Chief Constables of Derbyshire and Nottinghamshire, to confirm our bona fides.

Another example of police discretion concerns the number of 'official pickets' that are permitted to stand at colliery entrances to speak to working miners, as they go in. In most cases that we have observed, six 'official pickets' are permitted, and they are usually accompanied by two or three police. In a minority of cases the number of 'official pickets' is restricted further and, based solely on our observations, it is as though the officer in charge has been instructed to 'think of a number between two and six'.

On several occasions it has been noted that police constables have not been wearing identity numbers. On 19 July, at Creswell Colliery, a constable wearing a first-aid arm band, was seen moving down the lines of Kent police collecting the insignia and number tags (normally worn on the left breast pocket, by Kent police) from each constable in turn. . . .

SYNOPSIS FROM MONTHLY SUMMARY REPORTS: JULY 1984 – FEBRUARY 1985

POLICING THE PICKET LINES

The nationally co-ordinated police action during the miners' strike manifested itself in Derbyshire in the presence of police from many different constabularies. These included Cambridgeshire, Cheshire, Cumbria, Devon and Cornwall, Essex, Hertfordshire, Humberside, Kent, Lancashire, City of London, Greater Manchester, Metropolitan (many different Divisions), Merseyside, West Midlands, Norfolk, Nottinghamshire, Suffolk, Thames Valley, Wiltshire, South Yorkshire.

Police were to be seen, frequently in large numbers, at all NCB establishments, coke works, and power stations that were visited by our observers, as well as at all local motorway intersections and various other locations. A slight reduction in the number of police road-blocks encountered was first reported in the latter part of August, but a significant reduction in the ratio of police actively deployed to the number of picket supporters present on the picket lines did not occur until December 1984 (see Table below).

Outside the collieries and coke works visited the picket supporters were usually closely confined by police who stood shoulder to shoulder, surrounding and facing the picket supporters. The numbers of police actively deployed in this way were routinely increased a few minutes before the buses carrying the working miners entered the colliery premises, thus exacerbating an already tense situation. The number of 'official' pickets allowed on any picket line appeared to be at the discretion of the senior police officer, and varied from 2 to 6.

In a variety of ways the striking miners were denied any opportunity to peacefully persuade those who were working not to cross the picket line and to join, or re-join, the strike.

1. A majority of working miners were picked up at locations some way from the collieries, then taken to work in buses which entered the colliery without stopping;
2. For some time before the bus(es) entered with the working miners, police took precautions to ensure that the entrance road was not obstructed in

any way and that any possibility of the buses being held up was eliminated;

3. The 'official' pickets were thus enabled to speak only to the minority of working miners who entered the colliery in their own transport, or who walked in;

4. When a car stopped for the driver to talk to the pickets, other vehicles coming behind were frequently diverted by a police officer on to the 'wrong' side of the road. This was clearly a hazardous practice and, on more than one occasion, a collision with a vehicle leaving the colliery was only narrowly avoided;

5. Nottinghamshire police, e.g. at Warsop Main Colliery, would not permit even this limited amount of picketing to take place. They insisted upon the 'official' pickets standing on the near-side pavement, so that they could not speak to the drivers of vehicles entering. When asked by our observers, the police Superintendent in charge stated that this action was in accordance with instructions issued by the Chief Constable of Nottinghamshire: '. . . so as not to impede the free flow of traffic'.

From an examination of the detailed daily reports, it is clear that, during the final three months of the strike, increasing numbers of working miners preferred to use their own transport, or to walk in, rather than to go to work in the vehicles provided by the NCB. It is significant that this period, during which policing was generally rather less heavy, also saw an increase in the number of working miners who chose to turn around at the colliery gates, rather than cross a picket line. This trend continued, even into the closing weeks of the strike.

Our observers went out on 94 occasions, between 9 July 1984 and 26 February 1985, visiting 164 picket lines, mostly at collieries within the North Derbyshire area. Less frequently, collieries in South Yorkshire and Nottinghamshire were visited, and NCB area workshops, coke works, and electricity power stations. Throughout the strike the media coverage on NUM picket lines concentrated almost exclusively on reporting instances where violence had occurred. An analysis of the detailed reports submitted by our observers shows a very different picture, and has been summarized, on a monthly basis, in the Table below.

ADDITIONAL NOTES AND COMMENTS UPON DATA PRESENTED IN TABLE

1. Our observers always tried to insist upon standing on 'neutral' ground, some distance away from the main concentration of picket supporters and police.

2. This enabled our observers to gain the best possible overall view of events. It was, however, not possible in most cases to assess whether pushing had been initiated by police or by picket supporters.

3. Nevertheless, in at least four cases, it was quite clear that an inappropriate amount of violence was perpetrated by the police. These instances occurred:
   • On 11 July 1984 at Shirebrook Colliery, when police resorted to violently pushing picket supporters and NCCL observers alike (although the latter were wearing prominent NCCL tabards) as they were walking quietly

Month	One or more stones were thrown	Concerted pushing occurred between police and picket supporters	No violence of any sort was reported	Percentage of non-violent picket lines	Ratio (no. of police actively deployed to no. of picket supporters present)
1984					
July	1	4	20	80	1:1 to 1:5
Aug.	2	7	32	82	1:1 to 1:4
Sept.	nil	3	17	85	1:1 to 1:4
Oct.	nil	4	21	84	1:1 to 1:4
Nov.	1	5	27	82	1:1 to 1:4[a]
Dec.	nil	nil	5	100	1:4 to 1:7
1985					
Jan.	nil	1	5	80	1:4 to 1:7
Feb.	nil	nil	11	100	1:4 to 1:30

Note: [a] Ratio rose to 1:6 and 1:7 occasionally, in November.

from Shirebrook village down the lane leading to the colliery entrance;
- On 31 August, at Kiveton Park Colliery, when police violently frog-marched one of our observers across the road, into a police 'pen', with NUM picket supporters – all of whom were released some minutes later;
- On 19 September, at Whitwell Colliery, when police pushed about 150 picket supporters (standing on the pavement, in front of a turreted brick wall, with iron railings in between) with such force as to demolish about 12 yards of the brick wall and railings;
- On 25 January 1985, at Markham Colliery, when police pushed into picket supporters with such force that at least one fell to the ground.

4. On numerous other occasions police officers were heard to be verbally restraining the over-zealous violence being used by the close-knit ranks of police constables against picket supporters.

5. The monthly percentages of totally peaceful picket lines show a remarkable degree of consistency, at 80 per cent or above.

6. It was only during the last three months of the strike that the ratio of police actively deployed on picket lines, to the number of picket supporters present, showed any significant reduction. NB It should be stressed that, throughout the strike, very significant numbers of police remained on site, sitting within their coaches or minibuses. These numbers were not included in those 'actively deployed'.

7. Was it coincidental that, during the final three months of the strike, when policing was much lighter, violence on the picket lines virtually disappeared?

ADDITIONAL COMMENTS ON POLICING OF NUM PICKET LINES

1. Within Derbyshire the senior officer in charge of the policing of individual picket lines always appeared to be from the Derbyshire Constabulary. Nevertheless considerable variations in attitude were apparent as between different senior officers and in the general attitude of police from different constabularies. Some preferred to 'play it cool'; others preferred 'a show of force'. This comment from the general report covering the period 13–30 August is still relevant:

> A clear example of the increase in the number of arrests made when strong-arm tactics are adopted by the police occurred at Markham Colliery on 16 August. Our observers reported about 300 picket supporters present (by no means an excessive number at this colliery, which previously employed more than 2,000 miners) 'being walled in by two rows of police, who surrounded them' and 'picket supporters packed tightly together'. According to our information not less than 12 arrests were made that morning. This number may be contrasted with a total of 5 arrests made at two other collieries (on 17 and 30 August) and the 25 other occasions on which our observers were present during this period, at which more relaxed methods of policing were generally adopted, when no arrests were made.

2. Over a fairly extended period the policing at Kiveton Park Colliery, in South Yorkshire, with mounted police, police dogs, and police wearing riot-gear much in evidence, was much heavier than normally seen in Derbyshire.

3. Many policemen seem to use quite unnecessary violence when making an arrest. A blatant example occurred at Whitwell Colliery, on 30 August, when a youth of 17 was arrested (subsequently found 'Not Guilty'). A series of photographs taken on this occasion show three burly policemen making the arrest: one holds the youth by his hair, while two others twist his arms as they march him away.

4. Throughout the period of the miners' strike constables were seen wearing no identification numerals. Also throughout the strike persistent rumours were heard of Service-personnel being used to augment police numbers. Whilst no hard evidence in support of these rumours was available, the persistent flouting of police regulations in this manner can only help to give a semblance of justification for the rumours.

5. Reference is made elsewhere (p. 180) to apparently arbitrary and inconsistent police rulings at road-blocks. Similar arbitrary rulings were given by police attending picket lines. Frequently at Shirebrook and Warsop Main Collieries, and sometimes at Markham Colliery also, picket supporters were permitted to pass through the surrounding police ranks only at points which could be varied from time to time by the police themselves. Such rulings cannot be expected to encourage cheerful and willing co-operation from striking miners.

6. Sophisticated electronic methods of crowd surveillance were noted at Bolsover and Arkwright Collieries. These methods, which impinge equally on guilty and innocent alike, are naturally resented.

7. Whilst, in general, all necessary co-operation was given to our observers

by the police and striking miners alike, nevertheless isolated instances of harassment both verbal and physical, from the police only, did occasionally occur.

POLICE ROAD-BLOCKS

A month or so before our members first went out to observe events connected with the miners' strike, a letter was sent to the Chief Constables of Derbyshire and Nottinghamshire, informing them of our intention to put out teams of observers, who would submit factual reports. An acknowledgement of receipt of this letter was received from the Assistant Chief Constable of Nottinghamshire. A xerox copy of this, together with a copy of our original letter, was provided for each team of observers.

Our observers' cars were frequently stopped by police at road-blocks, in a variety of locations but, having shown their credentials (including locally produced credential cards bearing the photograph of each observer) they were almost always permitted to proceed. Only on a few occasions were we asked to (a) go by a different route, or (b) park the car and proceed down the colliery lane on foot (the latter happened fairly regularly at Shirebrook and Whitwell Collieries).

Two occurrences, each of which was repeated with depressing regularity, served to undermine somewhat the respect for the police which our observers would normally accord to them:

1. The regular inconsistency of such rulings by the police (particularly at Southfield Lane, leading down to Whitwell Colliery) even though the material situation was precisely the same;
2. The bland lies which some police at road-blocks resorted to, quite gratuitously and quite unnecessarily, e.g. at M1 Motorway access point 22 (South) on 15 August, our observers were asked not to go to Bagworth Colliery, because large numbers of demonstrators were already present and any increase in numbers was likely to lead to a breach of the peace. Less than half an hour later, at 5 am, our observers reported not a single demonstrator or NUM picket present at Bagworth Colliery.

Appendix 3
Some major confrontations: Orgreave and the return to work in South Yorkshire

This appendix consists entirely of materials from the daily reports of Sheffield Policewatch. The first two are observers' accounts of events at Orgreave on the two days of maximum conflict, 29 May and 18 June. The other two are about the conflicts surrounding the first return of working miners at Brookhouse (28 August) and Cortonwood (8 November). The reports are reproduced in full by kind permission of Sheffield Policewatch and of their authors; footnotes are from the originals, and editorial comments (where included) are in italics.

ORGREAVE

SHEFFIELD POLICEWATCH REPORT
OBSERVATIONS MADE AT ORGREAVE, TUESDAY 29 MAY 1984
OBSERVERS: JENNY OWEN, JANET McDERMOTT

We arrived at 7.05 am, coming from the Handsworth direction, and at this stage there were already several hundred miners gathered along the road outside the plant. Most were concentrated in two large groups, one some way up the hill from the plant, and the other at least five hundred yards further down, on the other side of the road. Lines of policemen had them confined to sections of pavement. Soon after arriving we introduced ourselves to Chief Inspector McGuire. He advised us to keep well clear (although making no objection to our presence). A picket standing nearby commented, 'You'll be all right, love, unless the police charge.' Chief Inspector McGuire immediately asked him his name, which pit he was from, and whether he was making a complaint. When the picket declined to answer, Chief Inspector McGuire started to accuse him of not being a miner; we resumed our explanation about Policewatch and the picket moved away.

As more pickets arrived, they began to spread over the road, until there were crowds right across, both above and below the gate (i.e. where each group mentioned above was). At 7.35 am a group of mounted police trotted[1] briskly down the road, right through the group above the gate. Some of the mounted police took up positions in a field to the right of this group. Six to eight trotted on towards the second large group of pickets on the other side; they rode into this crowd, and, along with police on foot and some with dogs, forced the pickets into a car park to the left of the road. This group was then hemmed in by lines of police at least two deep, and backed up by the mounted police. From this time onwards, we also observed a dog patrol van stationed behind some trees in the field to the left of the road. This seemed to be waiting for any pickets who might be forced off the road and down the steep bank into the field.

At 7.40 am the police tried to clear the road above the gate. First, the mounted police previously waiting in the field on the right rode up the hill, through the crowd; then they rode back through again, followed immediately by several police vans. However, each time the crowd scattered, but then reassembled. So these moves failed to clear the road, but considerably increased tension and restlessness among the pickets. After this, a convoy of fifteen police vans and two dog patrol vans arrived from the motorway direction, and turned into the police headquarters opposite the plant gates. By this time, there were two lines of police and another of mounted police cordoning off the pickets above the gate. Another group of mounted police were again stationed in the field to the right.

At 8.20 am these mounted police trotted straight into the crowd, in wedge formation, for no apparent reason. Panic ensued, and people ran up the road and into the fields on either side. There was a lot of noise and confusion – including some confusion among the police themselves about what they were trying to achieve: we heard one policeman comment, 'That was a silly order', to another. Nobody moved very far away; when the police turned their horses around to go back to their original position in the field, there was a lot of jostling, shouting, and pieces of broken fence flying through the air.[2]

Tension was now greatly increased; there seemed to be a feeling among the pickets that a violent confrontation was inevitable because of this unprovoked demonstration of force by the police.

At 8.50 am another convoy of at least fifteen police vans drew up opposite the crowd down the road in the car park. Some two hundred policemen got out, and marched up towards the crowd above the gate. At this point we estimated that there were some three thousand people in the car park area, and the crowd above the gate was bigger than that, and still growing, as more pickets arrived from the Handsworth [*a suburb of Sheffield*] direction.

At 9.05 am, just before the coke lorries came up the road, someone let off a smoke bomb at the front of the crowd near the gate, and there was some movement in the crowd. Then, as the convoy of lorries approached up the road, the police pushed forward, up the hill, into the crowd. At this point we noticed that the front line of police had riot shields and helmets, as well as truncheons. They were followed by a line of mounted police; the police from the field on the right also rode into the pickets, and a further twenty or so lines of police also followed the men with riot shields.

Meanwhile, two police vans (minibus type) had reversed down the road, from the Handsworth direction; they took up position behind the crowd, which continued to face down the hill and towards the entrance to the plant.

Just below the vans, one of which had both doors open at the back, a single line of policemen was spread across the road. Thus the crowd was surrounded.

As the police pushed or rode into the crowd, as mentioned above, some fighting broke out among the pickets and the advancing police, and many miners ran back up the road, away from the plant. The police made at least three charges into the crowd; each time pickets scattered right back up the hill, over the railway bridge and towards Orgreave [*i.e. Orgreave Village*] and Handsworth. Some attempted to get away by running into the fields on either side of the road. We saw men being chased by mounted police right along the top of the railway embankment, in the field which adjoins the plant, and running down on to the line to escape. By this time, we had withdrawn to the far side of the railway line; even from this point, we could hear a lot of shouting and struggling, and we could see objects flying through the air above the crowd.

By now, miners were moving away from the plant in small groups, leaving the main body of the crowd. We walked on towards Orgreave and Handsworth, stopping by the first house in the village, above the railway. Here we observed four policemen searching the garden of the first house, which was uninhabited. They found three men in the back garden, and questioned them at length about which direction they had come from. The men said they were trying to get back to their car. The policemen were aware that the conversation was being overheard, and told the men to be on their way. They moved the men on up the road – we followed close behind, until we saw the men walk away, without further incident. We feel our presence was a restraining influence on the police, and this impression was shared by a miner's wife who was also standing nearby.[3]

After this, we went on to our own car and stopped observing.

Notes

1. 'Trotted' may sound mild, but don't underestimate the speed of a large police horse, even at the trot: they were moving fast.
2. NB before this point we had seen nothing thrown by people in the crowd, nor was there any sign of any other threat to the police.
3. Previously she had expected the policemen to arrest the three miners for throwing bricks earlier.

SHEFFIELD POLICEWATCH REPORT
OBSERVATIONS MADE AT ORGREAVE, 18 JUNE 1984
OBSERVERS: DR NICHOLAS RALPH, ANKI HOOGEVELT, BRIGITTE PEMBERTON

Approaching Orgreave from Handsworth direction (Orgreave Lane) about 9.45 am with Anki Hoogevelt and Brigitte Pemberton, we saw large numbers of miners leaving the area after the early morning clashes. We parked at the top of Orgreave Lane and walked down to the police lines which had been set up about 100–200 yds west of the coking works. We asked permission for Brigitte to be let through the police lines to observe from behind the lines but this was refused by a Superintendent. At this time some 700–900 police formed a human barrier (behind riot shields) right across the road and the adjacent field to the south. There were at that time perhaps 500–800 pickets in the immediate area between the railway bridge and the police lines. Many were lying in the sun or simply standing around chatting. We took up a position half way across the field next to some trees; this gave us a good clear view of the whole area.

Shortly after we arrived (and after I [*Dr Ralph*] had photographed the riot-equipped police line and a group of horses by the woods to the south) the police riot shields were removed and the mounted squad moved from the wood to a position behind the police lines, where they appeared to be exercising. For about half an hour little happened. Then a small group of miners towards the front of the crowd were involved in some sort of altercation with the police line. It was not possible to see precisely what happened; there was a good deal of yelling and shouting but no physical confrontation. However very soon afterwards a small number of pickets threw stones towards the police. Immediately the riot squads returned and the long riot shields reappeared on the police lines. This provoked further stoning by pickets, and eventually a small detachment of police in riot gear ran into the crowd. Stoning was intensified and the police returned to their line. The pickets retreated some 50–60 yds up the hill away from the lines as riot squad police started to hammer their truncheons on their shields – a very frightening sound and sight. Some stone throwing continued. I would guess that not more than 5–10 per cent of the 1,000–1,200 pickets now present were involved in the stone throwing. Police were constantly reinforcing the line with men in full riot gear and some 1,500 or more may by now have been present. Suddenly the police lines opened and some 8–12 mounted police charged into the pickets on the road. Behind them police with small round riot shields fanned out among the pickets. Both foot and horse police were using truncheons against the pickets. A hail of stones was sent up and the police horses turned back towards the police line, which meanwhile had taken the opportunity to move up the hill about 30 yards. An almost identical sequence of events was repeated on at least two occasions before it became clear to myself and the other observers that we would shortly be overrun by the advancing police line and would be in danger both from inadvertent violence from the police and from missiles from the retreating pickets. I have several photographs of this cavalry-led advance by the police.

In view of the danger we moved up the hill to a small electricity sub-station just east of the railway bridge. Until this point most of the police attack had concentrated on the pickets in the road area, where most of the stone throwing was occurring. However, as we reached the sub-station all hell broke loose with riot-equipped police running up the hill and attacking pickets in all areas. At this point I lost touch with the other two observers who had sought shelter between the buildings of the sub-station (I later saw one of the observers again – see below). I retreated with the pickets towards the steep bluff that led down to the railway line. At the top I turned around as a riot policeman approached me and shouted out that I was not a picket and was a Policewatch observer. He made it very clear that he couldn't have cared less who I was, and lunged towards me with his truncheon. I don't think he was trying to hit me – merely scare me, which it did! I then turned to descend the bluff, and as I turned I saw a policeman in normal uniform fling a large wooden stake down the bluff at descending pickets. I did not see whether it hit anybody because by this time I was hurrying to get down myself. I crossed the railway tracks and then stopped to look back (another photograph was taken at this point). Then I ascended the bluff on the west of the tracks and finally reached safety (temporarily). Looking back across the bluff I then saw Anki Hoogevelt being shepherded away from the area back towards the police nearer the bridge.

My escape from immediate danger was short-lived. The horse and riot squad charges now continued across the bridge and up into the area of the road where there are houses on one side and factories on the other. Wherever pickets ran they were followed by police on foot and horse. As I retreated through this area I continued to take photographs until my film ran out. By this time I had reached the junction with Orgreave Lane. The pattern of events was that each police charge was followed by a tactical retreat during which miners cautiously drifted back towards the police line (often stoning the police heavily as they did so); then a renewed charge would occur and pickets would run frantically away from the charging horses. At the junction of Orgreave Lane, I took temporary refuge in one of the factories and watched as police horses rounded the corner and headed up Orgreave Lane (by now nearly a mile from the coking plant). Incautiously I then left the factory and joined pickets in the road. Just as I reached the road a large second squad of horses and more riot police arrived from the east and I found myself pinned in a private garden next to the junction (NE Corner). Four or five pickets were with me and riot squad police entered the garden and attacked the pickets. As I turned to leap over into the field behind I was pushed against the wall by a riot shield. I turned round, shouted who I was, and was then let free to move back on to the road, where I rapidly moved about 50 yds up Orgreave Lane. The police horses were now returning down Orgreave Lane. I was very shaken and decided to rest briefly in the shelter provided by closely parked cars. It was about 11.35 am.

During the retreat from the bridge and before I took refuge in the factory, I did observe closely one attack by two riot police on one picket; he was hit with a truncheon by one officer while the other was holding him. I was running away from the advancing riot squads at the time, but I did attempt to photograph this event.

At about 11.45 a stalemate was reached with perhaps 30–40 mounted police occupying the junction area and preventing pickets moving back towards the plant. Many pickets drifted away up towards Handsworth at this point. After perhaps ten minutes, the police withdrew. I did not at once follow them, nor initially did many pickets. However near to 12.00 pm a sizeable group of pickets did move back along the road to the coking plant and eventually I followed them. I had been afraid of meeting yet another police charge, but I needn't have worried. By this time the pickets had built a substantial barricade of old wrecked cars from a breakers yard and had set it ablaze. As a result the police were now cut off from the pickets by a wall of flame immediately west of the railway bridge. At this point I was able to obtain some film from a news photographer, and I took a shot of this scene. The roadway was strewn with stones and burning debris. It was clear that no police behaviour would be observed in this area for some time and at about 12.30 I headed back to Orgreave Lane, where police vans had started to arrive from the Handsworth direction.

I, and many pickets, were afraid that a new police pincer movement would start coming down Orgreave Lane, and for about 15 mins I took refuge in a house next to the junction in the hope that, should such an event materialize, I would be able to observe it without serious danger to myself. Fortunately this did not happen and at about 1.00 pm I headed back up Orgreave Lane to Brigitte's car past a dozen or so police transit vans (perhaps 250 police – West Yorkshire Force).

It is difficult to summarize the events of the day or the feelings evoked. From the moment the police charges started to the time that their horses occupied the junction three-quarters of a mile from the plant, there had been a running battle; I had seen numerous attacks by police on individual pickets trapped by events among the houses and factories, and I had become very scared that the same fate awaited me. When the riot squads get going they are terrifying, and seem quite out of control; certainly some of their attacks appeared quite unwarranted. They simply grabbed those who could run least fast, or who reacted too slowly. No doubt in some cases they were arresting pickets who had thrown stones but many others were simply caught up in events they had not provoked or taken any active part in.

THE RETURN TO WORK IN SOUTH YORKSHIRE

SHEFFIELD POLICEWATCH REPORT
BROOKHOUSE PIT (S. YORKS), 28 AUGUST 1984
OBSERVERS: CAROLYN SPRAY, KILA MILLIDINE

5.05 Left Beighton Miners' Welfare for Brookhouse pit. The pickets had left for the pit already. (They have been picketing their own pit since yesterday because there are rumours that a man intends to go back. Until then, there has only been the official picket on duty.) When we got to the right-hand turning in to the pit lane (about ½ mile from pit), we were stopped by South Yorkshire police. We explained that we were Policewatch and we were finally allowed through after they had conferred with each other and checked with their sergeant.

5.15 We arrived at the pit entrance. There were 6 official pickets, watched by a small group of South Yorkshire police who stood a few yards away. The pickets said that the police were strictly enforcing the 6-picket guideline – unlike yesterday when there was a peaceful good-natured picket of about 50, and no police. From the picket line we can see a considerable police presence this morning – 3 transits and 3 small vans parked at the NCB buildings, and police officers in the buildings. The pickets say the police have taken over the office buildings and the canteen, and that there are many more police vehicles parked out of sight in the pit car park. This appears to be borne out by the fact that, as we arrived at the pit entrance, 6 police transits left the pit and an armoured vehicle arrived and disappeared out of view. As dawn broke, we could see a policeman on top of the tower which houses the pit lights – approx. 80–100 ft tall, an excellent look-out point.

We spoke to the police at the picket line – they said it was South Yorks police in charge of the pit but other forces were also involved. They did not know who the main officer in charge was.

A few vehicles drove in – managerial and maintenance.

5.40 We left the picket line and drove back towards Beighton village to see what was happening. As we turned left from the pit lane on to the main road there was an obvious police presence of 3 transits and odd groups of police patrolling the area. No pickets to be seen. This was explained as we drove towards Beighton. There was a police road-block opposite the Roper Group building and 4 more police vehicles and police stopping people as they approached the pit lane.

We drove back to the turning in to the pit lane. As we were stopped by the police, a solitary Brookhouse picket asked the police for permission to speak to us. We were allowed through the road-block, but the picket was not allowed to speak to us.

5.50 Arrived back at picket line – 6 men.

Police vehicles steadily coming and going. Noticed City of London police arrive. Some Metropolitan police arrived and told Pete Rose (Secretary of Brookhouse NUM and one of the official pickets) that they had a message for him from 'your assistant' – his assistant wished to speak to him at the end of the pit lane (½ mile away).

6.05 Pete Rose looked a bit bemused by this, but drove away with 2 of the official pickets (leaving 3) in the only picket van.

6.20 Pete Rose returned to the picket line on foot. He said nobody had wanted to speak to him and that it had been a police lie to get rid of the pickets' vehicle. The van had not been allowed to return to the picket line.

6.25 4 South Yorkshire police transits arrived with their wire-mesh screens down over the windscreens.

6.30 The official pickets told us that the police were using dog patrols to exclude pickets from the area. (When we had driven in to the village at 5.40 am we had seen a dog van parked on the left, just down a lane.)

6.35 We decided to drive down the pit lane again to see what was happening where there were more police and probably other pickets.

As we drove along the pit lane we saw police vehicles driving towards us. We pulled over and stopped. The following convoy drove past us, through the picket line and in to the pit:

A coach full of police.
A police motorbike.
4 police transits.
A police motorbike.
7 police transits.
A police landrover.
A police transit.
A police motorbike.
6 police transits.
4 police transits.

A police motorbike.
8 police transits.
A police car.
A police lorry.
7 police transits.
A police motorbike.
3 police transits.
A small van, colour navy*.
3 police landrovers
A police motorbike.
Total: 55 *vehicles!*

1. As far as we could see, this huge convoy was led by South Yorkshire police vehicles, then came about 9 Kent police vehicles, then
about 8 Cumbria police vehicles, then 4 South Yorkshire police
vehicles, then the navy-blue van, then 4 more South Yorkshire
police vehicles.
2. Some of these vehicles, at least, carried riot gear.
3. From what we were later told, the working miner was most
probably in the small, navy-blue van,* towards the end of the
convoy, flanked by South Yorkshire police.
4. We saw no aggressive behaviour by pickets.

6.44   After the convoy had passed us, we continued to the main road where
we saw 7 police transits and many groups of police. A policeman told
us that if we were intending to return to the picket line we would have
to do so without the car.
We turned on to the main road, to the right, away from Beighton
village. As we drove over the railway bridge, we saw police and pickets
grouped along the verge – perhaps about 50 of each. We saw a line
of pickets' cars parked, and a BBC camera crew. We parked the car.
6.50   As we walked back towards the bridge, 2 very big police horse-boxes
drove past (maybe 10 horses in each?). One was Avon and Somerset,
one was South Yorkshire police. As we crossed the bridge, the horse-
boxes came back towards us, driving away from the pit.
6.54   The pickets were loosely surrounded by some 20 police, whose helmet
crests seemed to be black and gold plastic. We asked one of the
policemen which constabulary these were, and he replied that they
were not a constabulary, they were City of London police.
We saw more press.
The pickets were not allowed to cross the bridge in the direction of
the pit. They did not challenge this – we saw no confrontation or
aggression.
We walked past the pit lane towards Beighton and spoke with 2
women who were standing at the bus-stop. They said that they had
been there for hours. They told us that at 4.30 am they had been told
by a policeman that if they did not catch the next bus they would be
arrested for obstructing the police and that they would appear in court
that afternoon.
They said that most of the convoy had come from across the bridge,

but the last part (South Yorkshire and the small unmarked blue van) had come from the Beighton direction and then followed the rest of the convoy down the pit lane, led by a motorbike with flashing lights.

7.15 As we spoke, a transit full of police drove out of the pit lane towards the bridge. The back doors were open and its occupants were loudly singing:

> Busy doing nothing
> Working the whole day through
> Trying to find
> Lots of things not to do . . .

In spite of this blatantly provocative behaviour a mere 35 minutes after the first working miner had crossed the picket line at Brookhouse Colliery, the pickets behaved impeccably.

7.20 The police vehicles began en masse to leave the pit. We walked back across the bridge to the car and drove back to Beighton Miners' Welfare.

7.35 As we returned, some 15–20 pickets were still at the bridge, surrounded by City of London police. Police were still stopping traffic at a block on the Beighton side of the pit lane.

7.50 We arrived at Beighton Miners' Welfare. We were told that Pete Rose, Branch Secretary, had been informed that one young man had crossed the picket line this morning. Pete Rose had not been allowed to speak to him or see him, despite requests. The official pickets at the entrance to the pit had not seen or spoken to him either. Morale seemed high – we were told that nobody else was expected to go back to work at Brookhouse, and that these pickets would soon be 'flying' again.

SHEFFIELD POLICEWATCH REPORT
CORTONWOOD, 8 NOVEMBER 1984
OBSERVERS: JAN SMITH, JAN SYMINGTON, ANNE BULMER

4.55 Parked in side-street on small housing estate. Left car to walk to where pickets gathering.

4.58 As we came on to the main road we could see a group of men ahead in the road and on the bank to the left. It was misty and flashing amber lights could be seen behind the group. Walked up to what turned out to be the back of a picket of about 100. We stayed up on the bank to the left where we could get a better overview. There are a group of 10 police with riot helmets on the bank making a line across a footpath which leads down steps to the road. Across the road at the front of the picket 28 officers stand with riot helmets. There is a van with its hazard warning lights behind the police lines. Behind and to the left a lane goes off which we are told is the pit lane. This lane runs a distance of 1 mile to the pit. Spoke to a police inspector (Inspector Peddrick) from Surrey. He is in command of 10 men and sergeant on the bank but says he honestly doesn't know what other forces are here. He tells us the man in charge is a Mr Marsh of S. Yorks police. Inspector Peddrick is friendly, co-operative, and chatty and allows us to observe from the position we have chosen at the top of the bank. All is quiet. There is a police transit with gull wings parked in the pit lane, 4 police with riot helmets by the van and one near and one by the entrance to the pit lane. There are 7 men not in uniform (presumably the official picket) in the entrance to the pit lane.

5.07   This is the first day someone has gone to work at this pit. We receive a few contradictory stories about how many, whether they are in yet, etc.

5.10   Police Range Rover arrives. Stands, engine idling, at back of picket. 3 vans can be seen parked down the pit lane. Vehicles come up to the back of the picket – some go through, some turn round.

5.17   Picket still 100 approx.

5.22   All quiet – situation the same. Inspector Peddrick continues to be friendly and helpful. Transit moves away up road from pit entrance (5.25).

5.35   A camera crew arrives. (Later identified as BBC.) The use of their lights causes a lot of anger and abuse within the picket.

5.40   Still 100 approx. pickets. Can see a flashing blue light to right up road.

5.45   Still all quiet. The police are now turning vehicles approaching the back of the picket.

5.47   Police van (with dent in side) makes its third turn in pit lane and goes back away up the road.

5.57   Police Range Rover comes out of the pit lane, backs up and parks. Two cars drive into pit lane (few shouts of 'scab'). A group of five police walk into pit lane. Now 25 across road plus inspector and officers in charge.

6.04   Inspector tells us every other man is to be sent for a cup of tea. Another group of 15 police with number 35 on the back of their helmets have come out and extended the line in front of us, down the bank to the end of the pit lane.

6.17   Still the same numbers of police and pickets. Car turns in and is talked to by the official picket.

6.20   Picket approx. 150, quiet and peaceful. Another car turns into the pit lane. Told it's the under-manager.

6.28   Picket now 250–300 in strength. This figure is independently corroborated by Inspector Peddrick.

6.30   Another 24 police (all riot-hatted) make a double line across the road. Now about 90 police visible from where we stand. The picket moves forward slightly as a police convoy arrives and sweeps into the pit lane. 2 Range Rovers, 1 small van.
(4 police run out to the back of the line from the pit lane. There is a push at the front of the picket.)
3 horse boxes, 4 transit vans, a big square box-shaped van from S. Yorkshire.
There is an officer with a megaphone who asks the picket to stop pushing. He orders a spotlight on the people on the top of the bank. There are some local women at the back of a bungalow. A police Range Rover has been parked behind what is now a line of officers three deep across the road. Another 14 come out to reinforce the line. Total officers visible over 100. The officer with the megaphone asks

if the bungalow is the property of the women stood at the top of the
bank and to move if it is not. Mr Nesbitt *[South Yorkshire Police]* has
arrived. Kaktus Leech and Jackie Field of Policewatch have arrived
and are pushed into the picket by Mr Nesbitt. We back off slightly
as we don't want to lose our observation spot. Inspector Peddrick
remains protective. A group of 20 more police officers are brought to
reinforce the line down the bank to the pit lane and our 10 Surrey
policemen turn at right angles to line the footpath at the top of the
bank. 2 Range Rovers and a gull wing transit are 3 abreast behind the
police lines.

6.40 There is a request from one of the women for the picketing members
of one family to go to their mother who is having a bad turn with
angina.

6.45 Beginning to get light. Still 100+ police and approx. 300 pickets. An
announcement is made over the megaphone as I speak. 'The working
miner is in this colliery – I want this road cleared. If the pickets do
not move the police will clear the road.' There are shouts of derision
and abuse from the picket. 'Come on. Let's have you on your way
now.' Immediately the police move forward and the horses are
brought through. The horses and riot police move the picket up the
road at a fast walk. Inspector Peddrick trys to slow it down on his side.
There are 10 horses (no 12). The vans put their sirens and blue
flashing lights on and move three abreast down the road at the picket
– pickets run. The dispersal was carried out in a frightening and
intimidating manner without any aggression from the picket. As we
reach the corner where a wall comes down on to the road the first
missile (made of glass) is thrown in retaliation. We retreat behind a
wall. The horses are withdrawn, the vans back up a bit. There is an
order for Mr Simpson with the shields. The horses form a line across
the road. Missiles are being thrown and the horses are retreating.
Insp. Peddrick runs past. 'Get back to the bloody gate' to his squad
of men. He yells to me to mind my head. The wings are out on the
gull wing van. The three vehicles move forward again into the picket.
The police horses follow up. There are three vans, a line of 100+ riot
police with shields and 12 horses. We have been separated from Jan
Smith. Two policemen walk a picket down the road. He is screaming
in pain as they have his arms up in the air behind his back and he is
unable to give us his name. 4CV plus a number on the back of their
helmets. The horses walk back; 5 on our side and 7 on the opposite
side of the road. They form a line across the road to our left. An
arrested miner is being walked backwards down the road past us. His
name is Jeff Howell, he says, from Ickleton Main. The BBC camera
crew leave through the line of horses. The riot police are in the road
to our right with the three vehicles, in front. There is a big gap, then
the pickets. Insp. Peddrick comes back alone with a riot shield.

7.00 More police run back for their shields (35 on helmets). They now have
six transit vans parked on the main road behind the horses. Some
police run back with four shields each. Some small square and some
large square.

7.04   A transit back. There are now 2 vans backed behind the men with riot shields and a gull wing van and two Range Rovers in front of them. Orders for personnel to drop back behind the long shields. Hear order for officers with keys for vehicles to right of road to move them.
I went back to where our car was parked to see if that was where was meant. In fact it wasn't.

7.07   Meet up with other observers.

7.10   We had to leave. There are still small groups of pickets scattered for a long way up the village street. We were concerned about the aggressiveness of the police dispersal technique which resulted in a very violent situation and phoned in what we had seen to Radio Sheffield in time for the 8.00 news. By 8.30 and on other bulletins on ITN, BBC, and radio the number of pickets was reported as 700 or 750, despite two Policewatch groups and a police inspector independently counting and agreeing on a figure of 300.

CONCLUSION

Between 5.00 am when we arrived and 6.45 we observed a peaceful picket of some 300 at Cortonwood Colliery policed initially by 40 officers. These numbers were reinforced to approx. 100 with the arrival of the working miner at 6.30. The police then dispersed the picket using horses, vans, riot police, and the presence of dogs. Instead of cooling the situation by a quiet, sensitive dispersal this tactic resulted in a violent confrontation between police and pickets. We were assisted in our observations by being allowed to choose our space to watch from by an Inspector Peddrick. He was an officer from an outside force and was friendly, helpful, polite, and concerned about observers' safety. Once again the media inflated picket numbers by 100 per cent.

Forces noted: Surrey, S. Yorks.

All officers, with exception of a few in charge, wore riot headgear throughout.

Appendix 4
Table of cases

Bradford v McLeod (1985) SCCR 379.
Broome v DPP (1974) ICR 74.
Brutus v Cozens (1973) AC 854.
Christie v Leachinsky (1947) AC 573.
Clarke v Chadburn (No. 2) (1984) IRLR 350.
Curlett v McKechnie (1938) JC 176.
Dibble v Ingleton (1972) 1 QB 480.
Duncan v Jones (1936) 2 KB 218.
Duport Steels v Sirs (1980) 1 WLR 142.
Express Newspapers Ltd v MacShane (1980) ICR 42.
Fisher v Oldham Corporation (1930) 2 KB 364.
Foss v Harbottle (1843) 2 Hare 461.
Hirst v Chief Constable of West Yorkshire (1986) The Times, 19 November.
Hubbard v Pitt (1976) QB 1.
Johnson v Phillips (1975) 3 All ER 682.
Jordan v Burgoyne (1963) 2 QB 561.
Kavanagh v Hiscock (1974) ICR 282.
Lyons & Co v Wilkins (1896) 1 Ch. 811; (1899) 1 Ch. 255.
Moss v McLachlan (1985) IRLR 76.
NCB v Ridgway (1987) ICR 641.
News Group Newspapers Ltd v SOGAT'82 (1986) IRLR 337.
NWL Ltd v Woods (1979) ICR 867.
Piddington v Bates (1960) 3 All ER 660.
R v Chief Constable of Devon and Cornwall, ex parte CEGB (1981) 3 All ER 826.
R v Fulling (1987) 2 All ER 65.
R v Hancock and Shankland (1986) 1 All ER 641.
R v Home Secretary, ex parte Northumbria Police Authority (1987) 2 All ER 282; affirmed Court of Appeal, The Times, 19 November 1987.
R v Home Secretary, ex parte Ruddock (1987) 2 All ER 518.
R v Howell (1982) QB 416.
R v Mansfield Justices, ex parte Sharkey (1984) IRLR 496.
R v Mason (1987) 3 All ER 481.

R v *Metropolitan Police Commissioner, ex parte Blackburn* (1968) 2 QB 118.
Richard Read (Transport) Ltd v *NUM (South Wales Area)* (1985) IRLR 67.
Ridge v *Baldwin* (1964) AC 40.
Simmons v *Hoover* (1977) ICR 62.
Taff Vale Railway Co v *Amalgamated Society of Railway Servants* (1901) AC 426.
Taylor v *NUM (Yorkshire Area)* (1984) IRLR 445.
Thomas v *NUM (South Wales Area)* (1985) 2 All ER 1.
Tynan v *Balmer* (1967) 1 QB 91.
Ward, Lock & Co v *OPAS* (1906) 22 TLR 327.
Wershof v *Metropolitan Police Commissioner* (1978) 3 All ER 540.

References and selected bibliography

Abdel-Rahim, M. (1985) *Strike-Breaking in Essex*, London: Canary.
Adeney, M. and Lloyd, J. (1986) *The Miners' Strike 1984–5: Loss without Limit*, London: Routledge & Kegan Paul.
Alderson, J.C. (1984) *Human Rights and the Police*, Strasbourg: Council of Europe Directorate of Human Rights.
Alderson, J.C. (1986) 'Gaining the peace', *Criminal Law Review* 708–18.
Allen, V.L. (1981) *The Militancy of the British Miners*, Shipley: Moor Press.
Bailey, S.H., Harris, D.J., and Jones, B.L. (1985) *Civil Liberties Cases and Materials*, 2nd edn, London: Butterworths.
Bailey, V. (ed.) (1981) *Policing and Punishment in the Nineteenth Century*, London: Croom-Helm.
Baxter, J. and Koffman, L. (1985) *Police, the Constitution and the Community*, Abingdon: Professional Books.
Benedictus, R. (1985) 'The use of the law of tort in the miners' dispute', *Industrial Law Journal* 14, 3: 176–90.
Bennett, T. (ed.) (1983) *The Future of Policing*, Cropwood Papers 15, Cambridge Institute of Criminology.
Bennion, F. (1985) 'Mass picketing and the 1875 Act', *Criminal Law Review* 64–72.
Benyon, J. (ed.) (1984) *Scarman and After*, Oxford: Pergamon.
Bercusson, B. (1980) 'Picketing, secondary picketing and secondary action', *Industrial Law Journal* 9, 4: 215–33.
Beynon, H. (1984) 'The miners' strike in Easington', *New Left Review*, Nov./Dec.
Beynon, H. (ed.) (1985) *Digging Deeper: Issues in the Miners' Strike*, London: Verso.
Bordua, D. (1967) *The Police*, New York: Wiley.
Bradley, D., Walker, M., and Wilkie, R. (1986) *Managing the Police*, Brighton: Harvester.
Brogden, M. (1982) *The Police: Autonomy and Consent*, London: Academic Press.
Bunyan, T. (1977) *The History and Practice of the Political Police in Britain*, London: Quartet.
Cain, M. (1973) *Society and the Policeman's Role*, London: Routledge & Kegan Paul.
Chadwick, E. (1829) *Preventive Police Organisation and Preventive Action*, London: Spottiswoode; reprinted in modified form from an article in the *Edinburgh Review*, 1828.
Christian, L. (1985) 'Restriction without conviction: the role of the courts in legitimising police control in Nottinghamshire', in Fine and Millar (1985): 120–36.
Clarke, R. and Hough, M. (1984) *Crime and Police Effectiveness*, Home Office Research and Planning Unit, London: HMSO.

Code of Practice (1980) *Code of Practice on Picketing*, London: HMSO.

Code of Practice (1982) *Code of Practice on Closed Shop Agreements and Arrangements*, London: HMSO.

Cohen, S. and Scull, A. (eds) (1983) *Social Control and the State*, Oxford: Martin Robertson.

Colquhoun, P. (1803) *A Treatise on the Functions and Duties of a Constable*, London: J. Mawman and T. Hatchard.

Coulter, J., Miller, S., and Walker, M. (1984) *State of Siege*, London: Canary.

Cowell, D., Jones, T., and Young, J. (1982) *Policing the Riots*, London: Junction.

Crick, M. (1985) *Scargill and the Miners*, Harmondsworth: Penguin.

Critchley, T. (1978) *A History of the Police in England and Wales*, 2nd edn, London: Constable.

Department of Employment (1987) *Trade Unions and their Members*, Cm 95, Green Paper, London: HMSO.

Dummett, M., Butler, R., Hall, S., Hewitt, P., Keys, W., Lestor, J., North, R., O'Higgins, P., Sondhi, R., Thompson, H., and Webb, P. (1980) – see NCCL (1980).

Ennals, M. (1984) 'The police and the public', in P.T. Wallington (ed.) *Civil Liberties 1984*, Oxford: Martin Robertson.

Evans, P. (1974) *The Police Revolution*, London: Allen & Unwin.

Evans, S. (1983) 'The labour injunction revisited: picketing, employers and the Employment Act 1980', *Industrial Law Journal* 12, 3: 129–47.

Ewing, K.D. (1982) 'Industrial action: another step in the "right" direction', *Industrial Law Journal* 11, 4: 209–26.

Ewing, K.D. (1985) 'The strike, the courts and the rule-books', *Industrial Law Journal* 14, 3: 160–75.

Ewing, K.D. and Napier, B.W. (1986) 'Labour law and the Wapping dispute', *Cambridge Law Journal* 185–214.

Field, S. and Southgate, P. (1982) *Public Disorder*, Home Office Research and Planning Unit, London: HMSO.

Fine, B. and Millar, R. (eds) (1985) *Policing the Miners' Strike*, London: Lawrence & Wishart/Cobden Trust.

Fisher, Sir H. (1977) *Report of an Inquiry by the Hon. Sir Henry Fisher into the Circumstances leading to the Trial of Three Persons on Charges Arising out of the Death of Maxwell Confait and the Fire at 27 Doggett Road, London SE6*, HC 90 (1977–8) London: HMSO.

Geary, R. (1985) *Policing Industrial Disputes: 1893–1985*, Cambridge: Cambridge University Press.

Gibbons, T.C. (1983) 'Obstructing a constable: the emergence of a new duty to co-operate with the police', *Criminal Law Review* 21–8.

Gifford, Lord (1986) *Report of the Broadwater Farm Inquiry*, London: Haringey Borough Council.

Glyn, A. (1984) *Economic Aspects of the Coal Industry*, Sheffield: NUM.

Hain, P. (ed.) (1980) *Policing the Police*, London: Calder.

Harrison, J. (1987) *Police Misconduct: Legal Remedies*, London: Legal Action Group.

Hart, J.M. (1951) *The British Police*, London: Allen & Unwin.

Heal, K., Tarling, R., and Burrows, J. (eds) (1985) *Policing Today*, Home Office Research and Planning Unit, London: HMSO.

Hohfield, W.N. (1923) *Fundamental Legal Conceptions as Applied in Judicial Reasoning*, New Haven, Conn.: Yale University Press.

Holdaway, S. (1979) *The British Police*, London: Edward Arnold.

Holdaway, S. (1983) *Inside the British Police*, Oxford: Blackwell.

Home Affairs Committee, House of Commons (1985) *Special Branch*, 4th Report, Session 1984–5, HC 71 (1984–5) London: HMSO.

Home Affairs Committee, House of Commons (1986) *Racial Attacks and Harassment,* 3rd Report, Session 1985–6, HC 409 (1985–6) London: HMSO.

Home Office (1980) *Review of the Public Order Act 1936 and Related Legislation,* Cmnd 7891, London: HMSO.

Home Office (1981) *Racial Attacks,* London: HMSO.

House of Commons Select Committee on Energy (1982) *Second Report 1982–3: Pit Closures,* HC 135 (1982–3), London: HMSO.

Hutton, J. (1984) 'Solving the strike problem: Part II of the Trade Union Act 1984', *Industrial Law Journal* 13, 4: 212–26.

Jefferson, T. and Grimshaw, R. (1984) *Controlling the Constable,* London: Frederick Muller.

Kahn, P., Lewis, N., Livock, R., and Wiles, P. (1983) *Picketing: Industrial Disputes, Tactics and the Law,* London: Routledge & Kegan Paul.

Kahn-Freud, O. and Hepple, B.A. (1972) *Laws against Strikes,* Fabian Research Series 305, London: Fabian Society.

Kettle, M. (1985) 'The National Reporting Centre and the 1984 miners' strike', in Fine and Millar (1985): 23–33.

Kettle, M. and Hodges, L. (1982) *Uprising!,* London: Pan.

Kidner, R. (1983) *Trade Union Law,* 2nd edn, London: Sweet & Maxwell.

Kidner, R. (1985) 'Picketing and the conspiracy and protecion of Property Act 1875', *Journal of Criminal Law* 49: 77–83.

Kinsey, R., Lea, J., and Young, J. (1986) *Losing the Fight against Crime,* Oxford: Blackwell.

Lambert, J.L. (1986) *Police Powers and Accountability,* London: Croom Helm.

Law Commission (1983) *Offences Relating to Public Order: Report No. 123,* HC 85 (1983–4) London: HMSO.

Leonard, T. (1985) 'Policing the miners' strike in Derbyshire', *Policing* 1, 2: 96–103.

Lloyd, J. (1985) *Understanding the Miners' Strike,* Fabian Tract 504, London: Fabian Society.

Lustgarten, L. (1986) *The Governance of Police,* London: Sweet & Maxwell.

McCabe, S. and Sutcliffe, F. (1978) *Defining Crime,* Oxford: Blackwell.

MacCormick, D.N. (1987) 'Access to the goods: a review of Joseph Raz's "The Morality of Freedom"', *Times Literary Supplement* 599.

MacGregor, Sir I. (1986) *The Enemies Within,* London: Collins.

McIlroy, J. (1985) 'The law struck dumb? – Labour law and the miners' strike', in Fine and Millar (1985): 79–102.

Mackenzie, G. (1986) 'Bitter lessons in the battle for coal', *Times Higher Education Supplement* 20 June.

Mainwaring-White, S. (1983) *The Policing Revolution,* Brighton: Harvester.

Marshall, G. (1965) *Police and Government,* London: Methuen.

Martin, J.P. (1974) 'The scope of police manpower studies', in R. Hood (ed.) *Crime, Criminology and Public Policy,* London: Heinemann.

Melville-Lee, W. (1901) *A History of Police in England,* London: Methuen.

Mesher, J. (1985) 'Social security in the coal dispute', *Industrial Law Journal* 14, 3: 191–202.

Metropolitan Police (1986) *Report by Assistant Commissioner M.D. Richards to the Chairman and Members of Haringey Police/Community Consultative Council 'Broadwater Farm, October 1985',* London: Metropolitan Police.

Monopolies and Mergers Commission (1983) *Report on the National Coal Board,* Cmnd 8290, London: HMSO.

Moody, S.R. and Toombs, J. (1982) *Prosecution in the Public Interest,* Edinburgh: Scottish Academic Press.

NCCL (1980) *Southall, 23 April 1979: Report of an Unofficial Inquiry,* London: National Council for Civil Liberties.

NCCL (1984) *Civil Liberties and the Miners' Dispute: First Report of the Independent Inquiry*, London: National Council for Civil Liberties.

NCCL (1986) *No Way in Wapping*, pamphlet, London: National Council for Civil Liberties.

Newbold, A.L. (1985) 'Picketing miners and the courts', *Public Law*, 30–4.

Oliver, I. (1986) *Police, Government and Accountability*, London: Macmillan.

Parker, T. (1986) *Red Hill, a Mining Community*, London: Heinemann.

Partington, M. (1980) 'Unemployment, industrial conflict and social security', *Industrial Law Journal* 9, 4: 243–53.

Pearson, G. (1983) *Hooligan: A History of Respectable Fears?*, London: Macmillan.

Police Complaints Authority (1987) *Annual Report 1986*, HC 295 (1986–7) London: HMSO.

Police Complaints Board (1985) *Annual Report of the Police Complaints Board for 1984*, HC 359 (1984–5), London: HMSO.

Policy Studies Institute (1983) – see D.J. Smith and Gray (1983).

Powis, D. (1977) *The Signs of Crime: a Field Manual for Police*, London: McGraw-Hill.

Rees, Rt Hon. M., MP and Brown, G., MP (1985) Unpublished report to the Leader of the Opposition on the policing of the miners' strike and matters arising therefrom, dated 9 May 1985.

Rees, W.M. (1985) 'The law, practice and procedures concerning redundancy in the coal mining industry', *Industrial Law Journal* 14, 3: 203–14.

Reiner, R. (1978) *The Blue-Coated Worker*, Cambridge: Cambridge University Press.

Reiner, R. (1985) *The Politics of the Police*, Brighton: Wheatsheaf.

Reiner, R. and Shapland, J. (eds) (1987) 'Why police', *British Journal of Criminology* 27, 1.

Reiss, A.J. (1971) *The Police and the Public*, New Haven, Conn.: Yale University Press.

Reith, C. (1943) *The British Police and the Democratic Ideal*, Oxford: Oxford University Press.

Riddall, J.G. (1984) *The Law of Industrial Relations*, 2nd edn, London: Butterworth.

Rideout, R.W. and Dyson, J. (1983) *Rideout's Principles of Labour Law*, 4th edn, London: Sweet & Maxwell.

Roach, J. and Thomaneck, J. (eds) (1985) *Police and Public Order in Europe*, London: Croom Helm.

Roberts, R. (1971) *The Classic Slum*, Harmondsworth: Penguin.

Rogaly, J. (1977) *Grunwick*, Harmondsworth: Penguin.

Royal Commission (1908) *Report of the Royal Commission on the Duties of the Metropolitan Police*, Cd 4156, London: HMSO.

Royal Commission (1929) *Report of the Royal Commission on Police Powers*, Cmd 3297, London: HMSO.

Royal Commission (1962) *Final Report of the Royal Commission on the Police* (Chairman Sir Henry Willink QC) Cmnd 1792, London: HMSO.

Royal Commission (1981) *Report of the Royal Commission on Criminal Procedure* (Chairman Sir Cyril Phillips) Cmnd 8092, London: HMSO.

Samuel, R., Bloomfield, B., and Boanas, G. (eds) (1985) *The Enemy Within: Pit Villages and the Miners' Strike*, History Workshop Series, London: Routledge & Kegan Paul.

Scarman, Rt Hon. Sir L. (1977) *Report of a Court of Inquiry into a Dispute between Grunwick Processing Laboratories Limited and Members of the Association of Professional, Executive, Clerical and Computer Staffs*, Cmnd 6922, London: HMSO.

Scarman, Lord (1981) *The Brixton Disorders, 10–12 April 1981*, Cmnd 8427, London: HMSO.

Scraton, P. and Gordon, P. (eds) (1984) *Causes for Concern*, Harmondsworth: Penguin.

Select Committee Report (1982) – see House of Commons.

Sheffield Policewatch (1984) *Taking Liberties: Policing during the Miners' Strike, April–October 1984*, pamphlet, Sheffield: Sheffield Policewatch.

Simey, M. (1982) 'Police Authorities and accountability: the Merseyside experience', in Cowell, Jones, and Young (1982).

Simey, M. (1984) 'Partnership policing', in Benyon (1984).

Skolnick, J. (1966) *Justice Without Trial*, New York: Wiley.

Smith, A.T.H. (1987) 'The Public Order Act 1986 Part I: the new offences', *Criminal Law Review* 156–67.

Smith, D.J. and Gray, J. (1983) *Police and People in London*, four vols, vol. 3 *A Survey of Police Officers*, vol. 4 *The Police in Action*, London: Policy Studies Institute.

Smith, I.T. and Wood, Sir J.C. (1986) *Industrial Law*, 3rd edn, London: Butterworths.

South Yorkshire Police (1980) *Report of the Chief Constable of South Yorkshire on the Policing of the Steel Strike*, Sheffield: South Yorkshire Police.

South Yorkshire Police (1985) *Policing the Coal Industry Dispute in South Yorkshire*, Report of the Chief Constable to the South Yorkshire Police Authority, Sheffield: South Yorkshire Police.

South Yorkshire Police Authority (1985) *Policing Policy during the Strike of the National Union of Mineworkers (Yorkshire Area) 1984: Report of an Inquiry by the Special Sub-Committee of the South Yorkshire Police Committee*, Sheffield: South Yorkshire Police Authority.

Spencer, S. (1985a) *Police Authorities during the Miners' Strike*, Cobden Trust Working Paper 1, London: Cobden Trust.

Spencer, S. (1985b) *Called to Account: The Case for Police Accountability in England and Wales*, London: National Council for Civil Liberties.

Storch, R. (1975) 'A plague of blue locusts', *International Review of Social History* 20.

Sunday Times Insight Team (1985) *Strike: 358 Days that Shook the Nation*, by Peter Wilsher, Donald Macintyre, and Michael Jones, London: Coronet.

Supperstone, M. (1981) *Brownlie's Law Relating to Public Order and National Security*, London: Butterworths.

Thornton, P. (1985) *We Protest: The Public Order Debate*, London: National Council for Civil Liberties.

Thornton, P. (1987) *Public Order Law*, London: Financial Training.

Waddington, P.A.J. (1985) 'The effects of manpower depletion during the NUM dispute', *Policing* 1: 149–60.

Wallington, P.T. (1976) 'Injunctions and the "right to demonstrate"', *Cambridge Law Journal* 82–111.

Wallington, P.T. (1985) 'Policing the miners' strike', *Industrial Law Journal* 14, 3: 145–59.

Wallington, P.T. (1987) 'The Public Order Act 1986: some implications for the policing of industrial disputes', *Criminal Law Review* 180–91.

Ward, G. (1978) *Fort Grunwick*, London: Temple Smith.

Watts-Pope, D. and Weiner, N. (eds) (1981) *Modern Policing*, London: Croom Helm.

Wegg-Prosser, C. (1986) *The Police and the Law*, London: Longman.

Welsh Council for Civil and Political Liberties (1985) *Striking Back*, Cardiff: WCCPL/NUM (South Wales Area).

West Midlands Police (1985) *Handsworth/Lozells, September 1985: Report to the Home Secretary*, Birmingham: West Midlands Police.

Whitaker, B. (1979) *The Police in Society*, London: Eyre Methuen.

Williams, D.G.T. (1987) 'Processions, assemblies and the freedom of the individual', *Criminal Law Review* 167–79.

Young, J. and Lea, J. (1984) *What is to be Done about Law and Order?*, Harmondsworth: Penguin.

Index

DATE DUE

DEMCO NO. 38-298